# Before the GOLD RUSH

## Flashbacks to the Dawn of the Canadian Sound

NICHOLAS JENNINGS

VIKING

VIKING
Published by the Penguin Group
Penguin Books Canada Ltd, 10 Alcorn Avenue, Toronto, Ontario, Canada M4V 3B2
Penguin Books Ltd, 27 Wrights Lane, London W8 5TZ, England
Viking Penguin, a division of Penguin Books USA Inc., 375 Hudson Street, New York, New York 10014, U.S.A.
Penguin Books Australia Ltd, Ringwood, Victoria, Australia
Penguin Books (NZ) Ltd, cnr Rosedale and Airborne Roads, Albany, Auckland 1310, New Zealand

Penguin Books Ltd, Registered Offices: Harmondsworth, Middlesex, England

First published 1997

1 3 5 7 9 10 8 6 4 2

Printed and bound in Canada on acid free paper ∞

**Canadian Cataloguing in Publication Data**

Jennings, Nicholas, 1953–
Before the gold rush: flashbacks to the dawn of the Canadian sound

ISBN 0-670-87381-0

1. Popular music – Canada – 1961-1970 – History and criticism. 2. Subculture – Ontario – Toronto. 3. Yorkville (Toronto, Ont.) – Social conditions. I. Title

ML384.J54 1997 781.64'0971'09046 C96-932222-4

Visit Penguin Canada's web site at **www.penguin.ca**

to all the players
—especially domenic troiano—
whose music both inspired
and fuelled the writing of this book.

VILLAGE CORNER
PEARS AVE.
DAVENPORT
NIGHTOWL
THE CELLAR
WEBSTER'S
WEBSTER AVE.
HAZELTON
NIMBUS 9 STUDIOS
THE HEAD SHO
ST. PAULS CHURCH
RECORD WORLD
MONT BLANC
AVENUE ROAD CLUB
HAMBURGER JOINT
BLOW-UP
THE GRAB BAG
COSMIC VISITOR
UPPER CRUST
PENNY FARTHING
THE MOUSEH
THE MYNAH BIRD
SAMMY'S
HALF BEAT
GATE OF CLEVE
BORIS'
PURPLE ONION
RIVERBOAT
GAS
CHETWYND APTS.
JACQUES' PLACE
CAFÉ EL PATIO
OLD YORK LANE
GAS LIGHT
HARLEQ HOUSE
NORMAN ELDER STUDIO
PARK PLAZA
HAMPTON COURT APTS.
COTSWOLD COURT APTS.
CHARLIE BROWNS
KIKI ROUGE
UNIVERSITY THEATRE
AVENUE ROAD
CHURCH OF THE REDEEMER
MAP IS NOT TO SCALE!
YORKVILLE VILLAG
1960 - 1969

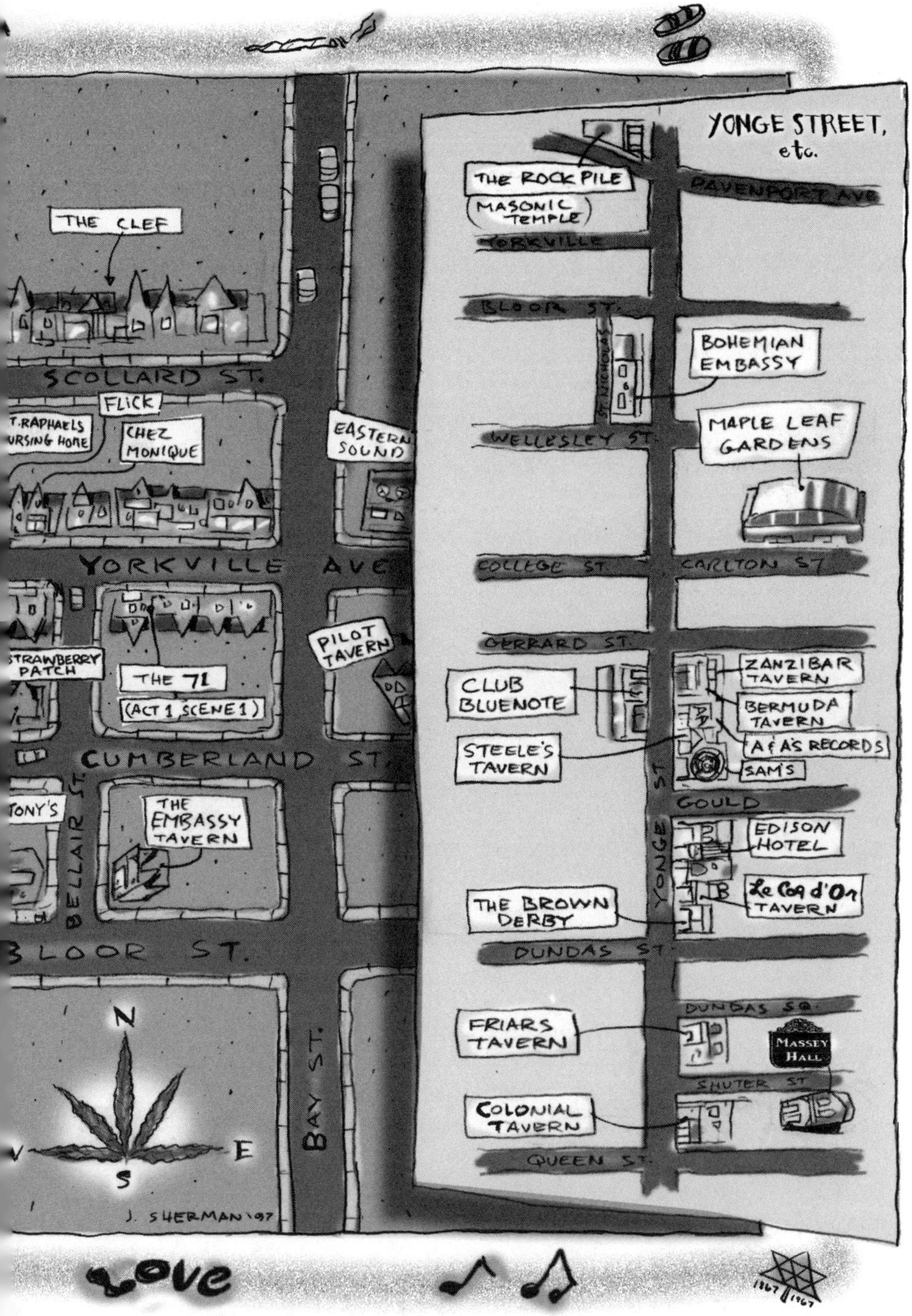

YONGE STREET, etc.
THE ROCK PILE
MASONIC TEMPLE
DAVENPORT AVE
YORKVILLE
BLOOR ST.
ST. NICHOLAS
BOHEMIAN EMBASSY
WELLESLEY ST.
MAPLE LEAF GARDENS
COLLEGE ST.
CARLTON ST.
GERRARD ST.
CLUB BLUENOTE
ZANZIBAR TAVERN
BERMUDA TAVERN
A & A'S RECORDS
STEELE'S TAVERN
SAM'S
GOULD
YONGE ST
EDISON HOTEL
Le Coq d'Or TAVERN
THE BROWN DERBY
DUNDAS ST.
DUNDAS SQ.
FRIARS TAVERN
MASSEY HALL
SHUTER ST.
COLONIAL TAVERN
QUEEN ST.
THE CLEF
SCOLLARD ST.
FLICK
ST. RAPHAELS NURSING HOME
CHEZ MONIQUE
EASTERN SOUND
YORKVILLE AVE
PILOT TAVERN
STRAWBERRY PATCH
THE 71
(ACT 1, SCENE 1)
CUMBERLAND ST.
TONY'S
BELLAIR ST.
THE EMBASSY TAVERN
BLOOR ST.
BAY ST.
N
E
S
J. SHERMAN '97
Love
1867 1967

# Contents

# PROLOGUE

My friend Peter and I missed out on Woodstock. In the summer of '69, we were simply too young to make the trek. But we did get to go to an all-Canadian version of that historic festival. Held in a campground near Orangeville, Ontario, over the Labour Day weekend, the Freak Out at Rockhill Park featured no fewer than twenty-one of Canada's best bands on three stages, including one on a small lake.

My parents drove us up from Toronto, actually right into the campground, which proved to be both a curse and a blessing. On the one hand, as sixteen-year-olds, we were mortified that we needed a parental escort at all, when most people had driven themselves or hitch-hiked. On the other, being in the company of an older, suburban-looking couple neatly avoided the drug-frisking at the gate: the security guards took one look at my parents and quickly waved us through.

Once we'd said goodbye to my folks, Peter and I set up our pup tent and rolled our first joint. Let the "Freak Out" begin. Sitting back under the sun, we soaked up some great music that weekend by the likes of The Guess Who, Lighthouse, The Five Man Electrical Band and Motherlode. To us, those bands were home-grown heroes, local acts that had gone on to become stars. In fact, many of them had begun their careers in Yorkville before graduating to the international stage.

Yorkville was the music mecca of Canada, the magnet that drew musicians from every corner of the country. To suburban kids like us, however, it was the forbidden zone, strictly off-limits as decreed by our parents because of the sensational news accounts of free love and drugs. But as soon as I was able to borrow the family car, another friend, Joel, and I snuck down to the village—as spectators, not participants. We did the Yorkville Crawl in bumper-to-bumper traffic, gawking like every other tourist at the kaleidoscopic sights and sounds. Music, I remember, poured out of every doorway into the street.

At its peak, about 1966–67, Yorkville had more than forty clubs and coffee houses featuring live music. On any given night, you could stroll westward from Bay Street to Avenue Road and catch a dizzying number of bands and folk-singers. At the Chez Monique, The Sparrows (later Steppenwolf) would be holding forth with their distinctive brand of blues-rock. The Flick would be featuring the paisley sounds of The Stitch 'n' Tyme or the zany antics of The Lords of London. Past the old folks' home, you'd see the go-go dancer in the glass booth at the Mynah Bird, the club that gave Rick James and Neil Young the name for their band. The Penny Farthing would be swinging to the folk-rock sounds of The Dirty Shames or The

Let the Freak Out begin

Stormy Clovers, while the Café El Patio had the fabulous, pre-psychedelic Paupers. And the Riverboat was the bastion of folk and blues, where you could hear anyone from Gordon Lightfoot and Murray McLauchlan to John Lee Hooker and Sonny Terry & Brownie McGhee.

Up around the bend, on Avenue Road, was the Purple Onion—home of Yorkville's thrilling Luke & the Apostles. Next door, the Gate of Cleve featured folkies like Phil Ochs and Eric Andersen, while the nearby Avenue Road Club hosted Toronto's r & b sensations Jon and Lee & the Checkmates. Across the street, the Night Owl had The Rock Show of the Yeomen and further up the road stood the venerable Village Corner, where it had all started with the harmonies of a youthful Ian & Sylvia back in 1960. Imagine the musicians performing in that close-knit community. How could they be anything but deeply inspired, especially when the high musical standards of Ronnie Hawkins & the Hawks (later The Band) loomed over everyone?

I caught only the tail-end of that scene, after Yorkville's make-over by developers and City Hall had succeeded in driving most of the music away. As a college student, I landed a part-time job at Bernie Fiedler's Riverboat, washing dishes and making cappuccinos. There, I watched an adolescent Colin Linden absorb every guitar lick he could from visiting bluesmen, and an eager Dan Hill (from my old neighbourhood) beg Bernie for a chance to play. From the kitchen, I saw many talented performers, including gifted songsmith John Prine, the foot-stomping Mendelson Joe and the irrepressible Steve Goodman. All the while, the club's fabled past and that of the village resonated, pointing me to its timeless contributions.

In 1996, while interviewing inductees to the Canadian Music Hall of Fame for *Maclean's*, Yorkville's significance became fully apparent to me. Each of the five inductees—David Clayton-Thomas (Blood, Sweat & Tears), Denny Doherty (Mamas & Papas), John Kay (Steppenwolf), Domenic Troiano (Mandala) and Zal Yanovsky (Lovin' Spoonful)—told me in separate interviews of the magical role that the village had played in their lives. I knew then that I had to write about this strangely ignored chapter in Canadian music history.

As music critic for *Maclean's*, I've written about another wave of Canadian artists, from Bryan Adams, Jann Arden, Sarah McLachlan and Jane Siberry to Cowboy Junkies, Barenaked Ladies, Blue Rodeo and The Tragically Hip. In doing so, I've seen how the singer-songwriter tradition—born in Yorkville with Ian & Sylvia and Gordon Lightfoot—lives on in their music. Arden, McLachlan and Siberry owe much of their autobiographical style to Joni Mitchell's stark confessional compositions, while the Junkies, Ladies and Blue Rodeo have each lovingly covered songs by David Wiffen, Bruce Cockburn and Ian Tyson. Still others have paid tribute to Lightfoot, Leonard Cohen and Neil Young.

It's easy to think of Canadian music in the '60s as just another hit of nostalgia for baby boomers in the '90s. But beyond the retro, golden-oldie aspect of the story lies a telling history lesson for today's musicians and music fans. Back then, there was no MuchMusic or Juno Awards, no seminars on how to shop your demos to the majors or Web sites to launch your debut album. The Canadian music scene was highly regionalized, still-virgin territory, and cross-country tours were practically unthinkable. There were only a handful of independent labels. And bands existed in their home towns on the strength of their fan clubs and word-of-mouth reputations. Back then, music was simply an adventure, a fly-by-the-seat-of-your-pants experience with absolutely no templates to follow.

This is the story of how it was then, when one short street, jammed with a plethora of clubs and coffee houses, became the rocking cradle for a myriad wondrous sounds. This is the story of how Canadian pop was born.

N.J.
Toronto
June 1997

# 1 Bound for Moving On

The gauntlet had been thrown and Ian Tyson wasn't about to back down. Here he was in Greenwich Village in the early 1960s, a veteran of rodeos and now one of the new stars of the folk boom, and some young pup who sang off-key and played an out-of-tune guitar was upping the ante—in fact, changing the goddam rules of the game on him.

Tyson and his singing partner, Sylvia Fricker, had come out of Canada like a bracing northern breeze, turning heads with their chilling harmonies and stirring ballads. They even had one critically acclaimed album under their belts and a long-term contract to boot. But Ian & Sylvia's repertoire, like that of any good folkie in those days, was all drawn from traditional sources: blues and country records and old

English songbooks. Hardly anyone was writing his own songs then.

Bob Dylan changed all that. When Tyson witnessed the scruffy folk singer, eight years his junior, get up and sing his "Blowin' in the Wind" one autumn night at Gerde's Folk City, it was like being kicked in the head by a bronco. This was the same "obnoxious little jerk" he had come across in the Village before, bumming cigarettes and crashing on people's couches. To see Dylan singing his impassioned anthem, its lyrics rich with poetic inquiry, and notice the audience hanging on his every word like he was some sort of messiah, well, the whole thing just bugged Tyson something awful. "I saw this raggedy-ass kid up on stage," he recalls, "and thought, 'boy, if this guy can write a song like that, I can too.'"

*The Crew-Cuts hit the Top Ten in the 1950s with "Sh-Boom"*

Tyson took up the challenge the very next day. Sitting in his manager's office, overlooking a rainy Central Park, he penned his first composition. The words that poured out of him had to do with the changing seasons. Tyson later described its meaning in the liner notes for the next Ian & Sylvia album: "Canada has many seasonal workers," he wrote, "and when the weather turns harsh they must move on and find a different type of work. Many of these people cross the country every year—from the tobacco harvest in Ontario to the wheat harvest on the Prairies to apple picking in British Columbia. With the advent of fall they move on, perhaps to return with the spring." There was also a hint in the song of a failed, bittersweet romance.

Little did he know, but with his

simple lyrics about good times gone and being "bound for moving on," Tyson had, like Dylan, written a classic. "Four Strong Winds" was one of the first and most successful songs to come out of Canada in the 1960s. It made Ian & Sylvia a household name and bought Tyson his first ranch. But most important, the song helped to usher in a whole new era of Canadian music.

Canada was still a musical wasteland at the dawn of the 1960s: plenty of talent, but no industry, no network, no scene. There had been a flurry of success stories, including vocal quartets The Four Lads, The Crew-Cuts and The Diamonds, all of whom had scored Top Ten hits in the U.S. in the previous decade. They had done this by taking songs by black artists and recording them, à la Pat Boone, as smoothed-out pop tunes for white audiences. Ottawa-born crooner Paul Anka had also made a name for himself south of the border, joining Fabian and Frankie Avalon as a teen idol with his song "Diana."

But in 1958, middle-of-the-road pop was being rudely sidelined by the driving force of rock 'n' roll and rockabilly, especially by that of a good-looking, former truck driver named Elvis Presley. In Canada, the Pelvis had made his presence felt a year earlier with sold-out concerts at Vancouver's Empire Stadium and Toronto's Maple Leaf Gardens. Presley's popularity was so strong that it convinced Toronto's CHUM 1050, the country's most powerful AM station, to adopt an all-rock programming policy. When the station issued the first of its influential CHUM Charts on May 27, 1957, the song in the number-one position was Elvis's "All Shook Up."

The other force that nudged doo-wop and teen idols off pop's highway in 1958 was "Tom Dooley." Sung by the San Francisco–based Kingston Trio, the song, based on a nineteenth-century ballad about a convicted murderer named Tom Dula, shot straight to the top of the charts late in the year. Unlike the more politicized sounds of Woody Guthrie or The Weavers, The Kingston Trio's clean-cut, folky strains were perfectly suited to North America's airwaves and "Tom Dooley" sparked a folk boom that would be heard well into the 1960s.

In Vancouver that year, twenty-five-year-old Ian Tyson had already been bitten by the rock 'n' roll bug and would soon feel the resounding effects of the folk boom. Along with riding in rodeos and studying commercial design at the Vancouver School of Art, the cowboy-loving Tyson had started playing guitar, something he'd learned to do while recovering from a serious rodeo accident. There were only a handful of coffee houses in the city at that time, including the Inquisition on Seymour Street, and they tended to favour established folk and jazz acts. So Tyson made his performance debut at the Heidelberg Café, which was known more for wiener schnitzel than music. For a while, he played rhythm guitar with The Sensational Stripes, a local rockabilly group. And he sang for his supper with the house band at Chinatown's New Delhi Chop Suey Parlour. By the time he graduated from art school, Tyson was ready for a steady wage in the workaday world—only trouble was, he couldn't find any work in his field.

*The first of the influential CHUM charts, issued May 27, 1957*

Even before Tyson knew where his fortunes would take him, Sylvia Fricker already had her mind set on becoming a folk singer—no mean ambition for a girl from Chatham, Ontario. While there was plenty of rock 'n' roll to be heard on nearby Detroit radio stations, there

*The Pelvis made his presence felt at Maple Leaf Gardens*

was not a trace of folk music. And certainly the town's record shop had no albums by Pete Seeger or The Weavers. Still, she was determined. With a $25 guitar her parents bought her from the Eaton's mail-order catalogue, she taught herself to play old English folk songs from books she borrowed at the library. By 1958, the eighteen-year-old Fricker had already performed at the community centre and was craving bigger challenges.

In the rest of Canada that year, other hopeful musicians were either getting their first instruments or playing their first gigs. Out in Halifax, Denny Doherty, also eighteen, was singing in a rock group called The Hepcats. Although he had worked with local bands during high school as a trombonist, his mellifluous tenor—not to mention his three-octave range—was pegging him as a vocalist. In Montreal, twenty-four-year-old Leonard Cohen didn't possess a fine singing voice. But he was a published poet and had begun reading his work, beat-style, with jazz accompaniment, at clubs like Dunn's Progressive Jazz Parlour on Ste. Catherine Street. One of his first accompanists was guitarist Lenny Breau, who later also backed Joni Mitchell when she passed through Breau's home town of Winnipeg.

**CHUM CHART TOP TEN JULY 6, 1959**

*The Battle of New Orleans*
Johnny Horton

*Waterloo*
Stonewall Jackson

*Lonely Boy*
Paul Anka

*Forty Days*
Ronnie Hawkins

*My Heart Is an Open Book*
Carl Dobkins Jr.

*Frankie/Lipstick*
Connie Francis

*Hushabye*
The Mystics

*Bongo Rock*
Preston Epps

*Mona Lisa*
Carl Mann

*Forty Miles of Bad Road*
Duane Eddy

In 1958, Mitchell was still Joan Anderson, a fifteen-year-old living in Saskatoon. That year, she purchased her first instrument, a $36 baritone ukulele, with money she earned from modelling. The ukulele was an alternative to a guitar, which her mother had strictly forbidden. But it enabled her to accompany herself, singing Kingston Trio songs and other folk material of the day. Coincidentally, Neil Young also received a ukulele from his parents around the same time, while living in Pickering, Ontario. The thirteen-year-old Young, who, like Mitchell, also suffered a childhood case of polio, had been inspired by seeing Elvis perform on TV's "Ed Sullivan Show."

Gordon Lightfoot was twenty and still living at home in Orillia, north of Toronto. Already, Lightfoot had sung in barber-shop quartets and vocal groups like The Collegiate Four and The Teen-Timers, acts influenced by The Crew-Cuts and The Four Lads. He then formed his first duo with Terry Whelan, The Two-Timers. By 1957, Lightfoot had even written his first composition and driven his father's car to Toronto to pitch it to Harold Moon, head of the BMI song publishing association. Although no "Tom Dooley," his "Hoola Hoop Song" marked the beginning of what would become a celebrated songwriting career. But first, the ambitious Lightfoot was heading to Los Angeles to study piano, orchestration and musical theory at the Westlake School of Modern Music.

Two other musicians, both later prominent in Canada, were living in the United States in 1958. Buffy Sainte-Marie, a Cree Indian born on a reserve outside Regina, had been adopted and raised in Maine, where she was studying languages and philosophy at university. But the seventeen-year-old Sainte-Marie was already aspiring to become a folk singer, performing at an off-campus coffee house. Ronnie Hawkins, a native of Fayetteville, Arkansas, had formed his first group while attending university, studying physical education. At twenty-three, Hawkins was fronting a rockabilly band and contemplating making his move to Canada, which he saw as a lucrative and crime-free alternative to the States.

While Hawkins was earning his reputation as a rockabilly showman, Robbie Robertson was already playing guitar at high-school dances for Toronto's Little Caesar & the Consuls, one of the city's earliest rhythm-and-blues bands. Although he was only fourteen and barely shaving, Robertson was about to lend his budding string-bending skills to Johnny Rhythm & the Suedes, and to such finely named outfits as Thumper & the Trambones and his own Robbie & the Robots.

All of these musicians would eventually converge on Toronto at the dawn of the 1960s, in the days before pop's gold rush. Canadian music then was still a brand new game, one without rules—and certainly without videos. The stakes weren't as high but the pay-off was infinitely richer.

## DISCS TO DISCOVER

*The 16 Most Requested*—The Four Lads (Sony imports, 1992)

*The Best of the Mercury Years*—The Crew-Cuts (PolyGram, 1996)

*The Best of the Mercury Years*—The Diamonds (PolyGram, 1996)

*Five Decades' Worth*—Paul Anka (EMI, 1991)

# 2

# On the Road

Ian Tyson wanted work. Although he had enjoyed playing music semi-professionally in joints and honky-tonks in and around Vancouver's Chinatown, Tyson was anxious to find employment in his chosen field, graphic design. However, despite his diploma, there was none to be found in Vancouver during the summer of '58. Tyson had a minor case of wanderlust anyway, having become a disciple of Jack Kerouac and his hipster bible, *On the Road*. So, with only a few dollars in his pocket and no particular destination in mind, he headed for the highway. His first ride took him all the way to Chicago. After a bus ride to Windsor, Ontario, across the border from Detroit, he decided to hitch-hike on to Toronto. Within a few days, Tyson was working as a paste-up artist for an advertising company.

Toronto at the time was still a little puritanical, still somewhat provincial, still deadsville. Aside from some lively bars on Yonge Street, which local temperance squares continually denounced as "hatcheries of hell," there was little in the way of new entertainment. This was in the bad old days of Toronto the Good. The only other new music to be found was in a few after-hours places that city by-laws forced to operate as private clubs. No liquor could be served, but if patrons bought a membership they could enjoy coffee, desserts and entertainment. Liquor laws were strict in those days and liquor licences scarce (rumour was you had to buy off the inspectors to get one). Since bars restricted drinking to those twenty-one and over, coffee houses found an instant niche market with students and hipsters.

**CHUM CHART TOP TEN SEPTEMBER 14, 1959**

*Sea of Love*
Phil Phillips

*I'm Gonna Get Married*
Lloyd Price

*Three Bells*
The Browns

*I Want to Walk You Home/Wheel*
Fats Domino

*Till I Kissed You*
Everly Bros.

*Mary Lou*
Ronnie Hawkins

*Kissin' Time*
Bobby Rydell

*Baby Talk*
Jan & Dean

*Broken Hearted Melody/Misty*
Sarah Vaughan

*Mack the Knife*
Bobby Darin

Tyson did well in his new job, developing a reputation as a first-rate designer and illustrator. After getting a few of his drawings published, mostly featuring his beloved cowboy or Western themes, he completed his highest-profile design: the logo for the Resdan dandruff shampoo bottle. Despite his success in the commercial art world, Tyson found himself drawn to the nascent coffeehouse scene. He soon discovered an after-hours jazz joint known as the First Floor Club, on Asquith Avenue in the Yonge and Bloor area. Housed in a former private girls' school, it featured some of the best of the local jazz scene: guitarist Ed Bickert, bassist Don Thompson, drummer Archie Alleyne and singer Don Francks. Tyson liked the atmosphere. People sat around and played chess, women with bohemian tastes hung out and the jazz was loud and progressive. A sign above the stage offered the stern, single-word instruction: "Listen."

Responding to the demand for folk music in the

wake of "Tom Dooley," the First Floor began featuring folk singers before midnight. Tyson quickly bought himself a guitar and started getting gigs almost right away, first with Francks, a charismatic fellow Vancouverite with whom he hit it off, and then on his own. Francks introduced him to blues and spirituals, while Tyson taught the jazz singer some of his favourite Western ballads, real honest-to-pete cowboy tunes like "Red River Valley."

*Ian Tyson, shortly after arriving in Toronto in 1959*

A small-town girl with big-city aspirations, Sylvia Fricker knew her destiny lay somewhere beyond Chatham, a small farming town just east of Windsor. Once the northern terminal of the Underground Railroad to Canada, Chatham may have provided refuge for runaway slaves but it held no beacon for Fricker. After saving $200 from her job at a local jewellery store, she made the first of what she called "field trips" to Toronto by train to see what the city had to offer.

On one of her initial visits, Fricker met Tyson through a friend who knew his boss at the ad agency. She sang for Tyson over the telephone, and he was immediately struck by her unique choice of songs and her knack for harmony. Fricker was a natural; she and her sister had sung a lot as kids and, thanks to their mother, had choir training growing up. Tyson suggested they meet.

Apparently, Tyson was also struck by Fricker's appearance. As she recalled many years later, "I was

*A teenage Sylvia Fricker near her home town of Chatham, Ont.*

wearing brown Bermuda shorts and one of those Yugoslavian embroidered blouses, which I had pinched from the costumes of the Chatham Little Theatre. Although that doesn't seem so peculiar today, Ian told me, years later, that it really blew his mind." Tyson remembers it differently—she was the one who had a crush on him. Whatever the dynamic of that first meeting, there was clearly a chemistry between the two.

Fricker went home to Chatham, full of plans to move to Toronto permanently and definitely to hook up with that handsome folk singer. But by the time she moved there in the fall of '59, she'd missed him. Tyson had headed out west to ride in a rodeo. Seizing her bull by the horns, Fricker began performing around town on her own. The first place she played was the Clef Club, a small Yorkville coffee house downstairs from a union hall. But soon, she became a regular at a hip new spot known as the Bohemian Embassy.

For some fans, rockabilly died on March 24, 1958, the day Elvis was drafted into the U.S. Army. In fact, the music never did recover from the king's induction. Still, for a while, it seemed like the whole field was left wide open by his departure. Jerry Lee Lewis, Carl Perkins and Johnny Cash—label-mates of Presley's at Sun Records—all stood in line to the throne. So too did Arkansas good ol' boys Conway Twitty and Ronnie Hawkins. Both were called over to Sun's Memphis studios to audition, although neither was signed.

Casting about for new opportunities, Hawkins learned from Twitty that Canada was still virgin territory for rockabilly. Twitty had just come back raving about all the places to play and money to be made. He even gave Hawkins the name of his Canadian booking agent: Harold Kudlets. Hawkins already had three musicians willing and ready to go. He just needed a drummer, and a skinny, blond-haired sixteen-year-old named Levon Helm was suggested. Although he didn't even have his own set of drums, Hawkins recognized instantly that the kid had as much blues as bluegrass coursing through his veins. Blessed with an innate sense of rhythm, Helm was in. But first, Hawkins had to convince Helm's sceptical dad who warned that Canada was a dangerous place, with "ten months of winter and two of bad sledding."

Heading north in a '55 Chevy with a double bass

**Yonge Street was a pearl in the city's oyster just waiting to be picked**

strapped to the roof, the Ron Hawkins Quartet made their Canadian debut at the Golden Rail club in Hamilton, Ontario, one night that spring. After a shaky start, the band packed the club with nearly a hundred rockabilly-starved fans by the end of the week—with line-ups outside. Another booking by Kudlets, at London, Ontario's Brass Rail, took them from $450 to $550 a week, and word spread about this raucous band from the south. By the time they rolled into Toronto the following week, to play at the Le Coq D'Or on Yonge Street, Hawkins and his boys were commanding a dizzying $700 for six nights' work.

To a hungry rockabilly rascal like Hawkins, Toronto's Yonge Street was a pearl in the city's oyster just waiting to be picked. The Strip, as the section of Yonge from Dundas to Gerrard was known, was a blaze of neon-lit bars. The Le Coq D'Or (always called *the* Le Coq D'Or by locals) stood next to the venerable Edison Hotel, while the Zanzibar and Bermuda taverns were just a little way up the street. But all these clubs featured country music. And the Brown Derby, on the corner of Dundas, had Vegas-style variety shows complete with comedians. That made the freewheeling Southern sound that Hawkins brought to town unique. "We were exotic," Helm admitted, "playing the most uninhibited, wildest rock and roll that Torontonians had ever heard."

The Strip was about as racy as Toronto got in the late 1950s. But it suited Hawkins just fine since it offered good crowds, good pay and plenty of prestige. The singer also liked the fact that the bars were ruled by the government-run Liquor Control Board. "That

*For Ronnie Hawkins, Yonge Street's Le Coq D'Or became home*

made it very professional and we got paid every week," he explains. "You didn't have to fight or lose money. With the honky-tonks in the States, you were often at their mercy. It was always some gangster who owned it but somebody else who operated it." Hawkins resolved to come back with his band, renamed the Hawks, as soon as possible.

Tyson returned from his rodeo out west to find coffee houses "sprouting like mushrooms" all around the neighbourhood known as Yorkville. Originally a prosperous village that lay to the north of Bloor Street, Yorkville had been annexed by the city in 1883. By 1960, entrepreneurs had begun moving into the area bounded by Yonge and Avenue Road after being pushed out of a bohemian district to the south. The first coffee houses were opened by English and German immigrants, who set up shop in Victorian build-

> **Coffee houses were "sprouting like mushrooms" all around Yorkville**

ings alongside their working-class residents. Werner Graeber opened the 71 Club, while John McHugh launched the Half Beat. Tyson, who met McHugh and found that they shared a taste for jazz and Goon Show–style comedy, eventually shared an apartment with the eccentric ex-RAF pilot.

Since the closest thing to entertainment initially offered at the Half Beat was chess, Tyson made his Yorkville debut at the Village Corner, a folk hot spot a short walk up Avenue Road. The Corner was an unassuming looking place from the outside, a quaint, two-storey house with a candle in a Chianti bottle flickering in the window. But inside, it was Hipster's Heaven: a smoky room with dark blue walls and a large mural of black slaves being unshackled.

The night that Tyson appeared, the club was full of beatniks all dressed in black. Some sat at tables, others stood in the wings or by the back door. Everyone's attention was fixed on the postage-stamp-size stage, where the handsome Tyson stood and sang. A newspaper account described him as "a clean shaven Vancouverite who performs in tight fitting blue jeans and a freshly laundered sports shirt open at the neck, singing about feudal England, the Great Depression and prison blues with a relaxed and easy manner." Tyson quickly became one of the biggest draws at the Corner.

**CHUM CHART TOP TEN MARCH 21, 1960**

*Beatnik Fly*
Johnny & the Hurricanes

*He'll Have to Go*
Jim Reeves

*Wild One/Little Bitty Girl*
Bobby Rydell

*Puppy Love/Adam & Eve*
Paul Anka

*Harbour Lights/Sleepy Lagoon*
The Platters

*Theme from a Summer Place*
Percy Faith

*Sweet Nothin's*
Brenda Lee

*Midnight Special*
Paul Evans

*Mama/Teddy*
Connie Francis

*Beyond the Sea/ That's the Way Love Is*
Bobby Darin

Meanwhile, Fricker was making a name for herself at the Bohemian Embassy, a club south of Yorkville that mixed folk and jazz with poetry and comedy. On many nights, Fricker sang English ballads and Appalachian mountain tunes as the musical break for readings by such writers as Margaret Atwood, Earle Birney, Gwendolyn MacEwen and the "people's poet," Milton Acorn, all of whom debuted their work at the Embassy. "I was the comic relief for all those terribly serious poets," Sylvia now quips.

As it turned out, her first appearance with Tyson wasn't anything to write home about. Fricker got a call from a CBC TV producer who wanted her to appear in a segment he was shooting at the First Floor Club. Excited, she jumped at the chance. Then Fricker, who was not yet a member of the musicians' union, discovered that union rules prevented her from accompanying herself. She called Tyson, who came down and played guitar and sang with her. It wasn't the breakthrough either of them hoped for.

But even then there were signs of the magic that was to follow—something about the way Fricker's voice blended with Tyson's to produce a sound that was warm and gentle, yet strangely unsettling, like a

Fricker and Tyson at the Village Corner

chinook in the dead of winter. It was a sound that was altogether impossible to ignore and quite unique within folk music at the time. Their song selection was equally striking. They were the first on the scene to perform traditional Canadian songs, a move that influenced others to do the same. One of the first songs they performed was "Mary Anne," an aching ode to love, collected from a Canadian trapper by musicologist Edith Fowke. Another number learned from Fowke's book *Canada in Song* was the melancholic French-Canadian ballad "Un Canadien Errant."

Tyson and Fricker began honing their sound, trying new harmonies and arrangements and adding Fricker's distinctive autoharp sound to Tyson's guitar. According to Sylvia, the secret to their success was simply hard work. "We did something that nobody else on the local folk scene did—we rehearsed," she says with a laugh. "In terms of what else was around, we were a pretty polished act." Before long, the two were the big-ticket attraction in the new, prospering coffee houses, working steadily and earning as much as $20 a night.

Robbie Robertson was a street kid who kept his eyes and ears wide open. Born to a Jewish gambler and a Mohican woman, he spent his youth in the twin worlds of downtown Toronto and the Six Nations Reserve near Brantford, Ontario. When his father deserted the family, Robertson began spending summers at the reserve, hanging out with his cousins.

*An early Hawkins album, featuring two of Robbie Robertson's first songs*

There, he learned the customs of his mother's people and got his first exposure to music, a "rural" style, he says, played on guitars, fiddles and mandolins. "It was the first time I'd heard music up close and I was really impressed," Robertson recalls. "I wanted some of it."

When he was in Toronto, the teenage Robertson soaked up music whenever he could—even late at night, listening to blues on radio station WLAC out of Nashville. He was already familiar with the sounds of Ronnie Hawkins and his band, having heard their first singles including an early version of "Bo Diddley," recorded at a tiny studio on Toronto's Kingston Road. And he could sense the excitement of their stage show as he hung around the Le Coq D'Or's entrance, catching glimpses of the musicians as the club's doors opened and listening to the music filtering out.

When he finally got to experience his musical heroes up close, opening for them at the Dixie Plaza as a member of The Suedes, Robertson couldn't believe his eyes and ears. The Hawks, he said, "played the fastest, most violent rock and roll I'd ever heard. It was exciting and exploding with dynamics. The solos would get *really* loud. Ronnie would come in and growl, then it would get quiet, then fast and loud again. It was these cool-looking guys doing this primitive music faster and more violent than anybody, with overwhelming power."

From then on, Robertson dreamed of becoming a Hawk. He loved everything about the band, right down to the look of their black mohair suits. His dream nearly turned into reality the day fellow Suede Scott Cushnie got a call from Hawkins at Robertson's mother's house where Cushnie was staying. Hawkins wanted Cushnie to play keyboards and asked him to come out to London, Ontario, where he was playing at the Brass Rail. On a whim, Cushnie took Robertson and Suede drummer Pete Derimigis along with him—hitch-hiking over 250 kilometres in the dead of winter. Their giddy plan was for all three Suedes to become Hawks. "I told Ronnie, 'If you want me, you have to take my pals as well because we're a team,'" a chuckling Cushnie now recalls. "But Ronnie said, 'Sorry, son, all's I needs is a piano player.'" Cushnie turned down the gig. In 20-below temperatures, the three Suedes hitch-hiked back to Toronto with nothing more than a case of frostbite to show for their troubles.

Cushnie eventually did join the Hawks, albeit briefly, and immediately set to work promoting Robertson's talent. Although Hawkins had already recorded two of Robertson's songs—"Hey Boba Lu" and "Someone Like You"—for his *Mr. Dynamo* album, he was sceptical of the kid's playing abilities. But when Hawkins needed a bassist during a tour of Arkansas, Cushnie urged him to consider his friend. "Can he play bass?" Hawkins wanted to know. "Sure he can," insisted Cushnie. "OK, let me think about it," said Hawkins. Cushnie rushed into the next room and immediately phoned Robertson, telling him to borrow Suede bassist Pete Traynor's instrument and start practising every Hawkins tune he knew. When Robertson finally got the call to go south, he had to pawn his Fender Telecaster for bus fare.

**CHUM CHART TOP TEN JULY 9, 1962**

*Roses Are Red*
Bobby Vinton

*Sealed with a Kiss*
Brian Hyland

*Remember Me (I'm the One)*
Gord Lightfoot

*I Can't Stop Loving You/ Born to Lose*
Ray Charles

*Palisades Park*
Freddy Cannon

*Limbo Rock*
The Champs

*Girls Girls Girls*
Eddie Hodges

*Speedy Gonzalez*
Pat Boone

*Little Red Rented Rowboat*
Joe Dowell

*Theme from "Dr. Kildare"*
Richard Chamberlain

As Robertson arrived in Arkansas, Gordon Lightfoot was returning from his music studies in California. Equipped now with composing and sight-reading skills, Lightfoot was determined to make it as a professional musician. With the blessing of his parents, he left Orillia for Toronto in an old Pontiac his father had bought for him. His dad also lined him up a teller's job at the Royal Bank which paid a weekly wage of $40. Lightfoot figured that handling other people's money during the day would enable him to pursue his music activities at night.

Initially, Lightfoot moonlighted at whatever music job came his way: freelance orchestrating for the CBC, back-up singing for demo recordings, arranging and producing commercial jingles. He even sang part-time in a group called The Gino Silvi Singers, which did some TV and jingle work, and, under the pseudonym

Charles Sullivan, played drums in a jazz revue called "Up Tempo '60."

But Lightfoot's financial fortunes rose in 1960 when he joined the chorus line of CBC TV's "Country Hoedown," a show starring, among others, a young Tommy Hunter. Second only to "Hockey Night in Canada" in popularity, "Country Hoedown" paid Lightfoot $100 a week as a dancing member of the show's Singing Swinging Eight—enough to quit his bank teller's job. But music school had not taught him to square dance, and the show's crew soon nicknamed him Gord Leadfoot. "I was the one who was always doin' a do-si-do instead of an allemande right," he once admitted. "The only reason they kept me was I was so bloody good at sight-reading."

Although he loved country music, what he heard on "Hoedown" provided little inspiration. Folk music, on the other hand, seemed to offer something fresh. He discovered traditional styles from listening to the *At Carnegie Hall* album by The Weavers, which also spurred him to buy a good guitar. Then one night at the Village Corner, Lightfoot heard Ian & Sylvia perform Merle Travis's coal-mining lament "Dark as a Dungeon" for the first time and a light bulb went on in his head. "When I saw that combination of folk and

country music," he said later, "I knew it was what I had been looking for. It was like seeing the light of day."

*opposite:*
*Gord "Leadfoot" (far right): is that do-si-do, or allemande right?*

*left:*
*Country Hoedown's Singing Swinging Eight (Tommy Hunter is back row, centre)*

Tyson and Fricker spent much of 1960 perfecting what Ian called their "strange duo sound." It was, indeed, the eerie combination of their distinctive voices—Tyson's warm and smooth as leather, Fricker's cool as the night air—that set them apart. When blended together, they produced a chilling effect, soaring joyously one moment and falling, wounded like doves, the next. And always their rich harmonies gave the impression that there were more than two voices at work. The secret to their sound, according to Tyson, was Sylvia's "unique concept of harmony." He added: "I couldn't sing harmony, and on the occasions I tried, I was out of tune. Right to the end, she was singing harmony to my lead, and whenever we tried it the other way around, it didn't work."

The couple sang with such a passion that few listeners doubted their convictions. "What counts with us," Tyson explained at the time, "is how emotionally involved we get with a song. First, of course, there is the learning period of years of the various traditions; but then each song becomes personal. Whether it's blues or an English ballad, we sing it for a couple of months or more. And then, unless we've really become wrapped up in the song, we discard it."

Quickly Tyson and Fricker found themselves in high demand. After packing the L-shaped Village Corner space, the pair moved to other stages as more coffee houses opened in and around Yorkville. Soon, they were attracting line-ups at larger venues like the Purple Onion as well. "People used to flock to hear them sing night after night," says the Onion's Sam Gutmacher, who now owns a copy shop in north Toronto. "No one ever seemed to get bored of them. And people liked the idea of seeing a couple perform. They thought it was very romantic."

Stepping off a Greyhound bus, Robertson stood by the banks of the Mississippi River and breathed in his exotic surroundings. Here he was, a sixteen-year-old Canadian boy in a strange new world, and his senses were working overtime. "There wasn't anything like it in Toronto," he recalled. "It smelled different and moved different. The people talked and dressed different. And the air was filled with thick and funky music." Robertson, who walked around wide-eyed and slack-jawed most of the time, was intoxicated.

*Ian & Sylvia: warm and gentle, like a chinook in the dead of winter*

His initiation into the Hawks was a trial by fire. While Hawkins and Helm flew to England for a TV appearance, they left Robertson in Arkansas to take a crash course in bass playing, with Cushnie and Hawk guitarist Fred Carter as his tutors. Hawkins was going to judge the new student when he got back. Robertson began practising day and night, dissecting Howlin' Wolf records and playing bass lines until his fingers were rock hard. When Hawkins and Helm returned, the head Hawk couldn't believe the kid's progress. "Robbie had a brain like a sponge and soaked everything up," recalls Hawkins. The kid was in.

Meanwhile, Robertson received a cultural tour of West Helena, a blues-rich town in central Arkansas, with Helm as his guide. Staying with the drummer's family, Robertson ate dishes with names he'd never heard of and listened to tall tales from Helm's relatives, an eccentric cast of characters of all ages. Later, he told Helm how much Arkansas had affected him. "I'd hear something at night," Robertson explained, "and not know whether it was an animal, a harmonica or a train. But it sounded like music to me." From that

*Little Caesar & the Consuls, one of the city's earliest rhythm-and-blues bands*

day on, vivid memories of the American South would colour the best of Robertson's songwriting.

With his youngest recruit now suitably groomed, Hawkins returned to Canada to seek his fortune. His decision deeply angered Morris Levy of New York's Roulette Records, who had signed the singer and believed he was destined for rock 'n' roll greatness. "You can't go back to Canada!" Levy shouted at Hawkins, Helm recalled. "You've got it all to yourself. Elvis is in the fuckin' army, and you're better than him anyway, now. Buddy Holly, Eddie Cochran—dead. There's a vacuum here, and you're the only one around who can take advantage of it. You're on the goddam verge! You can't just vanish on me."

But Hawkins had already made up his mind. He loved Canada. He'd built up a lucrative circuit in southern Ontario and Quebec and could work every night of the week if he wanted. Why would he want to give that up?

With the drinking age twenty-one, Toronto's bars only catered to older bands and an older clientele. Yet, the city's suburbs were full of teenagers with raging hormones, all desperately craving the latest sounds. Teen dances were the obvious solution. Held at high schools, community centres and hockey arenas around town, these sock hops not only satisfied pubescent urges for mixed company, but provided aspiring bands with much-needed stages to perform on. Where else did a group go once it had graduated from the garage or the rec room?

One of the first people to capitalize on the budding Toronto teen market was Ron Scribner, who was just eighteen himself when he began booking bands in 1960 for dances at his high school, sponsored by the local YMCA. Among the first groups he hired was Robbie Lane & the Disciples, one of the many bands influenced by Hawkins's group that later went on to record hits of their own.

Scribner's teen dances proved so successful that soon he was running his own shows, attracting large crowds to places like Masaryk Hall, Crang Plaza and the Balmy Beach Canoe Club. A local circuit developed that enabled bands to work every weekend and hone their skills. Scribner soon found himself in constant demand as a booking agent for the bands. He remembers how it happened. Little Caesar & the Consuls were one of the top acts at the teen dances, fetching as much as $75 for a night's work. Bruce Morshead (aka Little Caesar) had been handling his band's booking, but was finding it too time-consuming. Says Scribner, later Canada's first rock booking agent, "With me doing it, they could get $90 for a show which, even after my ten percent, was a better deal for them. It was one of those win-win situations."

The teen dance circuit became a breeding ground for local talent, an opportunity for young musicians to learn to play their instruments in front of a large audience. Hawkins and the Hawks provided a kind of schooling themselves whenever they appeared at Bloor Street's Concord Tavern. Their Saturday matinée performances drew budding musicians eager to study the stage moves and musical repertoire of what was then the city's top professional band. The kids sat in the non-alcoholic section where, for the cost of a Coke and a plate of fries, they could watch their heroes. Of particular interest was Robertson—himself a teenager—who was already on his way to becoming a guitar legend.

By the spring of '61, Ian & Sylvia were packing Yorkville's largest coffee houses. Ed Cowan, a friend who was booking concerts in town, provided a crucial connection—he introduced Tyson and Fricker to Pete Seeger before his appearance at Massey Hall. Seeger, a founding member of The Weavers and a folk legend, was impressed by the couple's knowledge of Canadian folk songs. During his show, he asked the couple to come up and sing a few of their songs. The crowd loved them. Suddenly, it was apparent that Ian & Sylvia needed to find a bigger stage for themselves. That meant heading to New York and Greenwich Village.

But before any migration plans were firmed up, Tyson and Fricker got wind of a plan to stage the first Canadian folk festival later that summer. It was the brainchild of Ruth Jones, a folk enthusiast from Lightfoot's home town, Orillia. The idea for the festival quickly gathered steam, drawing in a wide range of folkies, including Tyson and Fricker themselves, who all agreed that Canada needed something like the Newport Folk Festival. During meetings at the Clef Club, the working group mapped out plans for an event to take place during August in picturesque Orillia. The founding manifesto stated that an annual festival could help folk singers "make a career in Canada instead of having first to be recognized in the States." The mission statement added earnestly: "We also want to make the people of Canada familiar with their own folk songs." All that was left was to select a name. They chose Stephen Leacock's fictional name for Orillia—Mariposa.

## DISCS TO DISCOVER

*Greatest Hits* (2 CD set): Ian & Sylvia (Vanguard, 1970)

*The Roulette Years* (2 CD set): Ronnie Hawkins & the Hawks (Sequel, 1994)

*Made in Canada: Our Rock 'n' Roll History, Vol. 1, The Early Years* (1960→): Various artists (BMG, 1990)

# 3

# Hipsters & Hootenannies

Sitting in neatly arranged rows of canvas chairs, a buttoned-down crowd of 2,000 watched the inaugural Mariposa unfold one August weekend in 1961. The audience, mostly university students from Toronto, had travelled to Orillia on the shores of Lake Couchiching to hear an all-Canadian line-up headed by Fricker and Tyson, who'd also donated his artistic skills to create the stylized orange sun that dominated the festival's poster. On the opening Friday night, folk fans saw musicians ranging from Vancouver duo Alan McRae and Peter Wyborn to Newfoundland balladeer Omar Blondahl perform on a canopied, medieval-style stage. Afterwards, Orillia's main drag became a sea of bobbing crew-cuts and swirling summer dresses, as festival-goers partied at a "street jamboree" featuring bluegrass pickers The York County Boys. Townsfolk were not amused when a gaggle of beer drinkers spent half the night serenading the park's statue of Samuel de Champlain.

*The inaugural Mariposa Folk Festival, featuring an all-Canadian line-up*

As musically purist as Orillia was conservative, the first Mariposa tended to favour performers who adhered either to strictly traditional folk repertoires or to leftist singalongs, or both. That agenda excluded more commercial folk acts like The Two Tones, a duo made up of Orillia homeboys Gord Lightfoot and his barbershop singing buddy Terry Whelan. But it meant that, along with Ian & Sylvia, the stage was given over to The Travellers and Bonnie Dobson, two acts that got their start at a holiday camp for lefties. Located on a hundred acres west of Toronto, Camp Nivelt attracted families with ties to labour groups or Canada's Communist Party. When Pete Seeger visited there in 1952, he urged some of his Canadian "fellow travellers" to put together a folk group along the lines of his Weavers to popularize labour and activist songs. The Travellers, led by Sid Dolgay, scored a national hit when they Canadianized Woody Guthrie's "This Land Is Your Land" with such patriotic lines as "from Bonavista to Vancouver Island."

Bonnie Dobson had been a children's counsellor at Nivelt. But by 1961, the twenty-year-old Dobson was a rising folk star, thanks to her ballad "Morning Dew," a song that perfectly captured the fears of the new atomic age. The product of a sleepless night, "Morning Dew" came to Dobson after she watched the apocalyptic film *On the Beach*. The lyrics, she explains, "take the form of a conversation between the last man and woman, one trying to comfort the other while knowing there's absolutely nothing left." Although one reviewer pronounced it a "mournful dirge" after Dobson debuted it at Mariposa, "Dew" has enjoyed a lasting resonance. Recorded versions of the song by such artists as Jeff Beck, Lulu, Long John Baldry and, especially, the Grateful Dead—who made it a Deadhead favourite—have provided Dobson with substantial royalties.

Zal Yanovsky and Sharon Trostin, both red-diaper babies, were two other Nivelt campers who went on to musical fame: Yanovsky as a member of The Lovin' Spoonful and Trostin as Sharon Hampson, of preschool pop stars Sharon, Lois & Bram. Hampson remembers Friday nights at Nivelt always involved campfire hootenannies, sometimes with illustrious guests like Phil Ochs. Once, Hampson recalls, Pete Seeger performed a chain-gang song using an axe which he swung down forcefully as he sang. "Afterwards," she says, "we all ran around gathering up wood chips for him to autograph."

*Red-diaper baby Sharon Trostin, a folkie who found fame with preschool pop stars Sharon, Lois & Bram*

While Mariposa gave some folk musicians their biggest exposure to date, Hawkins was about to start doing his own bit to promote Canadian talent. As successive American Hawks began defecting south, returning to family and warmer temperatures, Hawkins was faced with having to find replacements. He'd lucked out with Robertson, who proved such a fast learner that he was soon able to move from bass to lead guitar, his first love. As for Cushnie, he would have gladly kept the key-

*Rick Danko, Richard Manuel, Hawkins, Levon Helm, Robertson, Garth Hudson*

boardist on had he not contracted a dose of the clap and become too weak to tour. With just Helm and Robertson as his steady Hawks, the indefatigable bandleader began casting about for new recruits.

Prospective band members had to meet specific criteria, as laid down by the head Hawk. "Naturally, they had to be able to either sing or play," explains Hawkins. "But just as important was how they looked. I tended to pick good-looking cats and made sure they were well dressed and could move with the ladies. That was the key. Part of their job was mixing and flirting with the girls in between sets. If you could get fifty girls hitting on the band, then you could get 250 guys hitting on the girls. It was simple mathematics."

By late 1961, Hawkins had found three musicians from across southern Ontario who fit the bill. First came Simcoe's Rick Danko, a handsome farm boy who sang sweet harmony. Although Danko couldn't yet play bass, Hawkins knew that would come with time.

Richard Manuel from Stratford was similarly recruited, not so much for his piano-playing ability as for his voice. When Hawkins heard Manuel sing with his band, The Rockin' Revols, he was immediately struck by his melancholic, Ray Charles–style vocals. London's Garth Hudson was the most surprising addition of all—a classically trained jazz pianist whose taste leaned more towards Bach and Brubeck than rockabilly. Still, Hawkins knew genius when he heard it.

Although a somewhat motley group, they all had potential—or POE-ten-shul, as Hawkins would say in his Southern drawl. To get them outfitted, he took the group to Lou Myles, the neighbourhood tailor, whose shop was just a few doors up from the Le Coq D'Or. Hawkins had matching black mohair suits made for each of the five band members. Dressed to kill, the band was now ready for Yonge Street.

Catering to all their needs, the Strip quickly became the Hawks' hang-out. They lived in one of the cheap hotels on Jarvis Street, and Hawkins and his boys usually ate at Tops, a greasy spoon full of a colourful assortment of late-night characters. "They were all guys who knew how to play the angles," recalls Hawkins. "They must've idolized Al Capone, or something, because they all had names like Squeaker, Dukie and Basher." Those wiseguys, or "rounders," became some of the Hawks' most hardcore fans at the Le Coq D'Or. The most dangerous among them, including hoods and thieves, appointed themselves the band's unofficial bodyguards. "You wouldn't want to lie to them or slap them or anything," laughs Hawkins, "but we were on the good side of most of them. If somebody got out of line and did something to the band, the rounders would take care of it. We were protected real good."

Hawkins worked his musicians hard, often having them practise until dawn after finishing playing at 1 a.m. With Hudson as their tutor and Hawkins as their coach in matters of behaviour and appearance, the Hawks quickly became the most sought-after act on the Strip. Their shows, legendary displays of musical pyrotechnics and physical gymnastics, were soon the talk of the town. Robertson, now using two banjo strings to get a more bluesy sound (a trick he'd learned from watching his predecessor, Fred Carter), had begun pulling notes from his guitar that many hadn't thought possible. Hudson was extracting eerie sounds out of his Lowrey organ, while Helm, Danko and Manuel were blending their voices in gorgeous three-part harmony. Hawkins, when he wasn't yelping or growling, was doing the splits and even backflips with wild abandon. Not surprisingly, he quickly earned the prefix "Rompin'." Says Hawkins, "I had the monkey act and I had a band that could play. We were new, we looked sharp and it worked."

Hawkins was right at home on Yonge Street—the proverbial big fish in a little pond. To him, Canada was "the Promised Land."

**CHUM CHART TOP TEN MAY 20, 1963**

*Summer Holiday/ Dancing Shoes*
Cliff Richard

*Surfin' USA/Shut Down*
Beach Boys

*Bachelor Boy*
Cliff Richard

*Two Faces Have I*
Lou Christie

*If You Wanna Be Happy*
Jimmy Soul

*I Love You Because*
Al Martino

*Da Doo Ron Ron*
The Crystals

*Bo Diddley*
Ronnie Hawkins

*Foolish Little Girl*
The Shirelles

*I Will Follow Him*
Little Peggy March

Unlike Hawkins, Ian & Sylvia weren't happy with the small pond; they were ready for larger waters. To the Canadian folk duo, the Big Apple was the big deal; Greenwich Village promised prestigious coffee-house bookings and record labels offered potentially lucrative recording deals. Armed with a four-song demo tape, Tyson and Fricker flew to New York in the fall of '61 full of hopes of securing both.

Wasting no time, the pair got an appointment to

see Harold Leventhal, manager of Pete Seeger and head of Folkways Records. Leventhal liked their sound, but his label was more interested in strictly traditional material by the likes of Seeger and the dulcimer-playing Jean Ritchie. They might do better with Albert Grossman, then managing folk singer Odetta, and putting together a trio that would find fame as Peter, Paul & Mary. In fact, Grossman loved Ian & Sylvia and wanted to sign the pair to a management deal right away. He boasted that he could get them a recording contract with the large, commercial Warner Brothers label. Tyson and Fricker demurred. They preferred the smaller Vanguard Records, home of The Weavers, Odetta and Joan Baez. "Albert tried very hard to talk us out of it," recalls Sylvia, "but we were adamant. We thought Vanguard was the label of honesty and integrity."

The deal was done. Ian & Sylvia signed with Vanguard and plans were made to record the duo's first album. To celebrate, Grossman took Fricker and

*Ian & Sylvia, with an unidentified banjo picker, at Mariposa*

Tyson for a night out in Greenwich Village, which was Yorkville magnified several times over, with dozens of coffee houses—the Gaslight, the Bitter End and Cafe Wha?, to name a few—lining MacDougal and other streets south of Washington Square Park. The premier Village nightspot was Gerde's Folk City, housed in a six-storey brownstone about a mile to the east. It was there that Grossman lined up his Canadian visitors to do a guest set. Recalls Ed Cowan, a Mariposa organizer who accompanied the pair to New York, "Sylvia went up and did a great blues song because she used to sing blues extremely well. Then she and Ian did several songs together and blew everyone away." Added Cowan, "It was obvious then that they were going to do well in America."

Before they left Gerde's that night, Tyson and Fricker met a young folk singer with a Huck Finn cap and a tattered corduroy jacket who mumbled when he spoke. Although Grossman mentioned that he was one of the Village's most promising poets, Ian & Sylvia were unimpressed. He seemed little more than a scruffy bum. That bum was Bob Dylan.

David Clayton-Thomas had only $20, some scars and a battered old guitar to show for himself when he walked out of Millbrook maximum security prison near Peterborough, Ontario, in the spring of 1962. The troubled son of a hydro worker, English-born Clayton-Thomas had actually come into the world as David Henry Thomsett. Growing up in the Toronto suburb of Willowdale, he left home at fifteen and moved like a vagabond from job to job. Trouble started when he stole a car in Hull, Quebec, and drove back to Ontario, where he was picked up by the cops near Barrie, north of Toronto.

For the next four years, he was in and out of Ontario's reformatories and prisons, including

Toronto's infamous Don Jail, the Guelph Reformatory and Burwash Industrial Farm. Clayton-Thomas was a bad ass. Big and brawny, he began fighting at the least provocation, developing what observers called an almost pathological paranoia. One of his stints in jail was for assaulting a police officer, another for intimidating a Crown witness. "My father didn't understand me at all," he once told a reporter, by way of explaining his problems, "but then neither did I. At that age, you leave the nest and rebel against everything and my parents were the most convenient target."

*Sylvia at Mariposa: not content with the small pond*

While in Burwash, spending ninety days in solitary confinement, Clayton-Thomas started singing to keep himself sane. There, in the cramped quarters, his voice echoed against the cold tiles. The other inmates, in the yard outside his window, obviously liked what they heard because they clapped along. Then, with a guitar loaned to him by a young Ojibway Indian, he learned enough chords to accompany himself. When he walked out of Millbrook for good, Clayton-Thomas headed straight for Yonge Street.

Just as the Hawks were beginning to take flight musically, Hawkins seemed more ready to settle down. In March 15, 1962, he married Wanda Nagurski, a former teenage beauty contestant whom he'd met in the "Coke-and-fries side" of the Concord. And he signed a contract to become the house act at the Le Coq D'Or, which meant stability for a twenty-seven-year-old newly-wed with family plans. For the band, however, it meant having to accept more of a routine. And along with routine came rules.

**CHUM CHART TOP TEN JUNE 24, 1963**

*Charlena*
Richie Knight & the Mid-Knights

*It's My Party*
Lesley Gore

*Indian Giver*
Bobby Curtola

*String Along*
Rick Nelson

*Blue on Blue*
Bobby Vinton

*Swinging on a Star*
Big Dee Irwin & Little Eva

*Summer Holiday/Dancing*
Cliff Richard

*On Top of Spaghetti*
Tom Glazer

*Surfin' USA/Shut Down*
Beach Boys

*First Quarrel*
Paul & Paula

There had always been rules in Hawkins's band—rules about women, personal habits, even hygiene. But now the head Hawk was actually *enforcing* them. Hell, he was even handing out fines to those who broke them. Although he loved his booze, Hawkins never drank during a performance and wouldn't allow his band to either. Cigarettes, as well, could only be smoked off-stage. A non-smoker himself, Hawkins absolutely forbade smoking in his car. The stories are legion about the fights over that rule being broken while on tour. Hawkins once offered to pay bonuses to get them to quit smoking, which resulted in a brief raisin-eating fad. But then he had to offer bonuses for them to quit raisins because they were messing up the upholstery in his beloved Cadillac.

Needless to say, pot, which Robertson and the others were starting to experiment with at the time, was officially off limits. Hawkins took a hard line against marijuana use. It'll only bring trouble, he said. Once, he'd discovered the group in the Le Coq D'Or dressing room, he claims, listening to Ray Charles at about 16 r.p.m. with an unusual scent in the air. They'd stuffed a towel under the door to hide the odour. Hawkins fined them big time for that one. He did allow the use of the little diet pills known as "orange hearts," which, although they were mild amphetamines, could be purchased over the counter at drug stores.

*Lightfoot's first album, recorded with barber-shop singing buddy, Terry Whelan*

One night, Hawkins used those orange hearts to trick Danko into playing lead guitar. Robertson was too sick to perform, and seeing that Danko clearly lacked the confidence to fill in for him, Dr. Hawkins simply prescribed him a couple of the orange pills—only what he gave him were two M & M candies with the lettering rubbed off. Danko went on to deliver a powerful performance. Chuckles Hawkins, "He thought he had taken the most powerful stimulant known to man, and there he was doing things he ain't never done in his life."

The Hawks were allowed girlfriends, as long as they stayed well away from the clubs. Their presence conflicted with the band's role as bait for female customers. Worse, they interfered with the clubs' financial operations. Explains Hawkins: "All their girlfriends would come in on Friday and Saturday nights and take up the tables right in front of the stage—the best seats in the house. The table loses money and, before you know it, the club owners and managers are on my case. I couldn't deal with that."

It was the beginning of the end of Hawkins's association with his promising protégés.

The purists' grip on Mariposa tightened with the second festival. Tried-and-true traditionalists like Ian & Sylvia, The Travellers and Quebec fiddler Jean Carignan all returned to dominate the Orillia program. But one commercial act slipped through the cracks. Maybe it was because they were home-town favourites, or perhaps because they now boasted an album, but no one was happier than Gord Lightfoot when his Two Tones joined the Mariposa '62 line-up.

Others were not as lucky. Alan McRae, who'd performed at the first festival in a duo, was snubbed when he returned as a member of The Chanteclairs. With their spiffy tuxedos and polished, supper-club repertoire of international folk tunes, the trio was deemed squaresville by Mariposa's blue-jeaned arbiters of cool. "They always felt that a song should be sung the way it was done 300 years ago," complains ex-Chanteclair Klaas Van Graft, now a landscape architect. "We found that very limiting."

Similarly, when Denny Doherty's group The Colonials arrived from Halifax that summer, they were turned away by Mariposa—despite having landed a major deal with New York's Epic Records. According to Doherty, it was a clear case of snobbery about his group's success as a bar-room act, making a good deal more money than their coffee-house counterparts. "We were way too successful for the Appalachian-nose-flute types or the hammered-dulcimer-with-a-feather types," deadpans Doherty. "Plus, we weren't

**This trio was deemed squaresville by Mariposa's blue-jeaned arbiters of cool**

performing Canadian folk songs, which was a huge faux pas. But mostly, there was a faction that resented us simply because we weren't starving artists."

Ironically, by the fall, the festival's favourite folk couple wasn't starving either. Following their appearances at Mariposa and Newport, Ian & Sylvia's self-titled debut album was released to critical acclaim. In particular, *The New York Times* praised the pair for their harmonies and repertoire, which included the traditional "Un Canadien Errant" and "Pride of Petrovar," by Yorkville folk singer Jim McCarthy. Suddenly, Ian & Sylvia were in heavy demand on the U.S. college tour circuit, earning a staggering $400 a week.

*"This little sucker's going to revolutionize the music business," Tyson claimed*

David Wiffen remembers Tyson striding into the Village Corner one night during the spring of '62, waving an album and announcing, "This little sucker's going to revolutionize the music business." The album was Bob Dylan's self-titled debut. Released in March, six months before Ian & Sylvia's, the album featured several of Dylan's own songs, including "Talkin' New York" and his Guthrie tribute, "Song to Woody." Tyson would soon be proven right. Everything was thrown wide open by Dylan's bold move. Suddenly, songwriting became the new standard for folk music everywhere.

Dylan visited Toronto himself later that year to check out the local scene. His appearance at the Bohemian Embassy one chilly night caused a stir among some of the club's younger, hipper regulars. Others failed to recognize the crown prince of Greenwich Village, or were at least unimpressed by his presence. Dylan had dropped by the club after hearing about its weekly poetry nights. Embassy owner Don Cullen recalls that the folk star, "looking like a kid in a fright wig," came with no intention of performing; he just wanted to sit undisturbed and watch some local poets at work.

But Cullen, who was sitting next to him, says Dylan got all uppity when it was announced that the Embassy would have a poetry contest the following week. "He turned to me and said, 'Hey, man, you can't

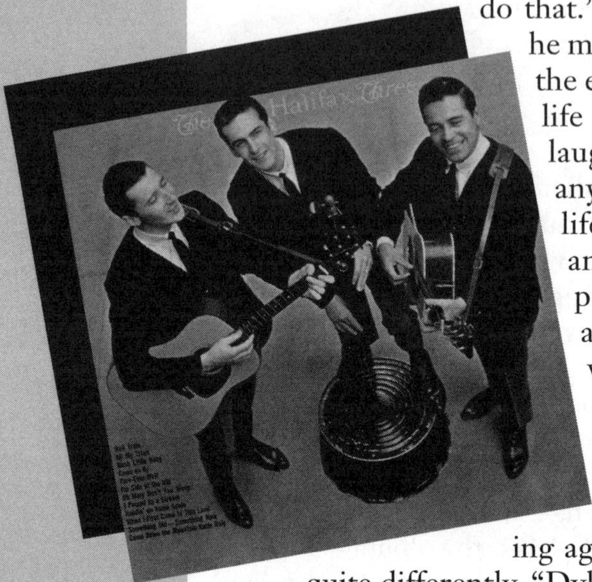

*The Halifax Three's Denny Doherty, Pat LaCroix and Richard Byrne*

do that.' When I asked him what he meant, he said something to the effect of 'Poetry is life, and life is poetry.'" Adds Cullen, laughing, "I'd never heard anything so corny in all my life. I reminded him that the ancient Greeks had held poetry contests back in about 500 B.C., so there was some historical precedent for it. But there was no talking to him."

Mitch Podolak, the Embassy's teenage booking agent, remembers the night quite differently. "Dylan was prepared to get up on-stage," says Podolak, who went on to found the Winnipeg Folk Festival in 1974. "But," he adds, still exasperated at the thought, "the guy running the poetry evenings didn't know who the hell he was and wouldn't let him go on."

Denny Doherty's group returned from their New York recording session with more than they bargained for: a name change. Epic felt that "Colonials" sounded old-fashioned and wanted something more contemporary, along the lines of The Kingston Trio. With two albums in hand, the rechristened Halifax Three landed a high-profile gig on Yonge Street. But in the midst of their engagement, the group lost its accompanist, guitarist Eric Hord. Quickly, Doherty enlisted Zal Yanovsky, then a denizen of Toronto's burgeoning coffee-house scene.

Yanovsky had been scuffling around Yorkville, becoming something of a local legend. Sometimes, he'd be working in the kitchen at the Purple Onion, cracking waitresses up with bizarre jokes. At others, he'd be stealing doughnuts or lending his idiosyncratic guitar style to a Bohemian Embassy jam. But most of the time, he could be found living in a laundromat next to the Dupont Street coffee house, the Gate of Cleve, struggling to make ends meet. Although Yanovsky now denies it, Jackie Burroughs, now one of Canada's foremost actresses, insists it's true. She should know—she was later married to the man, albeit briefly. "I met Zalman when I went in to do my laundry one day and he was asleep in one of the dryers," says Burroughs. "He looked like a deadbeat to me, with long hair, a bad complexion and green teeth. Why would I make something like that up?"

Doherty felt that Yanovsky was a vibrant addition to his group—even if his dishevelled appearance made him look like an unmade bed next to his clean-cut bandmates. "Zal was a crazy kid, a notorious practical joker who played guitar like he had twelve fingers," Doherty recalls. "I think he joined just after he got back from Israel, where he'd been thrown off a kibbutz for driving a tractor into a brick wall. Those sorts of things were always happening to him. But he had an incredible energy."

With Yanovsky in their ranks, the group—now called The Halifax Three Plus One—headed south and joined a touring folk-music show called "The Original Hootenanny USA" with The Journeymen, featuring future Mamas & Papas founder John Phillips. For Doherty, it would prove a fruitful connection.

*The Halifax Three with Zal Yanovsky (top)*

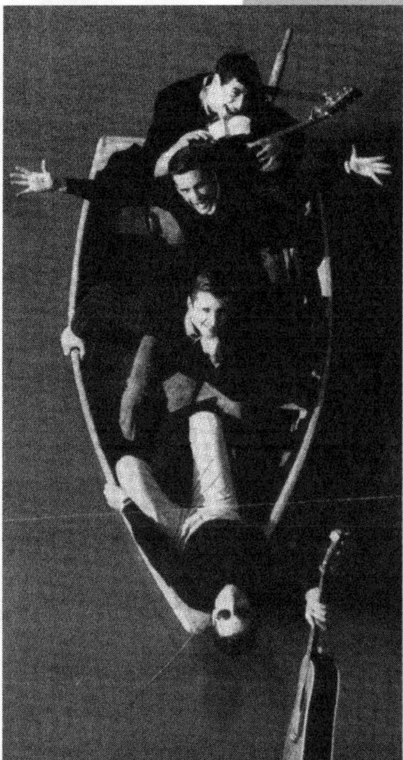

*Neil Young (left) with his Winnipeg band, The Squires*

Neil Young was making musical connections of his own in Winnipeg, where he moved with his mother after his parents divorced. While other boys devoted themselves to hockey or girls, Young spent most of his waking hours talking about guitars, bands and songs and forming a group of his own. He worshipped the British instrumental pop group The Shadows and admired its Winnipeg disciples, Chad Allen & the Reflections, featuring local guitar hero Randy Bachman. Young's musical obsession caused him to fail Grade 10, but that didn't stop him from launching his own Shadows-style band, The Squires, with his friend Ken Koblun. The group made its debut on February 1, 1963, at a Winnipeg-area community centre, playing instrumentals like "Tequila," "Telstar," "Walk Don't Run" and that drum-crazed classic, "Wipeout."

That summer, Young's ambitions took him into a Winnipeg recording studio. By September, The Squires had released a single for a Winnipeg outfit called V Records, featuring two instrumentals written by Young: "The Sultan" and "Aurora." Now a rare piece of vinyl, the record enjoyed considerable airplay on local station CKRC—perhaps because the station also owned the label. It also helped The Squires find regular work at community centre dances and at the Cellar, a seedy downtown club. Young was soon able to purchase a 1948 Buick Roadmaster hearse—affectionately nicknamed Mortimer—to transport the band and its equipment around. Perversely, funeral parlour vehicles would become a weakness for the budding musician.

Gordon Lightfoot wasn't thrilled about working on "Country Hoedown," but the experience did lead to other work. With the help of Art Snider, who had produced the *Two Tones at the Village Corner* album, Lightfoot was hired to emcee eight episodes of "The

**Perversely, funeral parlour vehicles would become a weakness for the budding musician**

Country and Western Show," a corny BBC TV variety series that critics derogatively called "Rancho Vegas." Together with his new wife, an ambitious publicist with the Swedish embassy, Brita Olaisson, Lightfoot flew to England in the summer of 1963 to begin work. Although hardly a gregarious host, the shy, soft-spoken singer stuck it out and tried to make the best of an awkward situation.

Curiously, Lightfoot was unaffected by Beatlemania or the Merseybeat wave of pop music sweeping Britain at the time. But his five-month stint in England did produce one significant result: it got Lightfoot's creative juices flowing. He returned to Canada armed with thirty new songs, a prodigious output for someone who had previously only written a handful, including the promising, Elvis-like "Remember Me (I'm the One Who Loves You)."

Back home, Lightfoot began performing at all the coffee houses springing up around Yorkville and listening to as much folk music as he could, including Ian & Sylvia. Like folk singers everywhere, he paid especially close attention to songs on the new *Freewheelin' Bob Dylan* album, and soon added several of them to his own repertoire of standard folk tunes. Dylan's protest anthems didn't strike a chord with either the politically conservative Lightfoot or Ian & Sylvia. They remained stubbornly non-partisan even at the height of the anti-war movement.

**CHUM CHART TOP TEN OCTOBER 28, 1963**

*Sugar Shack*
Jimmy Gilmer

*Be My Baby*
The Ronettes

*I Can't Stay Mad at You*
Skeeter Davis

*Deep Purple*
Tempo/Stevens

*A Love So Fine*
The Chiffons

*Maria Elena*
Los Indios T.

*Blue Velvet*
Bobby Vinton

*Fools Rush In*
Rick Nelson

*Four Strong Winds*
Ian & Sylvia

*Three Rows Over*
Bobby Curtola

With the birth of his first son, Ron Jr., Hawkins was spending less and less time with the band. Helm recalls that sometimes during week-long engagements, he and the other Hawks would only see their boss at one of the last sets at the end of the week. Fortunately, Hawkins had groomed his group well, training them so that each could take turns performing vocals, with the others adding harmony. Manuel took the high parts, Danko sang the middle, while Helm anchored with the bottom voice. "Three singers on one song," says Helm. "That became our trademark."

Frustration grew during the fall of 1963 as the band evolved musically beyond Hawkins. Money also became an issue when Helm and the others realized that Hawkins was making top dollar on the club circuit—as much as $1,000 for a week at the Le Coq D'Or—while they were still getting paid about $75 a week each. Hawkins's strict rules, meanwhile, only served to rub more salt in the wound. When Danko was caught with a girlfriend one night at the club and threatened with a $50 fine, he refused to pay because she had shown up on her own. Besides, he was already paying a fine for gambling on the job.

After a group meeting in the dressing room, Helm called Hawkins and told him the group was giving two weeks' notice. According to Robertson, Hawkins was intransigent. "Instead of saying, 'Let's go talk about it,' he put his foot down," says Robertson. "Part of it maybe was the heartbreak of the situation—trying to stand his ground."

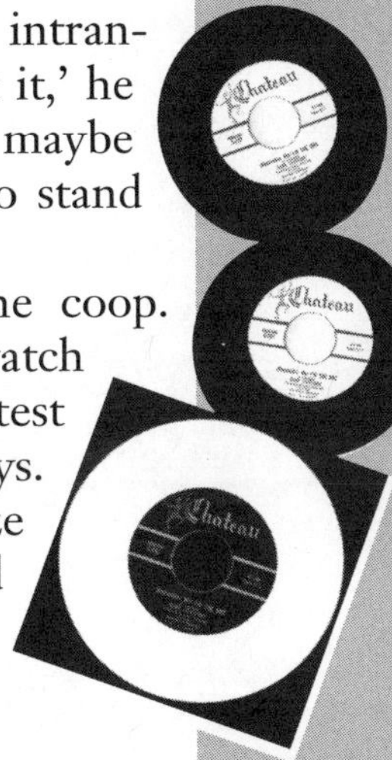

By November, the Hawks had flown the coop. Headmaster Hawkins admits it was hard to watch his best students leave. "It was seeing the greatest band ever put together moving on," he says. "But," he adds quickly, "you've got to realize that they were above bars by then—they had been for two years. If we'd had any kind of management at all, they'd have been on their way to the big time a lot sooner."

Says Robertson: "The band was becoming more knowledgeable about music and the old stuff we were doing was getting on our nerves. We were young and adventurous. We were on a musical journey, and this was the only way to explore it."

## DISCS TO DISCOVER

*Made in Canada: Our Rock 'n' Roll History, Vol. 4, More Great Stuff* (1961→): Various artists (BMG, 1991)

# 4

# ticket to Ride

During the early weeks of 1964, there was clearly something in the air. North America, still in a state of shock over the November assassination of John F. Kennedy, desperately needed a change. It came on February 9 with the televised appearance of an English band on "The Ed Sullivan Show." Time stood still that night as 73 million people across the continent watched The Beatles perform "I Want to Hold Your Hand" and "She Loves You" before a screaming studio audience. Even more tuned in to The Beatles' second appearance on the show the following Sunday. As Bob Dylan was telling everybody, the times were definitely 'a changin'.

But it was business as usual for Ronnie Hawkins. Just five days after his Hawks jumped ship, the Le Coq D'Or's captain recruited the next best-looking, best-playing back-up band he could find—Robbie Lane & the Disciples. Although they normally played rhythm and blues, the Disciples had no trouble joining Hawkins on ribald, rockabilly renditions of "Forty Days" ("the song that took me from the hills and the stills to the pills"), "Mary Lou" and "Who Do You Love"—all road-tested warhorses.

Before the year was out, family man Hawkins had cut a deal with the Le Coq's owners to open a second-floor teenage dance club, the Hawk's Nest, in exchange for free use of the building's third floor. There he held court with an office and a gym, complete with a boxing ring and his own Finnish sauna. The after-hours parties there and Hawkins's high spending in those days (among other things, he purchased a $6,000 king-size bed for his office and developed a penchant for Rolls-Royces, fully equipped with air-conditioning, colour TV and well-stocked bars) are the stuff of urban legend. No wonder Hawkins was soon dubbed "the underground mayor of Yonge Street."

Compared to the rest of Toronto, the Yonge Street Strip in 1964 was like a coarse and boisterous guest at a sedate dinner party. Neon-bright and incessantly noisy, the street boasted an explosion of retail outlets and entertainment houses that attracted bargain-hungry shoppers during the day and thrill-seeking gawkers at night. On a Saturday night, rubberneckers in cars checked out the sidewalk action all the way from the foot of Yonge, down near the lake, up to the tonier, midtown Bloor district. But the middle of the Strip was the source of most of the excitement since it contained the highest concentration of bars, late-night movie houses and twenty-four-hour cafés.

Robbie Lane & the Disciples had emulated the Hawks from the start. The band's guitarist, an Italian-Canadian named Domenic Troiano, was one of a number of Toronto teenagers who had studied Robbie Robertson's fretwork during afternoon "classes" at the Concord. John Kay, who emigrated from Germany as Joachim Krauledat and would soon gain fame with Steppenwolf, recalls how many kids saw Robertson as something of a god. "His disciples dressed like him," says Kay, "played blond Fender Telecasters like him and emulated his stinging staccato lead-guitar style." In fact, Robertson had a habit of selling his Telecasters at marked-up prices and buying new ones, leaving admirers to brag about how they owned Robbie's guitar.

Robertson and his bandmates continued to hold an almost irresistible sway over fans and musicians alike. One night during the summer of '64, Robbie Lane, Troiano and the other Disciples rushed out of the Le Coq D'Or during one of their breaks to catch Levon & the Hawks, who had returned from touring and were playing a short way down Yonge at the Friar's Tavern. Lane, for one, was shocked by what he saw. "I was still blown away by their musicianship," recalls Lane, "but they'd undergone an amazing transformation. They were playing for themselves, not even looking at the audience most of the time." Levon & the Hawks had discovered their own sound.

At the time, the Purple Onion—then Yorkville's most successful coffee house—was regularly booking American acts, including white blues singer John Hammond Jr. While in town, Hammond wanted to hear some good local music. Acting on a tip from Amos Garrett of The Dirty Shames, he caught Levon & the Hawks during their Saturday matinée at the Friar's. Hammond was immediately knocked out by their musicianship. "Each of them had their own little showcase spots," said Hammond, "doing Junior Parker and T-Bone Walker covers. And Robbie was the most intense, heavy-duty electric guitar player I had ever seen."

Hammond wasted no time in inviting Robertson, Helm and Hudson to play on his next album. Together, they recorded songs by Robert Johnson, Muddy Waters and Willie Dixon as well as a new rendition of Hawkins's signature tune "Who Do You Love." The result, *So Many Roads*, became Hammond's best-selling album. Ironically, the driving blues recording was on Vanguard, the same label which had released Ian & Sylvia's folk album. The experience whetted the Hawks' appetite to record themselves.

As The Canadian Squires, an alternate name they sometimes used, Levon & the Hawks went into a New York studio during the fall of '64 and recorded one standout track. "Leave Me Alone," sung by Helm, sounded like a swinging Chuck Berry boogie toughened with a streetwise attitude not unlike The Rolling Stones' "Satisfaction," which hadn't yet been released. The lyrics, written by Robertson, said it all: "I'm the talk of the neighbourhood / 'Cause I don't do what I should / I don't care what people say / I'm gonna do things my way." And the kicker was equally full of bravado: "I think I'm growing / I got my own thing going / Leave me alone."

Unfortunately, the Canadian music industry did exactly that. Despite the presence of another strong Robertson composition, "Uh Uh Uh," on the flip side, it flopped. Radio stations and record companies were still treating Canadian sounds with disdain,

**CHUM CHART TOP TEN OCTOBER 7, 1963**

*Blue Velvet*
Bobby Vinton

*Three Rows Over*
Bobby Curtola

*I Can't Stay Mad at You*
Skeeter Davis

*My Boyfriend's Back*
The Angels

*Cry Baby*
Garnet Mimms

*Sally Go Round the Roses*
Jaynettes

*If*
Little Ceasar

*Surfer Girl/Deuce Coup*
Beach Boys

*Sugar Shack*
Jimmy Gilmer

*Be My Baby*
The Ronettes

even though *RPM Weekly*, the influential music trade magazine founded that year by ex-Mountie Walt Grealis, had begun boosting local talent. As Hawkins told his former Hawks, the problem was their name. "Son, you're gonna have to forget this Canadian Squires thing," he said to Helm, "because they won't touch a Canadian group. Take my word for it. They know the Canadian market is so small they won't get their money back."

Disheartened, Levon & the Hawks returned to the club circuit. They regularly appeared at Quebec City's La Baril d'Huitres, Montreal's Café de l'Est and New York's Peppermint Lounge before going back to Ontario to play London's Brass Rail, Hamilton's Grange and Pop Ivey's Ballroom in Port Dover. Then they settled in for a month-long stint at Toronto's Embassy Club on Bellair Street near Yorkville. Although they were more casually dressed now (gone were the Lou Myles mohair suits), musically the group still thrilled and attracted a disproportionate share of female fans. One of these was Mary Martin, a Toronto native who worked for Bob Dylan's manager, Albert Grossman, and who couldn't sing their praises loudly enough.

*Helm (centre) and (clockwise, from top left) Manuel, Hudson, Robertson, Danko*

One of the many besotted young women drawn to the group like moths to a light bulb was Cathy Smith, a sixteen-year-old high-school dropout. Smith first saw the band at the Grange in her home town of Hamilton and caught Helm's attention with her teased hair, high heels and fishnet stockings. From then on,

Smith followed Levon & the Hawks to Toronto and was there at all their shows—and afterwards. One night in the Seahorse Motel on Toronto's Lakeshore Boulevard, she ended up in bed first with Danko and then with Helm. Although Smith eventually got pregnant by Helm, the paternity of the child was in doubt for a while and it was simply referred to as "the band baby." It was the start of Smith's long and infamous career as a groupie.

Like Smith, ex-con David Clayton-Thomas spent most of his evenings on Yonge Street studying both Levon & the Hawks and Hawkins himself, who was still spicing up his vocal work with acrobatics and speed-demon footwork. Occasionally, he'd get invited to sing a song or two. Blessed with a booming baritone, Clayton-Thomas impressed everyone who heard him. Although obviously influenced by Ray Charles, Clayton-Thomas—then performing under the name Sonny Thomas—had enough originality to set himself apart. For one thing, he attacked a song with fearless gusto, rising to the challenge of the most daunting crescendos. And he seemed willing to sing almost anything—from rock and blues to r & b. He could even throw some Hawkins-style twists, turns and leaps into his own performances. All that was missing was his own band.

Promoter Ron Scribner, who was booking bands through his new Bigland Agency, knew of a group that needed a vocalist. He suggested that The Shays check out the singer during his guest set at the Bluenote club, Toronto's bastion of rhythm and blues. Scott Richards, The Shays' bassist, recalls, "Ron said, 'I want you to hear a fabulous singer, a Ray Charles–style vocalist, big, powerful, contemporary.' He wasn't fooling. Right away we asked him to join and started working on stuff together."

Duff Roman, then an influential DJ at radio station CKEY, remembers the first time he heard Clayton-

Thomas sing. Roman was running Brave New World, an after-hours club near Yorkville, and Clayton-Thomas walked in one night and bragged that he had a group that was "miles better" than his house band. All he needed was a chance to prove it. Says Roman, now an executive with CHUM, "I gave him that chance and, sure enough, he blew my guys away."

Roman knew a good thing when he heard it. David Clayton-Thomas & the Shays were, in his words, "simply outstanding." Aside from Clayton-Thomas's big, bluesy voice, The Shays boasted the rugged sounds of guitarist Fred Keeler and organist Gord Fleming. Like Domenic Troiano, the fifteen-year-old Keeler was another Robertson-influenced prodigy, known more for his raw energy than the fast, clean and thoughtful style of Troiano. Fleming, meanwhile, was an incendiary musician, capable of drawing shrieks from audiences with one moan of his organ.

Despite the growing excitement about the group, Roman couldn't interest any local record labels. Working with Sylvia Train, a Toronto talent agent

*Clayton-Thomas (far right)*

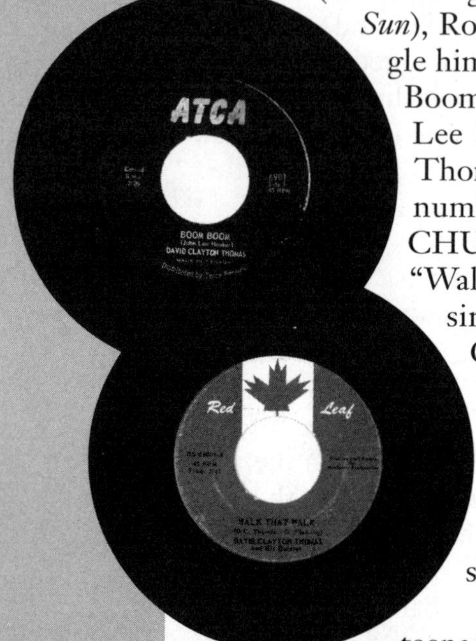


(and later gossip columnist for *The Toronto Sun*), Roman put out the group's first single himself on Train's Acta label. "Boom Boom," a driving rendition of the John Lee Hooker tune, featured Clayton-Thomas in full howl and made it to number sixteen on the influential CHUM chart in the summer of 1964. "Walk That Walk," the group's next single, caught the attention of Ottawa-born singing star Paul Anka, then booking talent for NBC TV's music show "Hullabaloo." Clayton-Thomas & the Shays got the call to come down to New York to appear on the show.

Seen by an estimated 50 million teenagers each week, "Hullabaloo" was huge, and an appearance on it was a major breakthrough for a Canadian band. Working with the show's producers, Anka decided to play up the group's Canadian-ness by surrounding them with young women sporting hockey gear. As Clayton-Thomas & the Shays did their best to impress, viewers were

**Girls in hockey uniforms brandished sticks and helmets in an unfortunate fit of patriotism**

treated to the bewildering sight of girls in hockey uniforms, brandishing sticks and helmets in an unfortunate fit of patriotism.

While testosterone filled the bars and fuelled the rock and r & b scenes, a more feminine sound dominated Canada's coffee houses in 1964. Donna Warner of Three's a Crowd thrilled audiences with her bluesy vocals in Vancouver nightspots like the Bunkhouse, while Kate and Anna McGarrigle of The Mountain City Four filled the air with intricate harmonies at Montreal's Café Finjan. In Yorkville, female folkies were inspired by the success of Buffy Sainte-Marie and Sylvia Tyson, who married Ian that year in Toronto and took his name.

Like Ian & Sylvia, Sainte-Marie had already conquered Greenwich Village and met Dylan at Gerde's Folk City where the protest singer had watched her perform and given his blessings. But Sainte-Marie was an original. She sang, wrote Vanguard Records' owner Maynard Solomon, with "a hint of blues-inflection, a trace of Indian song, a touch of Parisian chanson, an echo of beat, a bit of weird, but nowhere a direct or crucial influence." And she looked like no one else on the block. Sainte-Marie admits, "I was more beatchick than folkie, in a dress from Fredericks and a pair of spiked heels."

Yorkville and the Purple Onion became a favourite stop for Sainte-Marie in 1964, and she remembers how stimulating she found the whole scene: "The most influential thing in those days," says Sainte-Marie with a laugh, "was the caffeine. It was all talk, talk, talk and listen, listen, listen. It was really about exchanging ideas. People participated in what was going on on-stage, not clap-along or singalong stuff so much as talking about what an artist's set was all about. That led to a lot of original thinking."

*Clayton-Thomas, on "Hullabaloo"*

On her way to an Onion gig, Sainte-Marie's career took a fateful turn. While waiting for her flight to Toronto in the San Francisco air-

port, she encountered a group of wounded U.S. army recruits on their way back from Vietnam. The sight deeply affected Sainte-Marie. "All these soldiers came in pushing their friends in wheelchairs and on gurney stretchers," she recalls, "at a time when the newspapers were still insisting there was no war going on in Vietnam. But here was the proof. These guys were bandaged up and looking real bad."

Later, between sets at the Onion, she began writing. "It started with me wondering exactly who was responsible for war. I wondered was it those bandaged guys I'd seen and I concluded, 'Yeah, to a certain extent.' But then I thought about the military careerists who spend their whole lives pushing war. Then I thought about who sets one army against another, and it's the politicians. Finally, I asked myself who elects the politicians and, of course, it's us. That's exactly how the song came about." Adds Sainte-Marie, without a trace of insincerity, "I actually felt I was writing what everybody knew to be true. I had no idea it would be so controversial."

That controversial song was "Universal Soldier," a protest anthem to rival Dylan's "Blowin' in the Wind." It became a huge international hit the following year for British folk hero Donovan. But Sainte-Marie's original, included on her 1964 Vanguard debut album *It's My Way!*, packed a bigger emotional wallop. With her quavering, impassioned vocals, her rage was palpable. Joni Mitchell felt it and made plans to travel east and see Sainte-Marie at Mariposa that summer.

As the only child born to William and Myrtle Anderson in Fort McLeod, Alberta, Roberta Joan had grown up in Saskatoon—not far from Sainte-Marie's own birthplace on the Cree Indian Piapot Reserve in the Qu'Appelle Valley. A self-described "good-time Charlie," Joni first wrecked her stockings dancing to the jukebox jive of Chuck Berry, Elvis Presley and The Coasters. But at a certain point, like many teenagers in the early '60s, she traded rock's "jungle rhythms" for the more cerebral qualities of folk music. "Rock 'n' roll went through a really dumb, vanilla period," she recalled. "And during that period, folk came in to fill the hole."

At parties, Anderson began to lead singalongs, accompanying herself on baritone ukulele with chords she'd learned from a Pete Seeger instruction record. While performing at a local wiener roast in 1961, the eighteen-year-old caught the fancy of some people connected with Prince Albert's TV station, who promptly booked her as a one-time replacement for a late-night moose-hunting show. Two years later, while working as a waitress at Saskatoon's Louis Riel coffee house, Anderson ventured to the stage during one of the Riel's weekly "hoot nights." Sitting on a stool, the pigtailed performer screeched into the microphone and plunked away on her ukulele for some puzzled onlookers.

*Joni Anderson, Saskatoon debutante*

Indeed, her developing taste for folk music left more than a few people bewildered. "My friends who knew me as a rock 'n' roll dancer found this change kind of hard to relate to," she admitted recently. "The songs at that time [were] folk songs and English ballads, and English ballads are always [about] 'the cruel mother,' and there's a lot of sorrow in them. But they had beautiful melodies, that was the thing, and I always loved melody. Melody is generally melancholy and sad, and the text that accompanies it must be the same."

In the fall of '63, Anderson enrolled at the Alberta College of Art in Calgary to pursue her interest in painting. But she continued to entertain thoughts of becoming a folk singer and was soon showing up at Calgary's Depression coffee house. Will Millar, then a budding folk singer and later the leader of The Irish Rovers, recalls: "Joni came with her uke and tormented us all with a shrill 'Sloop John B' and 'I With I Wath an Apple on a Twee.'" But by the following year, Anderson had improved enough that the Depression paid her $15 to entertain weekend audiences of mostly fellow art students. She even got hired to perform at Edmonton's Yardbird Suite coffee house, which, along with the Depression and Vancouver's Bunkhouse, was a major stop on the folk circuit in Western Canada.

By late summer, the British Invasion had landed in Canada with the impact of the Allied troops at Normandy. The Beatles' concerts in Vancouver in August and in Toronto and Montreal the following month had established the initial beachhead, while tours by The Rolling Stones, The Kinks, The Animals and others solidified the takeover. The effect of all this was instantly noticeable on Canadian bands that began borrowing the look and sounds of the foreigners. Suddenly, musicians adopted Beatle haircuts and mod fashions and mimicked the latest British hits in the hopes of catching the new wave.

In Winnipeg, Beatlemania was rampant. Chad Allen & the Reflections performed Beatles songs and traded in their Fender and Gretsch guitars for the Rickenbacker favoured by John Lennon. Neil Young's Squires also started doing Beatles material and then turned mop-tops themselves, first wearing Beatle wigs and then, when their own hair was long enough, combing it over their foreheads.

English influences were popping up in all sorts of Toronto-area groups, from the obvious Merseybeat connection of The Liverpool Set to the brazen, Union Jack–sporting British Modbeats. But few Toronto bands borrowed more slavishly from the British Invasion than Jack London & the Sparrows. London was actually Dave Marden, a Toronto-born singer with a fondness for fur coats who went around town speaking in an English accent—even telling people he was from Liverpool. Two brothers in the Sparrows, Dennis and Jerry McCrohan, also adopted a new surname, Edmonton, because they thought it sounded more English (the name Sparrows was itself a homage to the Hawks).

The ruse worked. With the leader's phoney accent and the group's British-pop sound, Jack London & the Sparrows scored a prestigious deal with the Beatles' North American label, Capitol Records. As the first Canadian band signed to a major record company, the group released four singles in 1964,

*The British Modbeats*

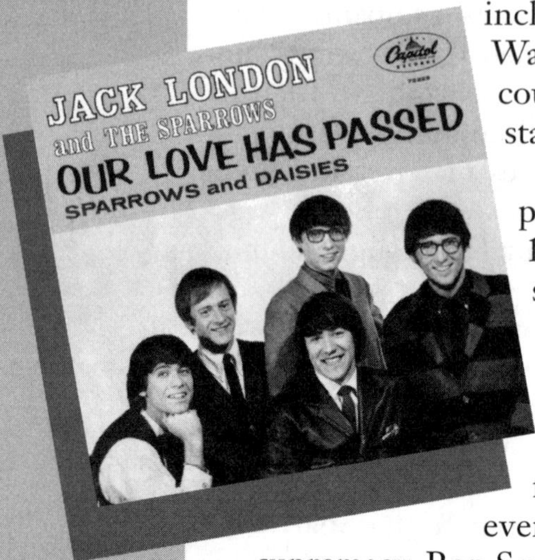


*Jack London (front, centre)*

including the hit "If You Don't Want My Love." Other bands could only look on with envy—or start talking Liverpudlian.

Merseybeat wasn't the only pop sound filling the airwaves in 1964. Motown came along that summer in the breezy form of The Supremes. Beginning with their "Where Did Our Love Go," which hit number two on CHUM in July, the glamorous female vocal trio challenged even The Beatles for chart supremacy. Ron Scribner had already started bringing Motown acts to Toronto for concerts. After the shows, the singers were lured over to the Bluenote club with the offer of earning a few extra bucks to perform with the house band. Stevie Wonder, Martha Reeves and, in the spring of '64, The Supremes themselves all treated regulars in the club to intimate performances.

**They lived up to their name as ruthless purveyors of blue-eyed soul**

Domenic Troiano clearly remembers the night The Supremes' Diana Ross, Florence Ballard and Mary Wells showed up. Troiano, fired from Hawkins's band for complaining about the lack of r & b in its repertoire, was playing guitar in the Bluenote's house band at the time. "They came in with charts for their songs," recalls Troiano, laughing, "which didn't help because none of us could read music. But we faked it and the show went over pretty well. The crowd absolutely loved them."

Troiano, singer George Olliver, bassist Don Elliot and drummer Whitey Glan performed as the

Bluenote's nameless house band for much of the year. Then, with the addition of keyboardist Joey Chirowski, they started calling themselves The Five Rogues. Donning pinstripe, gangster-style suits bought from tailor-to-the-stars Lou Myles, they began living up to their name as ruthless purveyors of blue-eyed soul.

With a guitar now in hand, Joni Anderson purchased a one-way train ticket from Calgary to Toronto and set out to attend Mariposa in July '64. She'd quit art college and, whether she knew it yet or not, was a couple of months pregnant—the result of a love affair with fellow art student Brad MacMath. Somewhere between the Prairies and the Lakehead, she penned her first song, "Day by Day," a bluesy piece written to the rhythm of the train wheels that she later described as a "feeling-sorry-for-myself song."

Joni arrived in Toronto and took a bus up to Orillia, only to find that Mariposa was in trouble. The previous year's festival had attracted such an unexpected flood of people that the town of Orillia had been overwhelmed. Although it was hardly a disaster of Woodstock proportions, there had been complaints of traffic jams, inadequate facilities and well-publicized acts of drunken debauchery. The local police chief had claimed that the festival had given Orillia "the worst forty-eight hours in its history." So even though Mariposa had been granted permission to use nearby

farm land for the '64 festival, a nervous town council blocked the move at the last minute—and the courts upheld the decision just one day before the festival was scheduled to open.

When Anderson and other early birds showed up, organizers were in complete chaos, faced with the monumental task of packing up and moving several tons of equipment and supplies back to Toronto, where the Maple Leaf baseball stadium had been lined up as a last-minute venue. According to the festival's Martin Onrot, Joni helped to load trucks along with other volunteers. Then, at the stadium by Lake Ontario, she and others braved the rain and cold temperatures to watch performances by blues legends Sonny Terry & Brownie McGhee, Mississippi John Hurt and others. In particular, Anderson studied the distinctive vibrato style of Sainte-Marie, who enjoyed no fewer than four standing ovations.

After the festival, the new girl in town had to find a place to crash. She discovered a rooming house in the Annex neighbourhood of the city and, to make ends meet, landed herself a sales job in ladies' wear at the Simpson's department store. Although Anderson must have figured it out by then, her pregnancy was still not evident. Eventually, her weekly wage would enable her to pay the dues required to join the musicians' union. In the meantime, she settled for playing several non-union coffee houses in Yorkville. The first to hire her was the Penny Farthing, which featured novice folk singers in its basement.

*The Penny Farthing's John McHugh with waitresses*

Owned by John

*Lonnie Johnson (far right)*

McHugh and his wife Marilyn, the Penny Farthing was housed in a grand old Victorian house in the heart of Yorkville. The McHughs, who had earlier operated the Half Beat coffee house, earned a certain notoriety by putting a swimming pool (the only one in Yorkville) in the Penny's backyard, allowing customers the chance to cool off in the summer months. Waitresses, John fondly recalls, sometimes took to wearing bikinis themselves while serving customers poolside. "We called it the Penny Farthing simply because of the Victorian era of the house," explains McHugh. But some people didn't know that the name referred to a type of bicycle. "We used to get letters addressed to Miss Penny Farthing."

Catering to his own tastes, John McHugh booked blues and jazz as often as he could, usually the Dixieland sounds of Jim McHarg's Metro Stompers. But he landed a legend when he brought in black bluesman Lonnie Johnson, who quickly became a regular. Johnson became so fond of Yorkville that he moved to Toronto and recorded a now-rare album with McHarg called *Stompin' at the Penny*. Johnson later operated his own Yorkville club, Home of the Blues. He died in 1970 at the age of seventy-one, but is still remembered as much for his geniality and graciousness as for his singular talent.

Blues, in fact, became such a staple of Toronto's club and coffee-house scene in the mid-1960s that the CBC had no difficulty gathering Muddy Waters and Sonny Terry & Brownie McGhee together with other major figures like Willie Dixon, Sunnyland Slim and Big Joe Williams in a downtown studio for a now-legendary film about the music called simply *The Blues*.

Bruce Cockburn had himself fallen under the spell of the blues while studying composition at Boston's prestigious Berklee College of Music in late '64. The Ottawa teenager had already written his first song, a comical blues number called "Baby, You're Not Leaving Me Out, Baby I'm Heaving You Out." Meanwhile, at Boston-area coffee houses like Club 47, he was checking out blues performers whenever he could.

Cockburn, who began guitar lessons at thirteen and piano lessons at seventeen, had actually made his own coffee-house debut back in Ottawa at Le Hibou on Sussex Drive. During the open-mike nights, the shy Cockburn would venture up to the stage to per-

**It was a perfect mid-'60s moment: a Toronto teenager imitating Dylan imitating Woody Guthrie**

form his repertoire of country-blues and ragtime—tunes by Big Bill Broonzy and Jelly Roll Morton—for anyone who would listen. At home, he spent a lot of time listening to late-night radio, catching the sounds of Ronnie Hawkins and his young guitarist Robbie Robertson.

Between high school and Berklee, Cockburn had also gained some performance experience during a backpacking trip around Europe. There, he overcame language barriers while singing for Swedish audiences at a Stockholm hootenanny and spent a night in jail for busking on the streets of Paris in a makeshift trad-jazz band with an American clarinet player and a French trumpeter.

Around the same time Cockburn was backpacking

around Europe, Murray McLauchlan was hitchhiking out west to British Columbia. Although the former art student had only a guitar and a few dollars in his pocket, he had plenty of romantic ideas in his head about the vagabond life—notions brought on from reading John Steinbeck and listening to Bob Dylan. Together with a buddy, he made his way across Canada, working in sawmills and logging camps, picking fruit and riding freight trains—all highly inspiring experiences for a wide-eyed sixteen-year-old.

Somewhere near Banff he wrote his first song, a wistful tune called "Murray's Mountain." It was a perfect mid-'60s moment: a Toronto teenager imitating Dylan imitating Woody Guthrie.

### DISCS TO DISCOVER

*The Best of Buffy Sainte-Marie:* Buffy Sainte-Marie (Vanguard, 1995)

*Stompin' at the Penny*: Lonnie Johnson with Jim McHarg's Metro Stompers (Columbia Legacy, 1994)

# 5

# No Direction Home

A revolution was under way. Led by the twin, transatlantic forces of Dylan and The Beatles, musicians everywhere began aspiring to more literate lyrics and experimental sounds. The once gaping chasm between folk groups and rock bands was blurring. Musicians moved freely from bars to coffee houses and switched comfortably from rock and r & b to folk and blues. Suddenly, shaggy troubadours in turtlenecks coexisted happily with groups of short-haired guys in suits. Détente had descended on the music world. This was the post-hipster, pre-hippie era of mod fashions and go-go dancers, where Beatle-influenced bands began wearing brightly coloured clothing and mop-top haircuts.

The crossover could be clearly heard in Vancouver. There, folk-rock groups like Three's a Crowd, The Painted Ship and The Tom Northcott Trio shared the scene with suit groups such as The Chessmen and The

Nocturnals, who packed clubs with names like the Grooveyard and Oil Can Harry's. In Montreal, the British wave had divided the city into two camps: those that supported the Beatle-ish M.G. & the Escorts and those that backed the more Stones-like Haunted.

In Winnipeg, meanwhile, the British-influenced Chad Allen & the Expressions underwent a significant transformation. In late 1964, the group had recorded "Shakin' All Over," a Merseybeat-style number, for Toronto's Quality Records. Quality's George Struth loved the new version of the song. But he knew that Canadian radio stations rarely played records by Canadian artists, and The Expressions were a known Winnipeg band. Ingeniously, Struth released the single in January without the group's name, using the cryptic words "Guess Who?" instead. The tease worked. Thinking that the record might be by The Beatles, radio programmers jumped on it. By March, "Shakin' All Over" had shot to the top of the charts across Canada, bumping off The Beatles' "Eight Days a Week."

"Shakin' All Over" went on to reach number twenty-two on the *Billboard* charts—a feat never before achieved by a Canadian-based rock group. Suddenly, Dick Clark wanted the band for an American tour. The name stuck and the group's career was launched. For The Guess Who, there was no looking back.

Meanwhile, Gordon Lightfoot was embarking on a crossover feat of his own. While other folk singers confined themselves to quiet coffee houses where they were usually guaranteed an attentive audience, Lightfoot spent the winter of 1964–65 paying

**Welcome to the post-hipster, pre-hippie era of mod fashions and go-go dancers**

his dues down at the noisy Steele's Tavern on Yonge Street. Sandwiched between Sam the Record Man and Sniderman's arch-rival A & A Records, Steele's was a bar-room hangout for college students from nearby Ryerson. Lightfoot had to compete for their attention with hockey games blaring from the TV over the bar. Still, he used his time there to practise his guitar picking while playing cover versions of his favourite folk and country tunes.

*Lightfoot in 1965*

Ian & Sylvia would drop in to hear Lightfoot at Steele's whenever they were in town. One night they brought along Ronnie Hawkins. The Hawk took an immediate liking to Lightfoot, to his down-home musical style and no-nonsense personality. Hawkins recalls, "Gordie had a good ear and played a good gee-tar. I used to go over whenever I could, and loved listening to him sing Marty Robbins songs."

Similarly, Lightfoot enjoyed Hawkins's company. They both liked to drink and shared a profound interest in women. The Hawk's celebrated humour obviously rubbed off on Lightfoot as well, because one of the songs he wrote and debuted at Steele's shortly afterwards was "Silver Cloud Talking Blues," an account of the time Hawkins shopped for a Rolls-Royce, kicking at the tires, asking to take the priceless vehicle for a quick test spin before buying it from a sceptical salesman with $15,000 in cash emptied out of an Honest Ed's shopping bag.

*Where Lightfoot got his start*

Although he was writing all the time, and had been deeply inspired by hearing Tyson's "Four Strong Winds" and "Someday Soon" as well as Sylvia's "You Were On My Mind," Lightfoot still lacked the confidence to perform his own material. One night, he got offered a gig over at the Toronto Teachers College. Steele Basil, the Yonge Street bar's Greek owner, let him off for an hour, and Lightfoot rushed over to do a guest set. He decided to try out a couple of his own songs. The crowd was delighted—much to Lightfoot's surprise. "The thing at the Teachers College was all me," he said later. "I went over well and I knew it. It *did* something to me."

From that point on, Lightfoot sang his own material as often as possible. When Ian & Sylvia next heard him, they were immediately struck by the quality of Lightfoot's songs, especially "For Lovin' Me" and "Early Morning Rain," which Ian said invoked "the old tradition of Canadians working in the Far North on construction jobs, then heading to the city to blow the money in." Sylvia was haunted by the line, "You can't jump a jet plane / Like you can a freight train," which she felt beautifully contrasted the rural past with the urban present.

Ian & Sylvia quickly introduced Lightfoot to their management company. After hearing a demo tape, Grossman's partner, John Court, flew up to Toronto that winter to see the singer perform at Steele's Tavern. Court remembers being struck immediately by Lightfoot's songwriting, especially the chilling imagery of "Early Morning Rain." "I felt he was a heck of a songsmith," recalls Court. "He had an unusual take on things, very original subject matter. And I was equally impressed with his voice. For a singer to be successful, people must trust the voice. They must be able to relax with it and go on the singer's journey with him. And Gord had one of those wonderful voices."

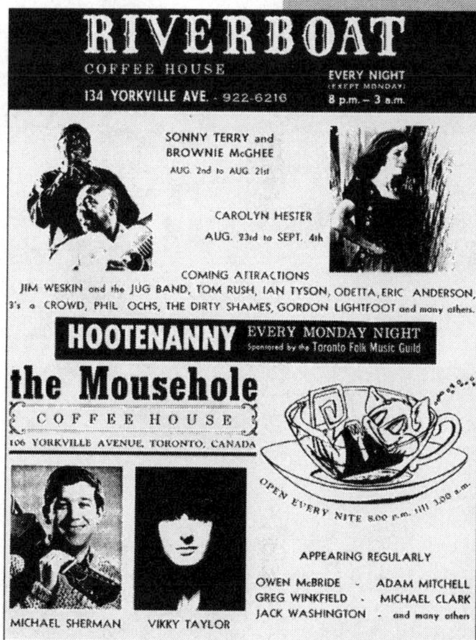


Court quickly signed him up and he and Grossman began shopping their new artist's material around. But they gave Lightfoot's "For Lovin' Me" (a song Dylan once said he wished he'd written) to their own act, Peter, Paul & Mary. It became an instant hit for the trio in February. Lightfoot the songwriter was on his way.

That same month, February '65, Joni Anderson gave birth to a daughter. A month earlier, she had moved out of the Annex rooming house and into an apartment above the nearby Lickin' Chicken restaurant with Vicky Taylor, another folk singer. Taylor remembers that Joni brought the baby girl home for a couple of weeks. But when she realized she could neither support the child financially nor get on with her singing career, she made the wrenching decision to place her daughter with foster parents. "That really tore her apart," recalls Taylor. "She knew that she couldn't be a single mum and do anything with her music. It was a really hard decision for her to make."

*Vicky Taylor, at a Riverboat hoot*

The decision haunted Joni for many years. She left clues about the baby, whom she had named Kelly, in some of her songs, including "Little Green" from her *Blue* album. The lyrics, in part, go: "Call her green for the children that have made her... / Child with a child pretending... / You're sad and you're sorry, but you're not ashamed / Little green, have a happy ending." In a fairy-tale ending worthy of a Disney movie, Mitchell and her daughter, whose adoptive name is Kilauren Gibb, met each other again in March 1997 in an extraordinary, media-hyped reunion.

Above the Lickin' Chicken, Joni began writing songs in earnest. Taylor remembers her getting up in the middle of the night and working, sometimes until dawn. "One morning," says Taylor, "she told me that she'd woken up with a tune going around in her head and couldn't go back to sleep until she worked it all out." That song turned out to be "Here Today and Gone Tomorrow," one of several that she later described as "lost-love pieces for a wandering Australian who really did me in."

In the spring of '65, Neil Young crammed The Squires into his beloved hearse Mortimer and set off for a gig on the Fourth Dimension coffee-house circuit—this one in north-western Ontario's Fort William. They were scheduled to open for an American folk group called The Company, which featured singer-guitarist Stephen Stills.

When The Squires took the stage at the 4D, Stills could barely believe his ears—electric versions of mouldy oldie folk standards like "Tom Dooley," "Oh Susannah" and "She'll Be Coming Round the Mountain." Now this was something new. "Neil was playing folk-rock before anybody else," Stills once declared. Young, in turn, was impressed by The Company's vocal arrangements—and, especially, by Stills's ability to sing harmony. Hitting it off instantly, the two fell into several beer-soaked jam sessions in Young's motel room. The Dirty Shames, a jug band from Toronto that was also passing through Fort William at the time, took part in one of them. "We sat around one afternoon playing bluegrass versions of Beatles songs," recalls the Shames' Chick Roberts. "It was pretty wild."

Young had become a fan of folk music the previous year. While hanging out at Winnipeg's 4D coffee house, he discovered Ian Tyson's "Four Strong Winds," which became a favourite song that he performed at parties and for friends. (Young later recorded "Four Strong Winds" for his 1978 *Come's a Time* album. That one version paid Tyson enough royalties to buy his second ranch.)

*Neil Young (centre): a weakness for funeral parlour vehicles*

Lightfoot was lured back to Yorkville by Bernie Fiedler, a one-time coffee salesman. Fiedler had switched from salesman to coffee-house owner at the suggestion of Yorkville pioneer Werner Graeber, who convinced Fiedler that there were greater dividends in selling coffee by the cup than by the bag. In October '63, Fiedler and his girlfriend (and future wife) Patti Tancock opened the tiny, rustic Mousehole, which did a roaring trade but sat only sixty people. With an eye to economic prospects as much as musical trends, Fiedler also opened the Riverboat in December 1964 and doubled his seating. With its brass portholes, pine walls and top-flight folk and blues entertainment, it quickly became a classy alternative to other coffee houses.

*Bernie Fiedler*

Almost immediately, Fiedler began hearing the buzz about town of a talented folk singer who was drawing line-ups down at Steele's. By then, Peter, Paul & Mary's recording of "For Lovin' Me" had hit the U.S. charts. When Fiedler found out that Steele's was paying Lightfoot $125 for playing four sets six nights a week, he offered to double Lightfoot's fee. The folk singer could hardly refuse. And when he debuted at the Riverboat in March, Lightfoot couldn't believe the difference: the audience was not only attentive, they seemed to hang on his every word. Fiedler quickly booked the singer for the following month. But when he tried to book him for May, Fiedler got a rude shock: with the Court/Grossman management muscle behind him, Lightfoot's fees had more than quadrupled.

By the spring of '65, Joni Anderson was back struggling to find work as a folk singer. She landed gigs at the Bohemian Embassy and the New Gate of Cleve where Mariposa's Estelle Klein saw her for the first time. "She wasn't doing all her own material," recalled Klein, "but she was a nice singer and had a very charming manner." Fiedler was not so quickly impressed, offering the folk singer a job in the kitchen when she first inquired about work at the Riverboat. She turned it down. (Fiedler has always denied this story, but she insists it's true.)

*Patti Fiedler*

Fiedler says he does remember saying to her, "So, Miss Anderson, I see you're going for the Baez sound," a comment that surely must have rankled her. Truth was, the more she wrote her own material, the less derivative she sounded. "Once I began to write," she admitted, "my vocal style changed. My Joan Baez / Judy Collins influence disappeared. Almost immediately, when I had my own words to sing, my own voice appeared."

You might say Joni Anderson was on the rebound from losing her daughter or maybe it was the wandering Australian. But when the older and wiser Chuck Mitchell blew into town that June, she was clearly vulnerable. He was the "star" folk singer from Detroit performing upstairs at the Penny Farthing, while she was the local girl on the basement stage. When he turned on the charm, the impressionable Joni found him hard to resist. "I was at an indecisive time in my life," she later admitted, "and he was a strong force. He decided he was gonna marry me. So he dragged me across the border, got me some work and we were quickly married."

Quickly is right. Vicky Taylor remembers the courtship as lasting all of thirty-six hours. The two were married in Mitchell's parents' backyard in

Rochester, Michigan. "I was totally shocked," says Taylor, "but I figured Joni knew what she was doing." She and Chuck moved into a cheap fifth-floor apartment on Detroit's Wayne University campus and Joni moved into her husband's world. Chuck was well known on the coffee-house circuit, and soon their apartment became a crash pad for visiting folkies, from Gordon Lightfoot and Buffy Sainte-Marie to Tom Rush and Eric Andersen. Andersen taught Joni some unusual open tunings on the guitar, which she quickly used to write new songs.

Chuck and Joni began touring together, playing Detroit's Chessmate coffee house and New York's Gaslight Café. Recalled Joni, "I wasn't very good, and I had a lot of trouble with the audience booing and hissing and saying, 'Take your clothes off, sweetheart.' Things like that really shook me up because I didn't know how to counter or act. I thought I'd bombed." Larry Leblanc, writing in *Rolling Stone* in 1971, described the Chuck & Joni show as a variety act, with him performing very theatrical, "Brechtian" shtick and Joni doing her own folky thing. When they did team up on duets, the songs they sang were often Lightfoot's.

**CHUM CHART TOP TEN APRIL 19, 1965**

*Mrs. Brown's Daughter*
Herman's Hermits

*The Birds and Bees*
Jewel Akens

*Game of Love*
Wayne Fontana

*Shakin' All Over*
The Guess Who

*King of the Road*
Roger Miller

*Stop in the Name of Love*
The Supremes

*Go Now*
The Moody Blues

*8 Days/Spoil the Party*
The Beatles

*I Know a Place*
Petula Clark

*Hear My Heartbeat*
Herman's Hermits

When Lightfoot was signed by Warner Bros. in early '65, a party was thrown at Steele's Tavern to celebrate. Organized by John F. Bassett, who published the *Toronto Telegram*'s "After Four" teen supplement, and Sam "the Record Man" Sniderman, the party was a modest affair with sandwiches paid for by Warner and beer supplied by Steele's. But Lightfoot, who was introduced by Ian

Tyson, brought the house down with a stirring performance of "For Lovin' Me." Sniderman recalled, "A lot

**Suburban girls in paisley dresses crammed into the Boat's red booths next to boyfriends with neatly pressed shirtsleeves**

of guys helped give Gordie his start because we believed in his talent. After that party, his career really took off."

Well, not right away. Although Lightfoot's next single, "I'm Not Sayin'," about a man's evasiveness towards commitment, made it to number seventeen on CHUM, Warner did little to promote it. As a result, the song bombed south of the border. In June of that year, Lightfoot made an eighteen-hour pilgrimage by train to Moosenee in Northern Ontario, "absorbing the whistle stops," as he put it. This would become a Lightfoot tradition—mining inspiration from the Canadian outdoors. One of the songs to come out of that trip was "Steel Rail Blues."

Lightfoot's management company, Grosscourt Productions, found him a new recording deal with United Artists after things went sour with Warner's. But for his next single they passed over his own compositions, choosing instead to have him record Dylan's "Just Like Tom Thumb Blues." For Lightfoot, it was a humbling experience—and the start of an uneasy relationship with the prolific U.S. folk star. Still, with the muscle of Grosscourt behind him, Lightfoot's own star did begin to rise in the United States. *Variety*, the U.S. entertainment bible, proclaimed: "Rangy, curly-haired Gordon Lightfoot, twenty-six, of Orillia, Ont. looks like he'll make it." Reviews like that, as well as Lightfoot's increased presence on the airwaves, helped to justify the new high fees he commanded for his performances.

Fiedler didn't mind paying the increased fee, which, by now, had reached $1,200 a week. "I was making money too," admits Fiedler bluntly. Indeed, during his first week in May at the Riverboat, Lightfoot brought in $4,000 worth of business, and nearly $7,000 the next. "This was unheard of at the time," explains Fiedler. The number of customers was equally staggering, with 885 people coming through on a Saturday night, suburban girls in paisley dresses crammed into the Boat's red booths next to boyfriends with neatly pressed shirtsleeves. To keep the fire marshall happy and to maximize the door receipts, Fiedler cleared the house after each show, squeezing in as many as five one-hour shows a night.

*Four to Go's Neil Young, Ken Koblun, Geordie McDonald*

Lightfoot was used to this sort of regimen at Steele's. But the intimacy of the Boat, a long, narrow room where no seat was more than fifty feet from the stage, demanded more of him. "I was doing a mostly traditional repertoire at Steele's," recalls Lightfoot. "When I got into the Riverboat, I felt compelled to introduce a lot more of my own stuff. Ultimately, I worked harder at the Riverboat than I ever did at Steele's because I was suddenly working to a very attentive audience. So the Riverboat really pushed me."

During the spring of '65, while Chuck and Joni were touring the 4D circuit, Joni started adding some of her own material into her sets, including "Both

Sides Now," a song she'd written about growing up. One night, after playing at Winnipeg's 4D, a tall kid with a Beatle haircut shuffled up, introduced himself as Neil Young and told her he'd written his own coming-of-age song. Later, as the café was closing, Neil played Joni the bitter-sweet "Sugar Mountain" which he'd written on his nineteenth birthday. Moved by its tale of a boy too old for the fairground, Joni wrote a response—"The Circle Game." In her song, which cleverly echoes the carnival imagery of "Sugar Mountain," she assures the boy that "there'll be new dreams, maybe better dreams and plenty."

For now, those dreams would take Young to Toronto where, he was certain, success lay in store. Arriving in June without The Squires—or Mortimer hearse, which had died en route—he stayed at the home of his father, journalist Scott Young, in the upscale neighbourhood of Rosedale. The jangly, folk-rock sounds of The Byrds' "Mr. Tambourine Man" were all over the radio that month, confirming for Young the musical direction in which he was heading. He badly wanted to start a new band. With ex-Squire Ken Koblun, whom he lured to Toronto, and drummer Geordie McDonald, Young put together a folk-rock outfit that began rehearsing at a theatre (steps south of Joni's old Lickin' Chicken pad), the rent paid for by his father.

*Joni Anderson, from the 1965 Mariposa program*

Acting on a tip from The Allen-Ward Trio whom he'd met on the 4D circuit, he contacted Martin

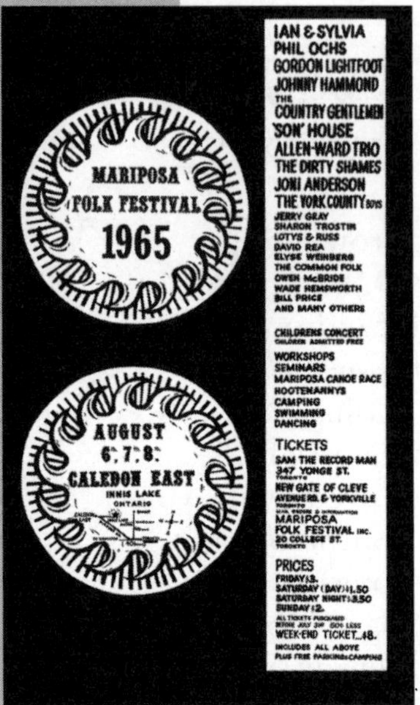


Onrot, the trio's manager and former Mariposa organizer. Onrot took the band on, suggesting the name Four to Go, and the group rehearsed in earnest whenever its leader wasn't working at his stock-boy job at nearby Cole's bookstore. Onrot was impressed by the group's sound but couldn't find them work. To Young's chagrin, Four to Go broke up without playing a single gig.

In August 1965 Joni took her new material to Mariposa, held for the first time at Innis Lake north-west of Toronto. On a weekend hit by heavy thunderstorms, she made her last appearance as Joni Anderson, sharing the stage with Ian & Sylvia, Phil Ochs, bluesman Son House and The Dirty Shames. (During a power failure one night, Ochs had to sing through a megaphone while illuminated by car headlights.) Joni went over well, both in concert and at a songwriters' workshop. But she insisted on singing only her own songs, which, at that point, were precious few apart from "Both Sides Now" and "The Circle Game." Some people complained, Estelle Klein recalled. "They said, 'She's really nice, but she's singing the same thing over and over again.' So when I invited her back for the next year, I said, 'Joni, I really like what you do, but could you expand your repertoire a little?' "

Throughout the spring and summer of '65, Levon & the Hawks began crossing the border fairly regularly to perform at Tony Mart's, a big nightclub in Somers Point, New Jersey. The group (now a quintet after saxman Jerry Penfound's departure) often headlined a bill that read "Over 110,000 Have Proclaimed Them Canada's Greatest." By this point, the band had released another single, containing two more Robertson tunes—"The Stones I Throw" and "He Don't Love You (and He'll Break Your Heart)." During one of these border crossings, the group got busted for marijuana possession ("Toronto Pop Group Seized," read the newspaper headline). It turned out to be a set-up. A jealous boyfriend of a girl Danko was seeing told the RCMP that the group was smuggling a trunkful of pot. In fact, Danko had an ounce of Panama Red in his jacket pocket.

*The gig Levon & the Hawks were playing when Dylan called*

With bail set at $10,000 apiece and with a court case likely to drag on for months, the whole thing looked as if it would seriously derail the group's momentum. Then Helm had a brainwave. In a move right out of an Iron Curtain thriller, he arranged for Cathy Smith to seduce the arresting officer. In a Toronto lakeshore motel, the seventeen-year-old gave the cop one hell of a blow job—then promptly told him she was only fourteen. Freaked at the thought of jailbait, the cop, who was the chief witness in the case, fled.

Meanwhile, Bob Dylan and Gordon Lightfoot were both scheduled to play at that summer's Newport Folk Festival. Lightfoot, who was introduced by Peter, Paul & Mary, went over well with his acoustic songs. But the audience seemed totally unprepared for what followed. Dressed in a polka-dot Carnaby Street shirt and shades, Dylan came out with an electric guitar, backed by members of The Paul Butterfield Blues Band. After playing three songs, he was driven from the stage by a chorus of boos and shouts of "sell out." He later returned to sing

"It's All Over Now, Baby Blue," a pointed kiss-off to the folk purists in the audience.

The uproar from the folk community was deafening, but it only toughened Dylan's resolve. By this time, he was looking for a band. Devoted Hawks fan Mary Martin, who had moved to New York and landed a job in Albert Grossman's office, had the answer: Levon & the Hawks. After checking them out at a New York nightclub, Dylan made the call. Actually, Martin made it for him. "Would the Hawks like to play the Hollywood Bowl with Dylan?" Martin asked Helm when she reached him at Tony Mart's. Helm, not exactly sure what this all meant, replied: "I'll discuss it with the boys and get back to you."

The boys, especially Robertson, didn't need much convincing. As Helm later put it, "Bob needed a group, we needed a break, and the two needs coincided." Initially, it was just Robertson and Helm who joined Dylan performing at Forest Hills Tennis Stadium in New York and the Hollywood Bowl in Los Angeles in late August. But when Dylan asked them to join him on a world tour, Robertson and Helm said they'd be happy to, but only if the rest of the Hawks came too. Dylan agreed.

With the tour scheduled to start at the end of September, Dylan was anxious to begin rehearsals. But Levon & the Hawks had one last commitment, a two-week engagement at the Friar's. Forced to accommodate his new band's schedule, Dylan flew up to Toronto on September 15 and checked into a midtown hotel. Then, for the next three nights, he had to wait until the band finished its Friar's sets before joining them at the club for jam sessions that usually lasted until dawn. There, on Yonge Street, Dylan and the Hawks forged a brave new sound.

While in town, Dylan got involved in the group's court case. According to Danko, Dylan testifed that the band was "indispensable to his artistic well-being and couldn't be replaced." Whether or not Dylan's eloquent testimony had any impact is unclear. But with the chief witness out of the picture, charges were dropped on everyone in the band except Danko, who received a year's suspended sentence. Time for celebration. The Hawks took Dylan to their old tailor, Lou Myles, who promptly outfitted him in a brown houndstooth check suit. A fitting souvenir of Toronto.

In the car ride back to Toronto from Mariposa in August 1965, Joni wrote a new lyric, "It's like running for a train that left the station hours ago / I've got the urge for going." Although she has explained that the song was written about the changing folk scene and the need for moving on, it also reflected what was happening in her relationship with Chuck.

*Hockey made it onto the charts via Toronto Maple Leaf goalie Johnny Bower*

"It was not a marriage made in heaven," she admitted. "He was relatively well-educated and in contempt of my lack of education. I was developing as an original, unschooled thinker [with] the gift of the blarney [and] the gift of metaphor. But he ridiculed me in the same way that Pierre Trudeau ridiculed his wife Margaret when she wrote her book. [Trudeau] said, 'My wife is the only writer I know who's written more books than she's read.' So there was this educated pride versus the uneducated and the marriage didn't last very long." Still, Chuck did give Joni something other than a married name. He advised her to protect her songwriting by forming her own publishing company, something she still gives him credit for.

Her marriage on the rocks, Mitchell ran into more chauvinism in October when she appeared on CTV's "Let's Sing Out" program with U.S. folk singers Dave Van Ronk and Patrick Sky. Mitchell felt inferior alongside these experienced performers and was looking to them for encouragement. But as she recalled, she didn't get it. "Van Ronk was saying things like 'Joni, you've got groovy taste in clothes, why don't you become a fashion model?'" she said, "and Sky was saying 'It sucks.'" But, she added, "David did like 'Urge

for Going' and he asked me for it, I remember. I wondered what ulterior motive he had in mind after saying all those dreadful things to me. I thought, 'He must just want to laugh at it or something.' I was that insecure about my writing."

Despite that insecurity—or maybe because of it—Mitchell threw herself into songwriting with a vengeance. At the same time, other artists began recording her songs. First "Urge for Going" got a country treatment by George Hamilton IV followed by versions by Tom Rush, Judy Collins and Van Ronk. Then Ian & Sylvia and Buffy Sainte-Marie covered "The Circle Game." Suddenly, Joni Mitchell's name was known on the U.S. coffee-house circuit, and her songs were earning her a tidy income to boot.

While Lightfoot was the Riverboat's biggest solo draw, folk groups like Three's a Crowd and The Dirty Shames started filling the club with a different sound in 1965. Formed the previous year in Vancouver, Three's a Crowd brought together the talents of Donna Warner, Trevor Veitch and Brent Titcomb in a Peter, Paul & Mary–style trio. After touring the western Canadian coffee-house circuit, the group moved east and began adding more theatrical and comedic touches to their act. With the help of man-

*Three's a Crowd's Brent Titcomb (left), Trevor Veitch, Donna Warner at the Riverboat*

ager and former Traveller Sid Dolgay, Three's a Crowd made some high-profile TV appearances and performed at Ottawa's Le Hibou. But they drew their biggest crowds in Yorkville—at the Penny Farthing and the Riverboat. Recalls Titcomb, "Yorkville was really the epicentre of the whole music scene in Canada, with an incredible energy all its own. And the Riverboat was its most prestigious venue."

The Dirty Shames were also taking folk in a new direction, captivating Riverboat audiences with humour and an infectious dose of jug-band music. Considered by many to be a folkier version of The Lovin' Spoonful, The Shames were actually closer in style to The Jim Kweskin Jug Band, an influential

*(bottom right, clockwise from top) Chick Roberts, Jim McCarthy, Carol Robinson, Amos Garrett*

American group that regularly toured Canada. Carol Robinson was the Shames' consummate entertainer. With her dark hair in pigtails and dressed in brightly coloured shifts, Robinson would ham it up while singing and playing autoharp and washboard. The red-bearded Chick Roberts, a former carnival barker from England, played her straight man and added kazoo and percussion. Jim McCarthy, meanwhile, was a handsome, captivating singer and twelve-string guitarist who had cut his teeth performing solo at the Village Corner. Among those he impressed in those early days was Lightfoot. "It was fantastic to watch him work," Lightfoot said of McCarthy. "He just hypnotized back then."

But the musical genius of the group was Amos Garrett, a lanky mandolin player and guitarist from Toronto. Garrett brought clever arrangements and an eclectic repertoire to the band, everything from blues and Dixieland to country and classic '50s rock. Together, the Shames were one of Yorkville's most popular groups. Even Beatlemania, which returned to Canada late in the summer of '65, couldn't shake their devoted following. While The Beatles packed Toronto's Maple Leaf Gardens the night of August 17, The Shames still managed to fill the Riverboat. Among their many fans was broadcaster Peter

Gzowski, who wrote that their refreshing, "rinky-dink, oopsie-doops" sound was "like no other group anywhere."

The new music in Toronto wasn't confined to the Yonge-Yorkville axis. At times it spread further afield, forcing city fathers to come to terms with its growing power and influence. In September '65, for example, Toronto threw a party to celebrate the opening of its new city hall. Jon and Lee & the Checkmates, a local blue-eyed soul band, opened for pop singer and TV personality Bobby Curtola. The group, fronted by singers Jon Finlay and Lee Jackson, was known by its followers for feverish, gospel-like performances. Drawing from its usual medley of r & b covers, from The Isley Brothers' "Shout" to Junior Walker's "Shotgun," Finlay's group worked the crowd of 60,000 into a frenzy. When the band hit its climax on James Brown's "Please Please Please," the audience suddenly surged forward and Toronto mayor Phil Givens tried to stop the show. The Soviet Union's Izvestia news agency, always looking for evidence of bourgeois decadence in the West, covered the event and reported, "The excited mayor tried to control the mob. [He] rushed to the stage and shouted at a wriggling singer and begged him to stop his gyrations."

Finlay also remembers the mayor jumping on-stage and grabbing drummer Jeff Cutler's cymbal. It didn't work. Cutler whacked the mayor across the knuckles and the band kept on

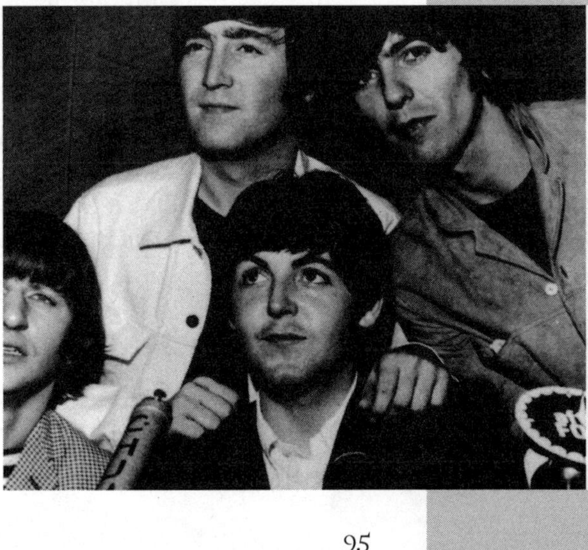

*The Fab Four, prior to their August 1965 appearance at Maple Leaf Gardens*

playing. After they finished, a hoard of screaming girls chased the band all the way to their rented limousine, grabbing at their clothing. Jon and Lee & the Checkmates had stolen the show that the media affectionately dubbed "Toronto A Go-Go." Admits Finlay, "Crazy things like that were always happening to us. Our shows were very spontaneous and emotional."

"How does it *feeel*...to be on your *ooown*...with no direction *hooome*...like a complete un*knooown* ...like a rolling *stooone*." With those lyrics, Dylan seemed to sum up what many kids were feeling that fall on both sides of the continent, from Haight-Ashbury to Greenwich Village and from Kitsilano to Yorkville—lost, alone, unprotected, seeking freedom while fearing isolation. If Dylan shared that sense of vulnerability as he and his band embarked on their world tour, he didn't show it. But he had good reason to feel abandoned as audiences and critics seemed to turn their backs—and their knives—on him. Booing greeted them at concerts in Boston, Chicago and Washington. Folk fans seemed offended that their biggest star had "gone electric."

It was the same thing when the Hawks returned home to Toronto with Dylan on November 14 to play Massey Hall. Far from an exultant homecoming, the concert was a humiliating experience for Robertson, Helm and the others, as members of the audience hurled indignant epithets at the stage. "Elvis, you're another Elvis," yelled one. "Let's hear the words, not the electronics," shouted another. Then came the most insulting of all: "Dylan, you're only doing it for the money."

To make matters worse, *The Toronto Star* ran a scathing review the following day that saved its harshest criticism for Levon & the Hawks. Antony Ferry, a news reporter sent to cover the show, wrote: "Here was a Bob Dylan who once was a purist, a folk-poet of

America in direct line to Woody Guthrie, now electronically hooked up to a third-rate Yonge Street rock 'n' roll band which he has now contracted. That great voice, a wonderfully clean poet's voice, is buried under the same Big Sound that draws all the screamies to a Beatle orgy at Maple Leaf Gardens."

Dylan soldiered on, like a diehard missionary, determined to take his new, folk-rock message to the masses. The band, fuelled by pills, grass and groupies, kept up a brave rearguard support. But by late November, Helm had had enough. "The whole booing thing was heartbreaking," he later said, "considering the effort Bob was putting out and how easy it would have been for him to play it safe. I was starting to get real pissed off. It was better for me not to be part of that."

*Blue-eyed soulmen Jon (Finlay) & Lee (Jackson), without their Checkmates*

The tour lasted another six months with a replacement drummer, ending the following spring at London's Royal Albert Hall. *Time* magazine later called Dylan's collaboration with Levon & the Hawks "the most decisive moment in rock history." And it clearly was a watershed, auguring all the grander, more ambitious rock that was to follow. It was as if the Hawks' passionate rock 'n' roll spirit, born in the bars on Yonge Street, had fused with Dylan's keen literary intellect to create a whole new world of musical possibilities.

## DISCS TO DISCOVER

*The Original Lightfoot: The United Artist Years* (3 CD set): Gordon Lightfoot (Capitol, 1992)

*Shakin' All Over*: Guess Who/Chad Allen & the Expressions (Legend/True North, 1997)

# 6

# flowers in a hothouse

On a spring night in 1965, a warm breeze was blowing along Yorkville Avenue, carrying with it a strange mixture of scents: rich coffee, pungent marijuana and noxious automobile exhaust. Cars crawled along the one-way street between Bay and Avenue Road, past sidewalks filled with teenagers in Beatlecuts and miniskirts. Some sat on café patios, others strolled along the tree-lined boulevard or hung out on doorsteps. Boys watching girls watching boys.

Like flowers in a hothouse, the musicians in the village's clubs and coffee houses were thriving on the responses of those who flocked to hear them. There was literally something for everyone: the traditional jazz of Jim McHarg & his Metro Stompers at the Penny Farthing, the delicate ballads of Joni Mitchell at the New Gate of Cleve, the bluesy folk of John Kay at the Half

*The cultural crossroads and musical mecca that was Yorkville*

Beat and the stirring songs of Lightfoot at the Riverboat, where Harry Belafonte, no less, dropped by to hear Canada's brightest new star.

Meanwhile, the new pop sound had infiltrated Yorkville, with go-go dancers at the Mynah Bird and British-influenced bands everywhere: The Ugly Ducklings at Charlie Brown's, Jack London & the Sparrows at Café El Patio and Dee & the Yeomen at the Night Owl. Even the venerable Purple Onion had recently switched from folk to feature the blues-rock sounds of Luke & the Apostles. The close proximity of all the venues meant that club hoppers could easily catch up to a dozen different acts a night. It also meant that musicians could readily check out what others were playing.

Such was the breeding ground that was fast making Yorkville a cultural crossroads, a musical mecca where talented guitarists, singers and songwriters from across Canada gathered. With its greasy spoons and crash pads, Yorkville was also becoming a haven for dropouts and draft dodgers, artists and eccentrics, a place where you could work, live and play, largely outside the conventions of straight society.

The exploding population in the confines of the

Yorkville district did not go unnoticed by Toronto's city fathers. City Hall, anxious to clamp down on the burgeoning street culture, began launching an offensive. Marshalling an arsenal of bureaucratic weapons, inspectors and police swooped down on coffee-house owners and landlords, hassling them with an array of new by-laws and city ordinances in a desperate bid to control Yorkville's growth.

Yorkville seemed the perfect place for Rick James. A black teenager from across the border, James was an aspiring singer who had formed his own harmonizing, Motown-style group in his home town of Buffalo, New York. After dropping out of high school at fifteen, he joined the U.S. Naval Reserve to avoid the draft. James was placed on active duty the following year and ordered to report to the U.S.S. *Enterprise*. But when he missed registration and faced disciplinary action, he fled to Toronto and soon found refuge in Yorkville.

It didn't take James long to capitalize on both his singing talent and his navy uniform. Forming a band called The Sailor Boys, he began appearing at the El Patio and other clubs. Then the group met Colin Kerr, a nervy entrepreneur who was looking for ways to promote his Bloor Street store which sold mynah birds exclusively. With Kerr as their manager, The Mynah Birds were launched as Yorkville's newest rock band.

*Belafonte and Lightfoot at the Riverboat*

*London took his moptop hairdo and English accent into jingleland*

Meanwhile, Jack London & the Sparrows were already Canada's first rock group signed to a major label, and their hit singles on Capitol had led to TV appearances and some big gigs. There were even plans for a full-length album. But then the Sparrows found out that Jack London was more interested in lining his own pockets than in looking after the band. According to the band's drummer, Jerry Edmonton, the group learned that the deal London signed with Capitol had most of the money going to him. Recalled Edmonton: "He would go in and collect the royalties and we'd see him the next day with a new fur coat, going out to restaurants. I don't ever remember getting a penny." The Sparrows staged a mutiny and continued on without London.

Around the same time, the group decided to swap bass players with The Mynah Birds, much the same way two hockey teams might do with defencemen. The Mynah Birds sent Nick St. Nicholas to The Sparrows in exchange for Bruce Palmer, a skinny nineteen-year-old kid who'd already been in several bands and was living in Yorkville with his girlfriend. No one was happier about the trade than Palmer. "I was sick and tired of all the phoney business around Jack London & the Sparrows," he says today.

**They wore black leather jackets and pants with yellow Beatle boots and turtlenecks**

"Besides, when I saw the singer of The Mynah

*The Mynah Birds' Bruce Palmer (second from left) and Rick James (centre)*

Birds, the way he sang and moved, I wanted to be a part of that. He was the closest thing to the real deal, as far as talent and soul was concerned, that I'd seen in Canada."

Kerr had his own pet mynah bird called Raja, and one of his first moves as manager was to have the band adopt Raja as its mascot. He even taught it to say "Hello, Ed Sullivan" in anticipation of an appearance on the American TV show. Kerr, who seemed to spend all his waking hours dreaming up new gimmicks, then devised the perfect outfit for the group: black leather jackets and pants with yellow Beatle boots and turtlenecks—mynah bird colours. All the attention-getting tactics paid off with a number of TV appearances, although Ed Sullivan wasn't among them. The band also recorded a single for Columbia Records. Written by Kerr's brother Ben, a country singer turned street busker (not to mention Toronto's perennial underdog mayoralty candidate), "The Mynah Bird Hop" failed to make the charts. But the raucous rock 'n' roll number (and its soulful B-side ballad "The Mynah Bird

*Colin Kerr, with Raja*

Song") remains a fascinating piece of Yorkville-era Canadian pop.

At a certain point, Kerr's publicity stunts became too much for The Mynah Birds. Recalls Palmer, "He'd organize these screaming teenage girls to chase us from our rented limousine through the Eaton's department store on Queen Street; it was crazy. This was his idea for getting media coverage. It was bad enough that he had us wearing yellow Beatle boots, but we drew the line when he asked us to shave our heads to look even more like mynah birds. That's when we decided he was out of his mind."

Without a band through which to stage his schemes, Kerr turned his attention to his Mynah Bird coffee house, which became famous for its go-go dancers who performed in a second-storey glass booth visible from the street. When that novelty wore thin, Kerr introduced topless dancing. The much-publicized launch, however, was "more or less a bust," as one newspaper quipped. "Fifty-one choking reporters stumbled about in semi-darkness as a faulty smoke-effect machine spewed murky clouds of carbon dioxide in all directions, and a half-nude, gagging go-go girl was trapped in her cage." Still, Kerr did continue regularly featuring topless dancers, body painting, porno films and, strangest of all, a nude male chef. The Penny Farthing's John McHugh lamented that Kerr's policy brought "the dirty-old-men-in-raincoats brigade" into the village, while Palmer says he now thinks of Kerr as "the

*The Mynah Bird club's nude chef*

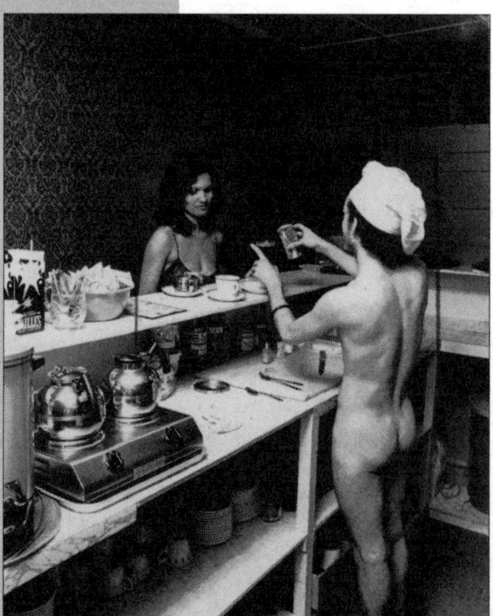

Larry Flynt of Yorkville."

According to John Robert Colombo's *Haunted Toronto*, "eerie presences and poltergeist-like effects" began to disrupt the dancing and showing of adult movies at the Mynah Bird. Lights went off and on, dancers heard angry, disembodied voices and chairs were thrown about unoccupied upstairs rooms. It turned out that, years earlier, the rooms had belonged to an artist who used them for his studio. Obviously, his ghost saw no artistic value in Kerr's nude policy.

Clayton-Thomas's appearance on "Hullabaloo" with The Shays boosted the singer to the forefront of Canadian pop. Following the success of "Boom Boom" and "Walk That Walk," the group released another hit single, "Take Me Back," and an album, *David Clayton-Thomas & The Shays à Go-Go*, on the Roman record label. According to label owner Duff Roman, the group's success was unprecedented. "We made the CHUM charts with every single we released," recalls Roman, now an executive at CHUM. "Nobody in the country enjoyed that sort of track record back then."

Although they boasted talent and a track record, David Clayton-Thomas & the Shays lacked one essential ingredient: an experienced manager who could take them to the next level. Instead, Clayton-Thomas and his band had to make do with the bar circuit in Toronto and around southern Ontario. The singer's tough image and pugilistic abilities preceded him wherever they went. Shays bassist Scott Richards

*Clayton-Thomas (centre), hanging out at Webster's restaurant*

recalls that often guys would take offence at their girlfriends' interest in the charismatic performer and would taunt Clayton-Thomas after a show. "David took on all comers," says Richards. "He never lost a fight."

Once, after a gig in Brantford, Ontario, The Shays were eating at a diner in the nearby town of Hagarsville when the local bully decided to torment the "fairies from Toronto," still dressed in their Lou Myles suits. According to Richards, Clayton-Thomas did a number on the guy that would make Arnold Schwarzenegger's moves in the *Terminator* movies seem feeble by comparison. "After he knocked the guy's teeth all over the restaurant and practically ripped his nose off his face," says Richards, "David calmly wiped his hands with a napkin and finished his dinner. He was that cool."

On yet another occasion, Clayton-Thomas got into a post-gig altercation with a kung-fu master in Toronto's Chinatown. Although the man had a seventh-degree black belt to his credit, Clayton-Thomas knocked him out cold for twenty-five minutes with one punch. "We never had a crowd-control problem at our shows," laughs Richards, now an instructor at Toronto's Harris Institute for the Arts. "But because of our nasty reputation, some bands didn't want to do double dates with us."

When the pugnacious frontman abandoned his band to fill in for Ronnie Hawkins for a few weeks, it ended his association with The Shays. The singer then drifted into Yorkville, where he found the free exchange of musical ideas that fuelled the scene irresistible. Occasionally, Clayton-Thomas would land a solo gig, performing his favourite John Lee Hooker tunes. But most nights, you could find him sitting on the steps of St. Paul's United Church on Avenue Road, singing the blues for anyone who would listen.

After the collapse of Four to Go in the fall of '65, Neil Young, looking shaggier than ever, decided to try his hand as a solo folk singer. Trading in his Gretsch electric guitar for a twelve-string Gibson acoustic, Young headed into Yorkville and played some hoot nights at the Riverboat and the New Gate of Cleve. Although his repertoire mostly consisted of Dylan, Ochs and Hamilton Camp covers, he also started singing a few of his own songs, howling in falsetto like a lonely prairie dog. At this point, "Sugar Mountain" was becoming his signature tune. The same autobiographical approach was behind "Nowadays Clancy Can't Even Sing," a song he'd written in Yorkville about a social misfit.

"Neil's songwriting, even then, was wonderful," recalls ex–Four to Go manager Martin Onrot. "Neil's an excellent communicator and each song told a story that, for me, touched a very responsive chord." But despite the high standard of his songs, Young had difficulty gaining acceptance as a folkie. One city newspaper reviewer even went so far as to call his material clichéd.

**CHUM CHART TOP TEN MARCH 21, 1966**

*These Boots*
Nancy Sinatra

*Nowhere Man*
The Beatles

*Listen People*
Herman's Hermits

*Green Berets*
Sgt. Barry Sadler

*Elusive Butterfly*
Rob Lind

*19th Nervous Breakdown*
Rolling Stones

*California Dreamin'*
Mamas & Papas

*Homeward Bound*
Simon & Garfunkel

*I Fought the Law*
Bobby Fuller Four

*Lightnin' Strikes*
Lou Christie

Still, Young was determined to record his songs. But, like Ian & Sylvia and Levon & the Hawks before him, that meant going to New York. Unlike England, where a recording industry was quick to capture the

*The Sparrows' Jerry Edmonton, Nick St. Nicholas, Dennis Edmonton, John Kay and Goldy McJohn at Chez Monique*

local sound on vinyl, few recording facilities existed in Canada, and those that did were inadequate even by the crude recording standards of the 1960s.

Young made two trips to New York in November '65. On one visit, someone (Young can't remember who) arranged for him to record seven of his songs, including "Clancy" and "Sugar Mountain," at Elektra Records' studios. On another occasion, Young travelled to the Big Apple to look up Stephen Stills, using the address Stills had given him after their Fort William jam session. By that point, however, Stills had moved on to California. Young did meet up with Stills's ex-room-mate and friend Ritchie Furay and played him "Clancy." Furay was so impressed that he took the song with him when he joined Stills in California a few months later.

One night, late in the summer of '65, The Sparrows were playing at the Devil's Den, a basement club in Yorkville. The band was still doing well without Jack London, living off the popularity of their hit singles. The group's repertoire consisted of Rolling Stones and Manfred Mann covers, some r & b numbers and a few ballads. Like Levon & the Hawks and other bands, The Sparrows had loosened up their image, trading in their suits for mod-style go-go gear, turtlenecks and corduroy pants. All they really lacked was a strong lead vocalist.

John Kay was a German-born singer who was playing folk-blues guitar and harmonica at the Half Beat and crashing above the Night Owl in an apartment belonging to Vicky Taylor, Joni Mitchell's ex-room-mate. One night, during an after-hours jam session above the Half Beat, some of the Sparrows came up, heard Kay and joined in. They loved Kay's bluesy edge and later suggested he drop by the Devil's Den and play some harmonica. The Sparrows then asked Kay to join—but not without a make-over. According to Jerry Edmonton, Kay's hair, for one thing, didn't look right. "It was all slicked back. He looked more like James Dean, black hair, greasy and combed back. He was a bit pudgy and was wearing white Levi's which I thought was odd. After [he] joined, I took him down to Cy Mann [rival to Lou Myles] for some decent clothes and we washed his hair."

If The Sparrows gave Kay some fashion tips, Kay, in turn, hipped the band to grass and acid. The real drug connoisseurs, however, were two waitresses—Jutta Maue and Solveigh Schattman. Originally from Germany, Maue and Schattman emigrated to Canada as au pair girls, and both worked at the 71 Club after meeting owner Werner Graeber. In short order, the two moved on to other Yorkville coffee houses, including the Penny Farthing, the Half Beat and the Riverboat, and became the most popular waitresses in the village. Using their tips to buy everything from amyl nitrates to acid and heroin, the pair began hanging out with what Maue admits was a dangerous crowd: "gamblers, older guys from Cabbagetown." Then Kay met Maue and they started double dating with Schattman and The Sparrows' Nick St. Nicholas (himself a German, born Klaus Karl Kassbaum). For Kay and Maue, still married after thirty

*Blues-rock in a Victorian-style row house*

years, it was the start of a life-long relationship.

Kay talks about that year in Yorkville as the best time of his life. "It was one of those rare situations where your private and professional lives totally merged. During the week, Yorkville was this isolated oasis of lifestyle and attitude. The Sparrows' gear was set up at the El Patio or Chez Monique, where we'd rehearse during the day and play at night. And the village was our home. We ate at the Mont Blanc restaurant and when we got the munchies, we'd go to the Grab Bag, which was sort of a hip 7-11. People lived above stores—it was a real community. And musically, you could check out what everyone else was doing because it was all right there."

*One-stop shopping for rolling papers, hookah pipes and late-night munchies*

Despite their love of Yorkville, The Sparrows knew that the big time lay in the States. A sugar daddy arrived in the person of Stanton J. Freeman, an executive with an audio equipment manufacturer who took a keen interest in the group. Freeman was a playboy who drove an Alfa Romeo, but more important, he had serious New York connections. He came through for the band, landing The Sparrows a booking at Arthur, a nightclub for New York's jet set.

The Sparrows loved the gig at Arthur and started mixing spacey, psychedelic rock with its more blues-oriented material. The songs and the sound appealed to producer David Kapralik, later manager for Sly & the Family Stone, who landed The Sparrows a deal with Columbia. The band's first single, featuring "Tomorrow's Ship" and the B-side "Isn't It Strange," had a deliciously dreamy, obviously drug-induced quality.

The new direction was not lost on *The Toronto Star*, which sent reporter Stan Fischler down to New York to cover The Sparrows' residency at Arthur. "Musical LSD" is how Fischler described the new sound. "A modern tonal thunderstorm." He added: "When the lads let loose with their tremerous sounds, the floor at Arthur resembles a St. Vitus dance convention." Throughout the summer the band, now simply known as The Sparrow ("to give a more hip ring to our name," explained Kay), also performed at the Barge on Long Island and at the Downtown Discotheque, a black club and home of The Chambers Brothers (where Bette Midler was a hatcheck girl).

*The Sparrows go high fashion, with models from Miss Chatelaine*

John Kay moved out of Vicky Taylor's Night Owl apartment just as Neil Young was moving in. In fact they met briefly and rapped about the New York scene. But, with Kay's future seemingly assured and Young's prospects looking dismal, they had little else in common. Young's prospects improved in early '66 when Bruce Palmer spotted him walking along Yorkville Avenue carrying a guitar and balancing an amp on his head like an African tribeswoman. Palmer was looking for a guitarist for The Mynah Birds and, in a brief Yorkville curbside exchange, asked Young if he wanted to join a band. Young said sure. "We actually needed a lead guitarist," Palmer recalls, "and he played rhythm on a twelve-string Gibson acoustic with a pick-up. And this, in a city full of Telecasters!

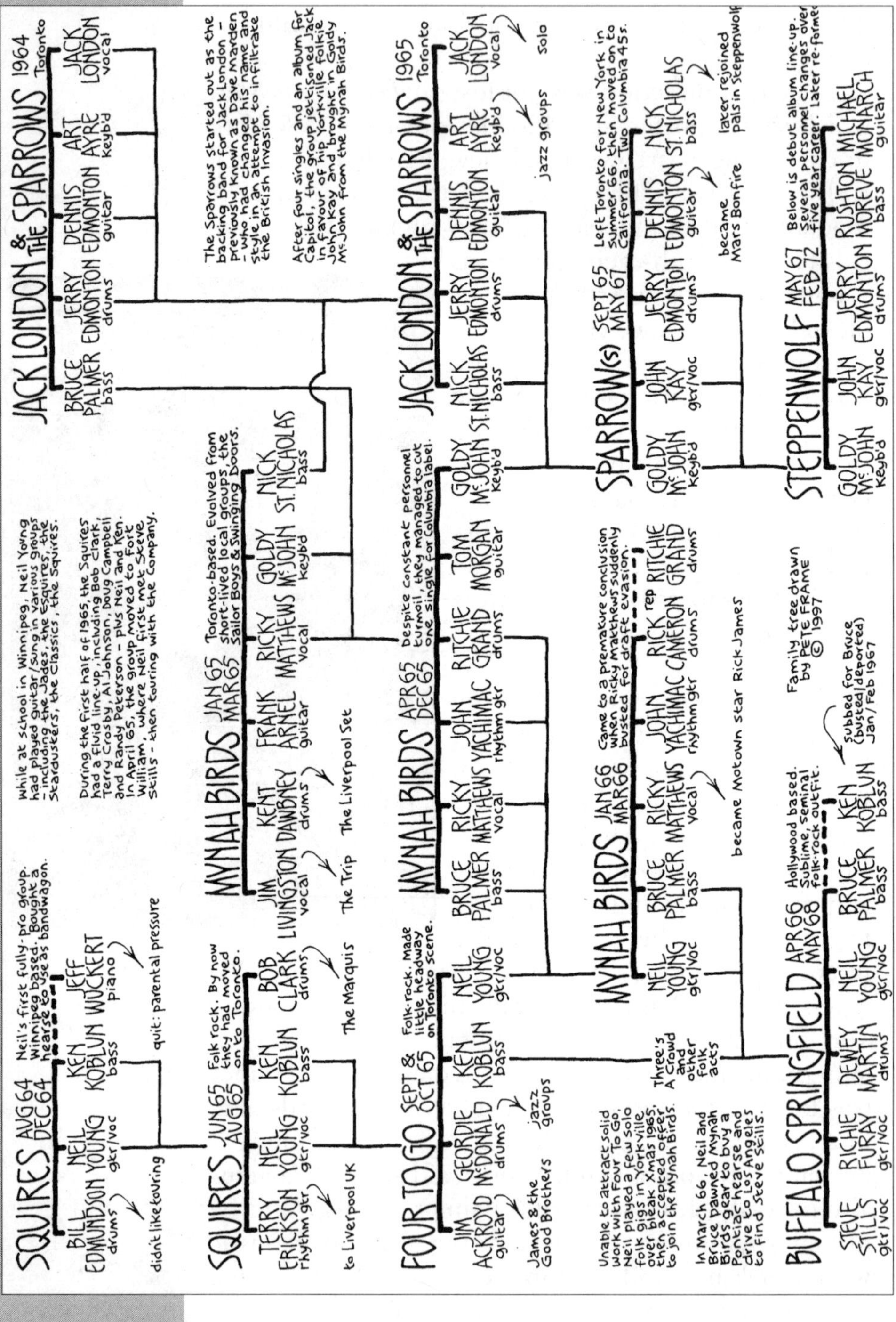
SQUIRES AUG64 DEC64
Neil's first fully-pro group. Winnipeg based. Bought a hearse to use as bandwagon.
BILL EDMUNDSON drums
NEIL YOUNG gtr/voc
KEN KOBLUN bass
JEFF WUCKERT piano
didn't like touring
quit: parental pressure
SQUIRES JUN65 AUG65
Folk rock. By now they had moved on to Toronto.
TERRY ERICKSON rhythm gtr
NEIL YOUNG gtr/voc
KEN KOBLUN bass
BOB CLARK drums
to Liverpool UK
The Marquis
FOUR TO GO SEPT & OCT 65
Folk-rock. Made little headway on Toronto scene.
JIM ACKROYD guitar
GEORDIE McDONALD drums
KEN KOBLUN bass
NEIL YOUNG gtr/voc
James & the Good Brothers
jazz groups
Three's A Crowd and other folk acts
Unable to attract solid work with Four To Go, Neil played a few solo folk gigs in Yorkville over bleak Xmas 1965, then accepted offer to join the Mynah Birds.
In March 66, Neil and Bruce pawned Mynah Birds gear to buy a Pontiac hearse and drive to Los Angeles to find Steve Stills.
BUFFALO SPRINGFIELD APR66 MAY68
Hollywood based. Sublime, seminal folk-rock outfit.
STEVE STILLS gtr/voc
RICHIE FURAY gtr/voc
DEWEY MARTIN drums
NEIL YOUNG gtr/voc
BRUCE PALMER bass
KEN KOBLUN bass
subbed for Bruce (busted/deported) Jan/Feb 1967
While at school in Winnipeg, Neil Young had played guitar/sung in various groups - including the Jades, the Esquires, the Stardusters, the Classics, the Squires.
During the first half of 1965, the Squires had a fluid line-up, including Bob Clark, Terry Crosby, Al Johnson, Doug Campbell and Randy Peterson - plus Neil and Ken. In April 65, the group moved to Fort William, where Neil first met Steve Stills - then touring with the Company.
MYNAH BIRDS JAN65 MAR65
Toronto-based. Evolved from short-lived local groups, the Sailor Boys & Swinging Doors.
JIM LIVINGSTON vocal
KENT DAWBNEY drums
FRANK ARNEL guitar
RICKY MATTHEWS vocal
GOLDY McJOHN keyb'd
NICK ST. NICHOLAS bass
The Trip
The Liverpool Set
MYNAH BIRDS APR65 DEC65
Despite constant personnel turmoil, they managed to cut one single for Columbia label.
BRUCE PALMER bass
RICKY MATTHEWS vocal
JOHN YACHIMAC rhythm gtr
RITCHIE GRAND drums
TOM MORGAN guitar
GOLDY McJOHN keyb'd
MYNAH BIRDS JAN66 MAR66
Came to a premature conclusion when Ricky Matthews suddenly busted for draft evasion.
NEIL YOUNG gtr/voc
BRUCE PALMER bass
RICKY MATTHEWS vocal
JOHN YACHIMAC rhythm gtr
RICK CAMERON
rep
RITCHIE GRAND drums
became Motown star Rick James
Family tree drawn by PETE FRAME © 1997
JACK LONDON & THE SPARROWS 1964 Toronto
BRUCE PALMER bass
JERRY EDMONTON drums
DENNIS EDMONTON guitar
ART AYRE keyb'd
JACK LONDON vocal
The Sparrows started out as the backing band for Jack London - previously known as Dave Marden - who had changed his name and style in an attempt to infiltrate the British Invasion.
After four singles and an album for Capitol, the group jettisoned Jack in favour of hip Yorkville folkie John Kay and brought in Goldy McJohn from the Mynah Birds.
JACK LONDON & THE SPARROWS 1965 Toronto
NICK ST. NICHOLAS bass
JERRY EDMONTON drums
DENNIS EDMONTON guitar
ART AYRE keyb'd
JACK LONDON vocal
jazz groups
Solo
SPARROW(S) SEPT 65 MAY 67
Left Toronto for New York in Summer 66, then moved on to California. Two Columbia 45s.
GOLDY McJOHN keyb'd
JOHN KAY gtr/voc
JERRY EDMONTON drums
DENNIS EDMONTON guitar
NICK ST. NICHOLAS bass
became Mars Bonfire
later rejoined pals in Steppenwolf
STEPPENWOLF MAY67 FEB72
Below is debut album line-up. Several personnel changes over five year career. Later re-formed
GOLDY McJOHN keyb'd
JOHN KAY gtr/voc
JERRY EDMONTON drums
RUSHTON MOREVE bass
MICHAEL MONARCH guitar

We must've been nuts."

Things were looking up for The Mynah Birds. They found a new guitarist, another manager, Morley

**Eaton would leave his sedate Rosedale mansion at night to come down to swinging Yorkville**

Shelman, and a serious investor in John Craig Eaton, the millionaire heir to the department-store empire. Eaton, like John F. Bassett, was bored with the family business and wanted to use some of its fortune to dabble in the new rock 'n' roll. He bought The Mynah Birds brand new equipment, gave them an expense account and allowed them free use of a company limousine. Eaton would leave his sedate Rosedale mansion at night to come down to swinging Yorkville to check out his charges and spur them on. Says Palmer: "He'd come into the dressing room in his trenchcoat looking like Knute Rockne. We were the football team and he was the coach. I guess it gave him something different to do."

*Mixing spacey, psychedelic rock with its more blues-oriented material*

Palmer also recalls an endless cash flow from Eaton. Most of it, he says, went on drugs, including amphetamines introduced by Rick James. For Young, it was a whole new experience. "We used to pop amyl nitrates before going on stage," said Young, "and walk on just killing ourselves laughing and rolling around from the things. I remember at a high-school gig I was so high that I jumped off the stage and pulled my guitar jack out in the middle of a song."

Young was happy playing sideman in a band that appeared to be going places. The strength of the group was really James, a dynamic performer who Palmer described as "a cross between James Brown and Mick Jagger" (much of The Mynah Birds repertoire, in fact, was based around Rolling Stones songs). But Young and James also began collaborating on original, folk-flavoured r & b material for the band, including a number called "It's My Time." It was this funky folk style that piqued the interest of Motown Records, home of such pop superstars as Stevie Wonder and The Supremes.

An all-black label owned by Berry Gordy, Motown had never signed a white rock band before, and certainly never one from Canada (though it did later sign Bobby Taylor & the Vancouvers, which included Tommy Chong, better known as half of the stoned-out comedy duo Cheech & Chong). Perhaps Gordy thought it a novelty to record a black singer backed by four white guys but, for whatever reason, Motown signed The Mynah Birds. In late February, the company flew the group to Detroit for a month-long recording session with Smokey Robinson as producer. They taped sixteen songs and Motown was excited.

*Fredrik Eaton, chairman of the board David Kinnear and Mynah Birds' investor John Craig Eaton (flanked by models)*

The album, however, never got released. The problem was that James was still technically AWOL from the navy, and with the Vietnam War moving into high gear with the first bombing of the North, Motown executives didn't want to get caught with a felon. They convinced James to turn himself in, and with the lead singer in the brig, the once-promising record deal was off. Bummed out big time, the remains of The Mynah Birds returned to Toronto only to find that Shelman,

The Mynah Birds' manager, had fatally overdosed on heroin, shooting most of the group's $25,000 advance straight into his arm. Talk about the needle and the damage done.

Meanwhile, the Riverboat was quickly becoming the premier showcase in Canada. Like the Bitter End in New York, the Yorkville coffee house was part of a circuit that regularly saw the top acts in folk and blues—from Eric Andersen, Tim Buckley and Tom Rush to James Cotton, John Lee Hooker and Sonny Terry & Brownie McGhee. Ottawa's Le Hibou booked many of the same artists, but the Boat was the more prestigious venue, partly because it was in Yorkville and partly because it developed a lore all of its own.

*Fiedler with Riverboat favourites Sonny Terry & Brownie McGhee*

Many of the best Riverboat stories stem as much from owner Bernie Fiedler's gift for self-promotion as from his entrepreneurial skills. Once, while in New York trying to book bluesmen Terry & McGhee, Fiedler was pressured by the agent to accept a one-week engagement with a largely unknown folk duo named Simon & Garkfunkel. In order to get Terry & McGhee, Fiedler agreed. As Simon & Garfunkel's Riverboat appearance approached, their singles "Sounds of Silence" and "Homeward Bound" shot up the charts, making the pair one of the hottest acts in North America. Suddenly, they wanted out of their Riverboat commitment. But Fiedler, sensing a potential windfall, held firm, threatening to sue unless the contract was honoured. A compromise was reached and Simon & Garfunkel performed a single legendary concert in the 117-seat club on March 29,

1966, at a time when they were filling large concert halls in other North American cities. Fiedler reaped a publicity bonanza.

The Riverboat may have been the place where U.S. protest singer Phil Ochs wrote "Changes," his finest song. Fiedler swears that the romantic tune, which Lightfoot covered on his debut album, was penned on his club's back steps one night between sets. But Joe Lewis, a Toronto folk-music broadcaster, insists it was at the New Gate of Cleve, which he managed at the time. Still others believe the song was composed at their own kitchen table. Perhaps Fiedler is right and everyone else just wants to share in the history of the beautiful ballad, or possibly Ochs, who committed suicide in 1976, really did write the epic in a number of different Toronto locales.

Cosy and intimate, the Riverboat perfectly suited a Lightfoot performance in early 1966. For one thing, it allowed an audience to enter the singer-songwriter's world without distance or distraction. At the same time, Lightfoot liked the intense response it generated. "For me, the Riverboat was my first taste of the big time," Lightfoot says. The singer also liked the whole mood that Fiedler had brought to the place. "It was very dark and had a wonderful ambience," he added. "And it really did give the idea that you were on some sort of boat."

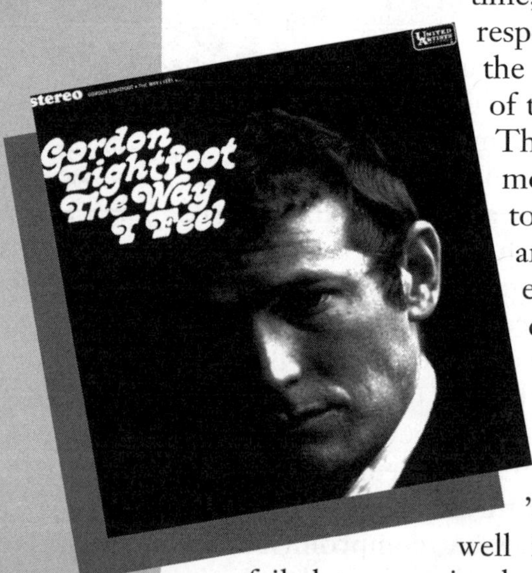


Lightfoot's debut album, *The Way I Feel*, finally appeared in the summer of '66. Although the album sold well in Canada, Lightfoot's star failed to soar in the United States. Part of the blame might be laid at the feet of Albert Grossman, Lightfoot's manager, who had already placed two of the album's strongest songs, "For Lovin' Me" and "Ribbon of Darkness," with other artists, depriving Lightfoot of a natural single for himself. The album won three Gold Leaf Awards (the forerunner of the Juno Awards, launched by *RPM* magazine), but Lightfoot was disappointed. "It came about several years too late," says the singer now. "It really needed an earlier start."

*Simon & Garfunkel at the Riverboat*

Timing is everything in the music business. Lightfoot's delayed debut meant that he lagged behind Dylan, folk's leader of the pack, who had already gone electric and toured with Levon & the Hawks a year earlier. Truth was, no songwriter, not even Lightfoot, who was fast becoming prolific himself, could keep pace with Dylan.

From the vantage point of the Bluenote, Domenic Troiano's Five Rogues looked over at Yorkville and decided they needed a facelift. The band disappeared briefly from the scene in 1966 and reappeared as The Mandala, choosing the name because of its mystic connotations. To the Buddhist, the mandala was a mind-expander, a way to communicate with his being, his soul. It was a perfect expression of the group's commitment to soul music as well as hinting at Eastern religions, then enjoying a vogue in the Western world.

Along with a new name, The Mandala boasted something few Canadian bands had in 1966: a smart,

*George Olliver's "dangerous" display of emotion at the Canadian National Exhibition*

aggressive manager. The group had been fired from the CNE for its "dangerous" display of emotion a year earlier, when singer George Olliver whipped his teenage audience into an emotional frenzy. Manager Randy Markowitz, who began his career as TV's Randy Dandy the clown, ensured it made headlines in all three Toronto newspapers. "It was amazing," says Troiano. "Randy was a master manipulator of the media. He saw the publicity potential in everything and exploited it." Markowitz upped The Mandala's fee dramatically. "Randy just decided that we were now worth $1,000 a night," says Troiano, "and we started getting it. Going from $150 to $1,000 a night is a quantum leap. It suddenly put us in an entirely new league."

At the same time, Markowitz introduced a revolutionary technique to Mandala performances. Where most bands used only standard spotlights, The Mandala began using coloured lights synchronized to the music and flashing strobe lights—among the first bands in Canada to do so. "The first night we used them with an audience," recalls Troiano, "people went nuts. They got disoriented and were staring at their hands and how it made them look. It was so weird." Later, the strobe effect was the talk of the town. Says Troiano, "Guys were asking us, 'What did you do to your audience, give them drugs?' It really made a big impression."

Although other acts mined similar musical terrain, none carried it off with such missionary zeal as The Mandala. Indeed, Troiano and his fellow evangelists, dressed in their brightly coloured, candy-striped suits, even dubbed their show a "soul crusade." "Our gigs started becoming more like events at that point," laughs Troiano. "We enjoyed trying to outdo ourselves."

Once, when The Mandala played the Hawk's Nest, the teenage dance hall above the Le Coq D'Or, Olliver decided to do a pied-piper number. Venturing out into the audience in mid-song, he ran downstairs and out onto Yonge Street with the whole crowd following. Then he raced around the corner, up the back stairs and re-entered the club. His audience, out of breath from the chase, was back at the stage with him as he resumed the song.

While Olliver won followers with his James Brown–inspired routines, right down to the acrobatic leaps and splits, Troiano wowed audiences with his fluid, inventive guitar solos. "I got away from the blues thing," Troiano admitted, "because it was pretty basic, three-chord, twelve-bar stuff. I liked a lot of harmonic things, chord changes and different time signatures." As a result, The Mandala's music

*Clockwise from front, centre: Mandala's Olliver, Whitey Glan, Joey Chirowski, Don Elliot and Domenic Troiano*

started taking on a sophisticated feel, with jazzier colours and mood shifts.

Bruce Palmer and Neil Young sat in Yorkville's Cellar club in March 1966 playing chess and talking about their career stalemate. Although they had an album in the can, Motown wasn't about to release it without the band's lead singer who was still in jail. (The Mynah Birds' recording remains unreleased to this day, with Motown claiming the tapes can't be found.) Young and his buddy began looking for distractions. "The club had bowls of sugar cubes," recalls Palmer. "Some were regular cubes, others were injected with LSD." He adds, with a laugh: "Ever tried to play chess on acid? It's a real journey." In that trippy head space, Palmer and Young decided it was time to move on. Young's instincts told him to go to California where The Byrds were based. Said Palmer, "It was like Neil had a compass in his head, a musical compass that told him to go west."

The next thing Palmer knew, Young was pulling up in front of the Cellar in another Buick hearse, this one a 1958. Palmer was his first passenger, but Young needed others to share the gas. He asked half of Yorkville, it seems. Guitarist Tony Quarrington remembers being in Vicky Taylor's apartment above the Night Owl. "Neil walked into the living room," Quarrington recalls, "and says 'Does anybody want to go to California?' I thought, no, I'll finish high school. But I've kind of regretted it ever since." Says Jeanine Hollingshead, a longtime Yorkville regular who made the trip with them: "It was really Neil's and Bruce's Excellent Adventure. The

*Troiano, the guitar superhero: able to pick two melodies with a single Telecaster*

rest of us were just along for the ride."

In the end, the passengers were Palmer, Hollingshead, a guy named Mike Gallagher and two women—Judy Mack and folk singer Tannis Neiman—who both had crushes on Young. Packed with musical instruments and an alarming amount of grass, the hearse headed north to Sault Ste. Marie where Young knew customs inspections were particularly lax. Where did Young get the money to buy the hearse in the first place? He sold all The Mynah Birds' equipment, which would've been fine except that it actually belonged to John Craig Eaton.

*Buffalo Springfield: a unique, cross-border creation*

After leaving Hollingshead, Neiman and Gallagher in Albuquerque, New Mexico, the remaining three ventured on to L.A., reaching the City of Angels on April Fool's Day, 1966. They dropped Judy Mack at the bus station—she'd had enough of her American adventure. That afternoon, Young and Palmer headed north along Sunset Boulevard en route to San Francisco. At a traffic light, the hearse and its Ontario licence plates were spotted by none other than Stephen Stills and Ritchie Furay. Stills knew the hearse could belong to only one person and in a nearby parking lot, the four musicians—two Canadians and two Americans—made plans to start a band. After adding a fifth, Canadian Dewey Martin, Buffalo Springfield was born.

A cross-border creation, the Springfield moved faster than flashing strobe lights. On April 15, the band went on tour, opening for The Byrds. In less than a year, they became one of the hottest bands on the West Coast circuit and signed a recording deal with Atco. As it turned out, the group's debut album featured several of Young's songs, including his Yorkville number, "Nowadays Clancy Can't Even Sing."

### DISCS TO DISCOVER

*The Best of John Kay & Sparrow: Tighten Up Your Wig*: John Kay & Sparrow (Columbia Legacy, 1993)

# 7

# a GO-GO '66

The sunny folk-rock sounds of California's Mamas & the Papas and New York's Lovin' Spoonful filled the airwaves across North America through the spring of '66. The fact that both acts had expatriate Canadians in their ranks was not lost on musicians back in the Great White North. But few others were aware that the honeyed lead vocals on "California Dreamin'" and "Monday, Monday" belonged to Halifax's Denny Doherty, or that the bristling lead guitar and manic energy of "Do You Believe in Magic" and "Daydream" came from Toronto's Zal Yanovsky.

After the Hootenanny U.S.A tour ended back in late '63, The Halifax Three had broken up and Doherty and Yanovsky both found work in a Washington, DC, club called Max's Pipe & Drum—waiting on tables. But it wasn't long before the two were on the Pipe & Drum's stage, in a surf group with a neophyte drummer, playing songs by The Ventures and The Surfaris. But all hell broke loose, Doherty recalls, the night that Hugh Rom-

*When Denny met Cass he gave her love bumps —called John and Zal and that was the Mugwumps*

ney, the future Wavy Gravy of Woodstock fame, dropped into the club. "We knew Hugh from Greenwich Village," says Doherty, "where he was a stand-up comedian. He had some pot with him and we turned the drummer on. But the kid, who'd never smoked before, freaks out and goes running home, screaming that he's losing his mind. The next day his father shows up at the club and starts getting heavy. It was basically, 'don't let the sun go down on you in this town.'"

Back in New York, Doherty and Yanovsky hooked up with singer Cass Elliot whom they'd met on the folk circuit. With Elliot's first husband, Jim Hendricks, they formed Cass Elliot & the Big Three, a folk quartet. Then Zal and Denny saw The Beatles on "Ed Sullivan" in Elliot's apartment. "Right away, Zal and I couldn't wait to get electric instruments," recalled Doherty. "We grew our hair—pretty soon Zal's was in his face, looking like an early version of Slash of Guns 'n' Roses." The four switched to folk-rock and changed their name to The Mugwumps (out of William Burroughs's *Naked Lunch*). According to Yanovsky, The Mugwumps also briefly recruited harmonica player John Sebastian because "he had the best grass in New York." As it turned out, The Mugwumps had a short life.

Sitting in his room at New York's Albert Hotel, Doherty got a call from John Phillips with whom he'd toured in Hootenanny U.S.A. Phillips needed Doherty's voice to round out the line-up for his Journeymen, which by then included his wife, Michelle, a stunning nineteen-year-old ex-model. Doherty agreed to join and threw himself into rehearsals. "I had to learn twenty-eight songs in less than a week," recalls Doherty. "John went down to the pharmacy on the corner—even at that time, he had special arrangements with pharmacists—and got diet pills to keep me up all night. I don't know how many of those I went through. It was pretty ridiculous."

After completing a ten-concert engagement, opening for comedian Bill Cosby, Denny, John and Michelle were sitting around one night in the Phillipses' apartment when Cass Elliot dropped in. Doherty recalls, "Cass had some LSD, which we all tried. At the end of a pretty wild night Michelle closed her eyes, spun around and pointed to the Virgin Islands on a map. We all decided to go there for a vacation." The Caribbean holiday was one riotous, drug-addled party. But whether influenced by dope or the hot sun they sang their hearts out—and, in the process, forged a distinctive vocal style—with their close-knit harmonies. Says Doherty, "With John and Michelle, we had a nice, sweet folk sound. But with Cass, we suddenly had power. When the windows rattled, we knew we were onto something good."

*The Mamas and the Papas' Michelle Phillips (second from left), Cass Elliot, John Phillips and Denny Doherty, with Ed Sullivan*

Meanwhile, in the damp, cockroach-infested basement of New York's Albert Hotel, Yanovsky and Sebastian were forging a unique sound of their own. Working with bassist Steve Boone and drummer Joe Butler, they began mixing Yanovsky's bluesy electric guitar with Sebastian's Appalachian autoharp. The four christened themselves The Lovin' Spoonful (after a song by bluesman Mississippi John Hurt) and took their acoustic-electric sound into Café Bizarre, where they worked for $35 a week and all the tuna-fish sandwiches they could eat.

By the summer of '65, the Spoonful had landed a breakthrough engagement at the Nite Owl café. After drawing line-ups and rave reviews for Sebastian's songs and Yanovsky's wild, on-stage antics, the group signed with Kama Sutra Records. The Spoonful's "good-time sound"—a mix of country, blues, rock and jug-band sounds—was a refreshing change from the protest music that had dominated the Greenwich Village scene. Yanovsky chuckled, "Both of my parents were Communists, so I had already stormed a lot of barricades. John and I just wanted to have some fun." The fun started when "Do You Believe in Magic" hit the charts—just seven months after the group had formed.

While the Spoonful's "Magic" was crystallizing, Doherty, Elliot and the Phillipses drove their beach-bum vocal sound across the country to California. Living in a Los Angeles crash pad (complete with eviction notices pinned to the door), the foursome struggled to find work. Car radios blared that summer with the surf sounds of The Beach Boys' "California Girls." John Phillips had written "California Dreamin'" back in New York and the band had worked out the harmonies in the Virgin Islands. On spec, they sang the song for Dunhill Records. They loved it. The record's release in November '65 launched The Mamas & the Papas. Recalled Doherty, "It came on the charts at forty with a bullet. David Crosby [then of The Byrds] stopped me on the street and said, 'Congratulations!' I didn't

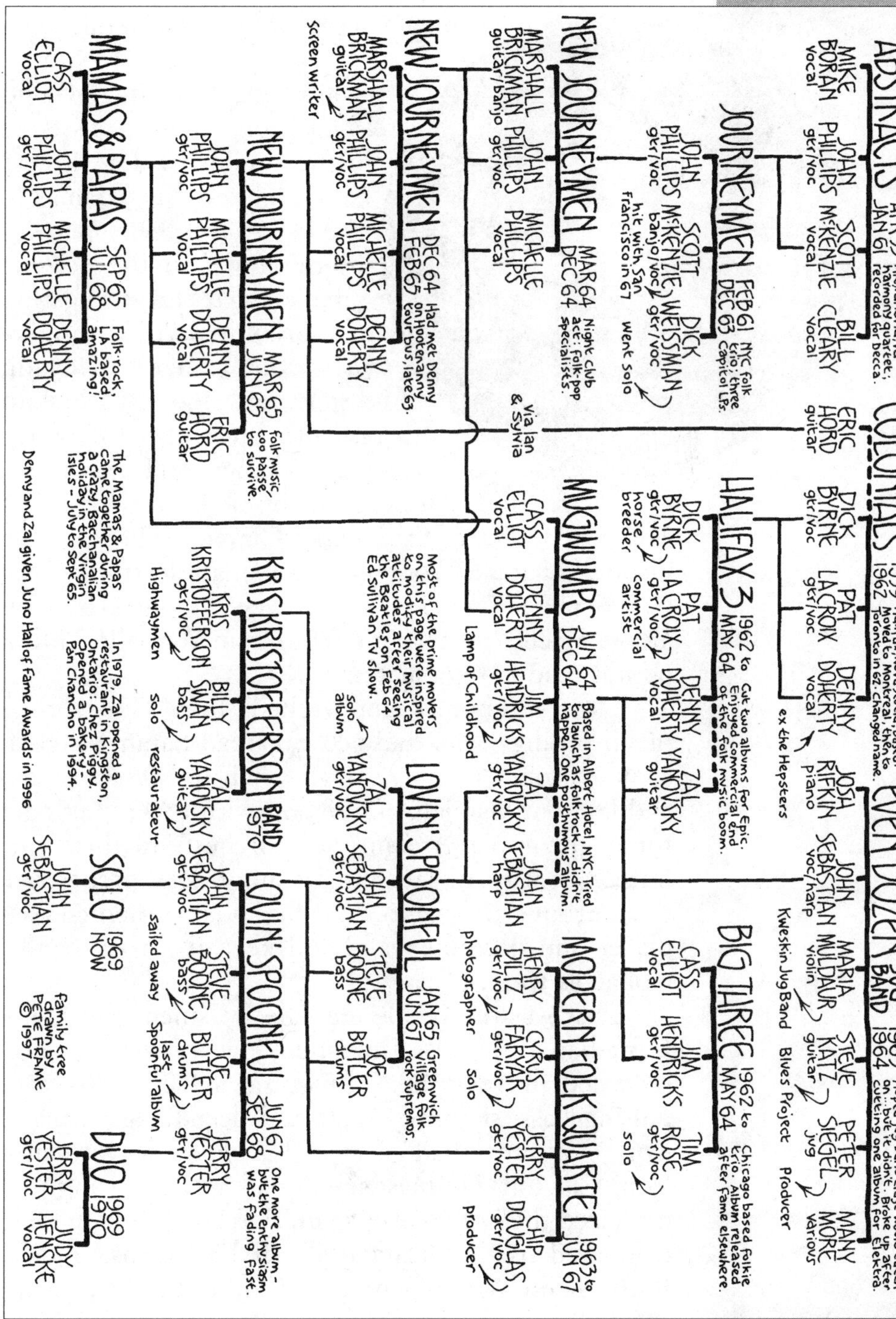
ABSTRACTS APR 59 JAN 61
Alexandria, Va harmony quartet; recorded for Decca.
MIKE BORAN vocal
JOHN PHILLIPS gtr/voc
SCOTT McKENZIE vocal
BILL CLEARY vocal
COLONIALS 1959 1962
Halifax, Nova Scotia, based. Moved to Montreal, then to Toronto in 62. Changed name.
ERIC HORD guitar
DICK BYRNE gtr/voc
PAT LA CROIX gtr/voc
DENNY DOHERTY vocal
ex the Hepsters
EVEN DOZEN JUG BAND 1963 1964
Hoped jug-band craze would catch on... but it didn't. Broke up after cutting one album for Elektra.
JOSH RIFKIN piano
JOHN SEBASTIAN voc/harp
MARIA MULDAUR violin
STEVE KATZ guitar
PETER SIEGEL jug
MANY MORE various
Kweskin Jug Band
Blues Project
Producer
JOURNEYMEN FEB 61 DEC 63
NYC folk trio; three Capitol LPs.
JOHN PHILLIPS gtr/voc
SCOTT McKENZIE banjo/voc
DICK WEISSMAN gtr/voc
hit with San Francisco in 67
went solo
HALIFAX 3 1962 to MAY 64
Cut two albums for Epic. Enjoyed commercial end of the folk music boom.
DICK BYRNE gtr/voc
PAT LA CROIX gtr/voc
DENNY DOHERTY vocal
ZAL YANOVSKY guitar
horse breeder
commercial artist
BIG THREE 1962 to MAY 64
Chicago based folkie trio. Album released after fame elsewhere.
CASS ELLIOT vocal
JIM HENDRICKS gtr/voc
TIM ROSE gtr/voc
solo
NEW JOURNEYMEN MAR 64 DEC 64
Night club act: folk-pop specialists.
MARSHALL BRICKMAN guitar/banjo
JOHN PHILLIPS gtr/voc
MICHELLE PHILLIPS vocal
Via Ian & Sylvia
MUGWUMPS JUN 64 DEC 64
Based in Albert Hotel, NYC. Tried to launch as folk rock... didn't happen. One posthumous album.
CASS ELLIOT vocal
DENNY DOHERTY vocal
JIM HENDRICKS gtr/voc
ZAL YANOVSKY gtr/voc
JOHN SEBASTIAN harp
Lamp of Childhood
MODERN FOLK QUARTET 1963 to JUN 67
HENRY DILTZ gtr/voc
CYRUS FARYAR gtr/voc
JERRY YESTER gtr/voc
CHIP DOUGLAS gtr/voc
photographer
solo
producer
NEW JOURNEYMEN DEC 64 FEB 65
Had met Denny on Hootenanny tour bus, late 63.
MARSHALL BRICKMAN guitar
JOHN PHILLIPS gtr/voc
MICHELLE PHILLIPS vocal
DENNY DOHERTY vocal
screen writer
Most of the prime movers on this page were inspired to modify their musical attitudes after seeing the Beatles on Feb 64 Ed Sullivan TV show.
LOVIN' SPOONFUL JAN 65 JUN 67
Greenwich Village folk rock supremos.
ZAL YANOVSKY gtr/voc
JOHN SEBASTIAN gtr/voc
STEVE BOONE bass
JOE BUTLER drums
solo album
NEW JOURNEYMEN MAR 65 JUN 65
folk music too passe to survive.
JOHN PHILLIPS gtr/voc
MICHELLE PHILLIPS vocal
DENNY DOHERTY vocal
ERIC HORD guitar
KRIS KRISTOFFERSON BAND 1970
KRIS KRISTOFFERSON gtr/voc
BILLY SWAN bass
ZAL YANOVSKY guitar
Highwaymen
solo
restaurateur
LOVIN' SPOONFUL JUN 67 SEP 68
One more album - but the enthusiasm was fading fast.
JOHN SEBASTIAN gtr/voc
STEVE BOONE bass
JOE BUTLER drums
JERRY YESTER gtr/voc
sailed away
last Spoonful album
MAMAS & PAPAS SEP 65 JUL 68
Folk-rock, LA based, amazing!
CASS ELLIOT vocal
JOHN PHILLIPS gtr/voc
MICHELLE PHILLIPS vocal
DENNY DOHERTY vocal
The Mamas & Papas came together during a crazy, Bacchanalian holiday in the Virgin Isles - July to Sept 65.
In 1979, Zal opened a restaurant in Kingston, Ontario: Chez Piggy. Opened a bakery - Pan Chancho in 1994.
Denny and Zal given Juno Hall of Fame Awards in 1996
SOLO 1969 NOW
JOHN SEBASTIAN gtr/voc
family tree drawn by PETE FRAME © 1997
DUO 1969 1970
JERRY YESTER gtr/voc
JUDY HENSKE vocal

know what he was talking about."

Back in Toronto, David Clayton-Thomas listened to the sounds of The Lovin' Spoonful and The Mamas & the Papas. But the singer was more drawn to the eclectic range of styles he was hearing in Yorkville. From singer-songwriters like Gordon Lightfoot and Joni Mitchell to the authentic blues of Sonny Terry & Brownie McGhee and the traditional jazz sounds of Lonnie Johnson and Jim McHarg's Metro Stompers, Clayton-Thomas was inspired by it all. "Yorkville was a major learning experience for me," he says now. "I went to high school on Yonge Street, but I went to college in Yorkville." Now, he was ready to graduate.

Clayton-Thomas approached Tony Collacott, a piano prodigy who had accompanied Sarah Vaughan at New York's Carnegie Hall when he was fourteen, and laid out his plan to fuse jazz with rock: "Let's get three guitar players and we'll orchestrate them like horns. Instead of strumming away, let's orchestrate them around the piano. And find a jazz-oriented bass player and drummer, and still keep it a rock band." Collacott was in.

That was the recipe for The Bossmen, whose big Canadian hit, "Brainwashed," was written and recorded in Yorkville. Three and a half minutes of pulsing bass, slashing guitar and fleet-fingered piano work, "Brainwashed" featured a gutsy performance from Clayton-Thomas, singing an anti-war song that criticized the U.S. presence in Vietnam. Though tame compared to the biting lyrics of Phil Ochs or even Buffy Sainte-Marie—the recording even bleeped out the word "damn"—it expressed a convincing rage about the politics of the day. "Brainwashed," bleep and all, raced to the top of the CHUM chart, dislodging The Beatles, The Rolling Stones and everything else for much of the summer of '66.

**Clayton-Thomas found a twelve-gauge shotgun in the arena manager's office and fired two rounds into the ceiling**

The Bossmen, however, went nowhere fast. American radio, deeply conservative, treated the single like a hot potato. Moreover, a tour of western Canada that summer was disastrous. Things fell apart in the northwestern Ontario city of Sault Ste. Marie when a motorcycle gang invaded the dance at a hockey arena where the band was playing, resulting in a massive brawl. The group's equipment got broken and Collacott was knocked out cold. Some semblance of order was restored only after Clayton-Thomas found a twelve-gauge shotgun in the arena manager's office and fired two rounds into the ceiling. "When the smoke cleared," he says, "the place was empty. Ever hear a shotgun go off in a metal arena? I couldn't hear for two days." But the jazz-rock sound The Bossmen had created resonated for Clayton-Thomas from then on.

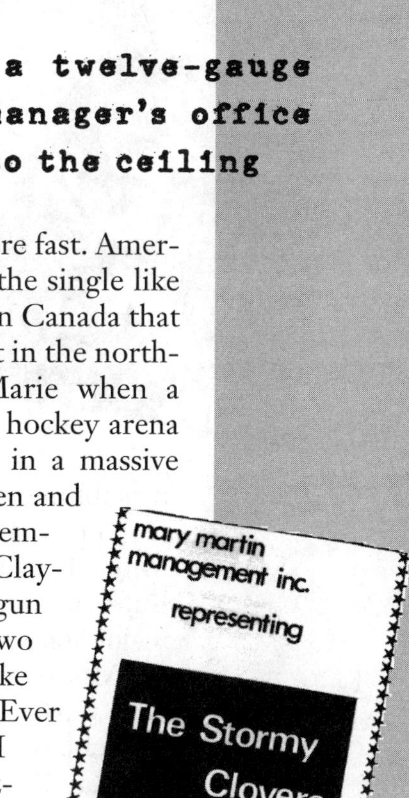


Joni Mitchell faced a much more receptive crowd at Mariposa that summer. In fact, Mitchell returned to the festival as one of its most popular attractions, joining a line-up that included Lightfoot, Doc Watson and The New Lost City Ramblers. Dressed in paisley and accompanied by guitarist David

Rea, Mitchell captivated audiences at both her evening and afternoon performances. This time, she brought a suitcase full of new songs, including "Both Sides Now" and "Night in the City" which she told her audience was inspired by Yorkville. "Music comes spilling out into the street," she sang, "colours go flashing in time."

Mitchell's appearance was a resounding triumph. "This girl has everything," enthused Ruth Jones (the Mariposa founder) in *Hoot*, the Canadian folk magazine, "looks, charm, personality, an inventive mind, excellent guitar and above all, a voice, which ranges from gutsy to sublime. My guess is that she will be a name to reckon with—and soon." Only two years earlier, Mitchell had come to Mariposa to hear her heroine Buffy Sainte-Marie. Now, she was one of the festival's major stars.

Montreal's Leonard Cohen also made an appearance at Mariposa that summer courtesy of The Stormy Clovers. A Toronto folk-rock group led by Susan Jains and Ray Perdue, the Clovers were the first artists anywhere to perform Cohen's songs, a full year before Judy Collins or even Cohen himself tackled his material. Cohen and the group shared a manager—Mary Martin—the same Toronto expatriate who'd been matchmaker for Dylan and The Hawks. It had been Martin who suggested that Cohen allow the Clovers to debut his songs, and the poet happily agreed.

With Jains singing Cohen numbers like "Suzanne" and "Sisters of Mercy," the Clovers travelled to Montreal to perform at the Venus de Milo coffee house on Sherbrooke Street. Cohen often dropped in to see them there. One night, in the intimate space of the Venus, the poet got up and joined them and sang his own songs for the first time.

Backed by the Clovers, Cohen made his first TV appearance on CBC's "Take 30" with Adrienne Clarkson. He sang both "Suzanne" and "So Long Marianne." Afterwards, Clarkson interviewed the poet-singer and asked, "And so you now want to sing instead of write poetry?" Cohen, in what Clarkson recalled was his "extreme politeness and sorrowful elegance," replied, "Well, I think the time is over when poets should sit on marble stairs with black capes."

The Penny Farthing's John McHugh remembers Cohen dropping in to his club during a Clovers performance. "I think he was in love with Susan [Jains]," speculates McHugh, "because she really was as cute as a button. She'd attach a big plastic daisy to her microphone stand and sing 'Suzanne' to all these dreamy-eyed men. One night, Cohen got up and sang a duet with her."

*The Stormy Clovers outside the Penny Farthing*

Playing covers was quite common, even for groups with strong songwriters. The Children, Ottawa's leading folk-rock act, played cover tunes at Ottawa high-school dances. But the group, comprising composers Bill Hawkins, Sandy Crawley and Peter Hodgson, who later became better known as Sneezy Waters, saved their original material for evenings at Le Hibou coffee house.

Bruce Cockburn had already written a number of songs by the time he joined The Children in

(from left) The Children's Bill Hawkins, Neville Wells, Richard Patterson, Sandy Crawley, Bruce Cockburn and David Wiffen

the summer of '66. But it was the influence of the group's Bill Hawkins, an established poet, that really inspired him. "Bill taught me about using words," recalls Cockburn. "I already had a sense of it because I always loved poetry, but he was more focused on that. He did a lot to get me to understand the importance of words, and was critical, in a useful way, of anything I wrote."

Initially, Cockburn just composed music for Hawkins's lyrics. And he estimates that there may be as many as a hundred of those songs "floating around out there." But writing with Hawkins gave Cockburn some much-needed experience, as did his performing with The Children, who got to open for The Rolling Stones. Later, the group would open for The Lovin' Spoonful at Toronto's Maple Leaf Gardens. There, Cockburn would meet Bernie Finkelstein, a budding music entrepreneur.

Bernie Finkelstein was pushing a broom, cleaning Yorkville's Café El Patio one afternoon, when he first heard The Paupers. The band was rehearsing for a week-long engagement at the club and Finkelstein, who made espresso coffees at night and cleaned the premises by day, began offering his opinions on everything from their Beatlesque singles "Never Send You Flowers" and "If I Told My Baby" to their Vidal Sassoon hairdos ("Batman-style" cuts, with the bangs trimmed to a conspicuous point in the middle). In particular, Finkelstein, a serious Dylan devotee, told the group that the best acts around were those writing original material. A natural manager,

*The Paupers' Bill Marion, Chuck Beal, Denny Gerrard and Skip Prokop in their "Batman-style" haircuts*

Like most Yorkville bands, the group had been handling its own affairs, with drummer Skip Prokop taking care of bookings and equipment rentals. With Finkelstein calling the shots, things started happening. When singer Bill Marion quit, Finkelstein promptly walked across the street to the Mousehole and recruited the red-haired Adam Mitchell, a folk singer performing there. "This is exactly the guy we need," Finkelstein told the band. "He not only sings and plays twelve-string, he writes his own songs!"

"Bernie could see that original material was what counted," says Mitchell, now a songwriter-producer living in Nashville. "At that point, very few local bands were doing their own songs, and it really helped to set us apart from the pack." Mitchell remembers him as both a visionary and a taskmaster. He really cracked the whip when it came to rehearsals, charging band members for infractions—much the same way Ronnie Hawkins had. "I got fined for having my gui-

*The hipper, Finkelstein-managed Paupers, with Prokop, Gerrard, Adam Mitchell and Beal*

tar capo in the wrong place during a song one night, and he fined me five dollars," says a still-incredulous Mitchell. "Since we were only making $50 a week at the time, it really hurt. I got so mad that I made another mistake and he fined me again!"

But Finkelstein's heavy-handed ways started paying dividends. With a sound that was becoming more folk-rock than pop, The Paupers quickly became one of the biggest draws in Yorkville, first at the El Patio and then at Boris's Red Gas Room on Avenue Road. The crowds came to hear Prokop's and Mitchell's songs, but also to watch the group's dynamic stage show built around earth-shaking drums, a wailing guitar and Denny Gerrard's mind-boggling bass. Mitchell and Gerrard joined a bearded Prokop to pound out thunderous rhythmic openings like a trio of Japanese Kodo drummers. Chuck Beal's guitar playing, meanwhile, was like an early version of U2's Edge, full of repeating, tape-looped notes and weird effects. As for the eccentric Gerrard—wearing his trade-mark Sluggo cap and performing frenetic, highly inventive bass solos—he was fast becoming a local legend.

*Finkel on the skins*

Finkelstein knew he had one of Yorkville's best groups. And he was beginning to enjoy the fruits of his labour, spending it on nickel and dime bags of grass. But the budding, nineteen-year-old impresario, whose office then was literally a pay phone opposite the El Patio, wasn't content to just sit back and get high. He had bigger plans for The Paupers, plans that involved following acts like The Sparrows into the larger, more lucrative U.S. market.

*An Ugly Ducklings board meeting: Robin Boers, John Read, Dave Bingham, (Brian Jones-clone) Glynn Bell and Roger Mayne*

The Ugly Ducklings would have gone nowhere if they hadn't started to write their own material. The Ducklings had started out as The Strolling Bones, a Rolling Stones clone band made up of singer Dave Bingham, lead guitarist Roger Mayne, rhythm guitarist Glynn Bell, bassist John Read and drummer Robin Boers. But none of the Ducks was as big a Stones fan as Bell, who consciously styled his long blond hair in a page-boy look to make himself a dead ringer for Brian Jones.

The Ducklings' first composition, a punchy piece of male bravado called "Nothin'," came about quickly one afternoon. "Like all of our songs," explains Bingham, "it evolved out of Roger or Glynn working up some riff on the guitar and me just singing along to it." He adds, "In those days, I'd make up the lyrics in like fifteen minutes. It was all pretty spontaneous stuff." The Canadian songwriting tradition, born in the folk era with Ian Tyson's "Four Strong Winds," had now taken hold in rock bands.

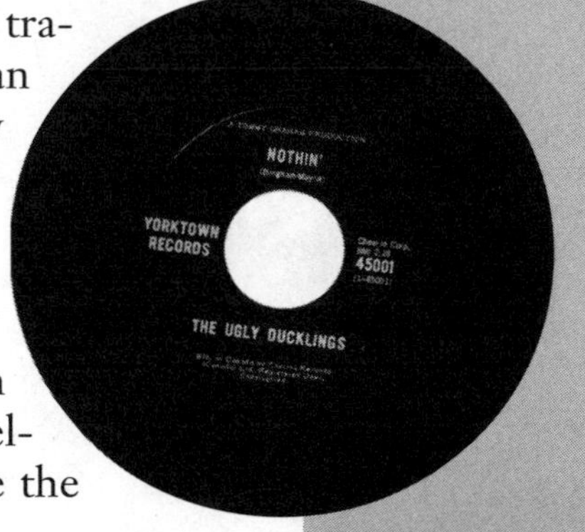


A few short weeks after it was recorded (on a two-track machine for just $300), "Nothin'" was playing on CHUM. Deejays had a lot of power in those days, and CHUM's Jungle Jay Nelson and Bob McAdorey helped to make the song a hit by pushing the record into heavy rotation. When "Nothin'" was entered in the station's weekly "battle of the bands" contest (where singles by local groups competed for listener votes), it won thirteen consecutive times.

The success of "Nothin'" led the Ducklings directly to the gig of their dreams—opening for the Stones at Maple Leaf Gardens on June 29, 1966. The thrill of playing with their heroes was offset only by the disappointment of not getting to meet them backstage.

"It was a real drag," recalls Bingham. "The Stones were our gods. But they had such heavy security around them that we couldn't even get close. We saw them arrive in a paddy wagon that drove right into the Gardens. Keith Richards was so drunk that he fell out onto the concrete floor. If their guys hadn't caught him, he wouldn't have played that night."

Tension mounted as show time drew closer. Bell caused near pandemonium by sticking his head through the curtains and staring out at the 15,000 Stones-hungry fans. "There's Brian Jones!" the crowd screamed. Bell retreated behind the curtain momentarily, grinning. Let's see if that works again, he thought. More screams this time, only louder. After he tried it the third time, getting a hysterical response, a worried Gardens staff put an end to his fun.

In a cheeky move, the Ducks kicked off their set with "Everybody Needs Somebody to Love," the very song the Stones were using in those days to open their shows. Afterwards Bell, Boers and a couple of girlfriends, determined to meet their heroes,

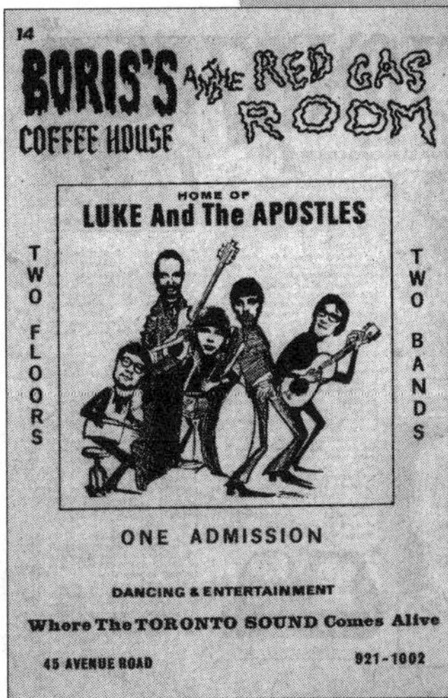


hung around the Stones' hotel long enough to get in to see them. Jagger, obviously in a generous mood, complimented Bell and Boers on "Nothin'," which he said he'd heard on the radio coming in from the airport. Several months later, Jagger told England's *Melody Maker* that The Ugly Ducklings were his favourite Canadian rock band. Somebody pinch us, the Toronto boys thought.

Looser and louder than any other band on the scene, the Ducks quickly became local heroes to a whole tribe of blues-rock lovers. Packed shows at tiny Charlie Brown's (where the band insisted on performing with the same massive Fender Showman

**On-stage, he was transformed into a writhing, shaking, screaming package of pure sexual energy**

amps they used at the Gardens) were legendary for their displays of body sweat and ear-splitting volume.

As "Nothin'" shot up to number eighteen on the CHUM chart that August, Luke & the Apostles—a quintet fronted by the Jaggeresque Luke Gibson—were packing the Purple Onion. Although guys were drawn to the Apostles' raw cover versions of songs like "Crossroads," "Good Morning Little Schoolgirl" and "Can't Judge a Book," girls were drooling over the sight of Gibson.

Off-stage, Gibson was shy and quiet, but on-stage, he was transformed into a writhing, shaking, screaming package of pure sexual energy. With his curly blond hair and boyish good looks, Gibson was the band's biggest asset. But the Apostles—guitarist Mike McKenna, keyboardist Peter Germyn, bassist Jim Jones and drummer Rich McMurray—sounded good enough to Paul Rothchild of New York's Elektra Records, the talent scout who later discovered The Doors.

In the midst of the band's year-long stand at the Onion, Rothchild arrived in Yorkville to check out what he'd heard was a happening music scene. After catching one set by Luke & the Apostles, he wanted to sign them. The next day, the talent scout showed up at the band's rehearsal at the Onion and asked them to play while he telephoned his boss, Jac Holzman. "We started doing our own song, 'Been Burnt,'" recalls Gibson, "and Paul hands me the phone and tells me to sing. That's how we auditioned."

The deal took Gibson and the group to New York where they recorded both "Been Burnt," a driving, incendiary number, and McKenna's "Don't Know Why." But in a cruel twist of fate, and a sign of the times, the record's release was put on hold for over a year while Rothchild served a prison sentence for marijuana possession. Luke & the Apostles then became victims of record company politics and were eventually dropped, leaving a recording legacy of just one classic single. Rothchild, who died in 1996, referred to the band as "the greatest album I never got to make."

The Paupers, The Ugly Ducklings and Luke & the Apostles were part of an explosion of new bands that filled the Toronto bar and coffee-house circuit in 1966. There were more than 1,400 rock bands in the city that year, 400 of them earning musicians' union scale. Despite the fact that Toronto had only a handful of studios at the time, those groups produced over 200 recorded singles in 1966 alone. Promoter Ron Scrib-

**CHUM CHART TOP TEN MAY 9, 1966**

*Monday, Monday*
Mamas & Papas

*Kicks*
Paul Revere

*Good Lovin'*
Young Rascals

*Shapes of Things*
Yardbirds

*Leaning on the Lamppost*
Herman's Hermits

*Sloop John B*
Beach Boys

*When a Man Loves a Woman*
Percy Sledge

*I Hear Trumpets Blow*
Tokens

*Secret Agent Man*
Johnny Rivers

*Lovedrops*
Barry Allen

*Luke & the Apostles*

ner described Toronto that year as "the New Orleans of rock and roll," while Bob McAdorey, musical director of CHUM, went even further: "It's just like Liverpool before The Beatles made it."

All the musical activity led to a catchphrase to describe the new sound coming from Toronto. Obviously borrowed from the Mersey Sound or the Motown Sound, the term "the Toronto Sound" was applied to the myriad bands performing on Yonge Street and in Yorkville. Although observers noted several characteristics—including a raunchy Robbie Robertson–style Telecaster guitar and a droning Hammond B3 organ—few musicians could actually agree on a definition of the music. "It's kind of whiny," offered Luke Gibson, whose band many thought epitomized the Toronto Sound, "a real screamingly dirty sound. Just about every lead guitar player plays that way." To Chuck Beal, lead guitarist for The Paupers, it was volume that set Toronto bands apart. "They all play louder, harder and with a more driving beat," he said. "Most U.S. groups seem soft compared to us."

Nor was there any agreement on the origins of the sound. To The Mandala's Domenic Troiano, Yonge Street influenced Yorkville.

But to Beal, it was Yorkville that contributed most to the explosion of Canadian music. "Yorkville, with its many clubs, gives a lot of bands a chance to work six nights a week," Beal observed. "It makes them compete every night against the band next door for the crowds. But it's not just the competition," he added. "The whole atmosphere, the whole way of life, the mood in Yorkville is so great. We've turned down jobs offering two and three times as much just to play there."

CHUM and the *Toronto Telegram*'s popular "After Four" section sponsored a massive concert at Maple Leaf Gardens in September billed as "The Toronto Sound." The home-grown extravaganza ("14 Hours—14 Big Groups in One Place at One Time!" read the posters) featured established acts like The Paupers, The Ugly Ducklings and Luke & the Apostles as well as such up-and-coming bands as The Spasstiks, The Last Words and The Trip. The concert sold out and thousands of teenage girls were suddenly screaming for local bands the way they had for The Beatles and The Rolling Stones. The Toronto Sound show also put the city on the map in the eyes of the American record industry, which sent along its top talent scouts.

*Clayton-Thomas*

In November '66, Joni Mitchell made her debut at Bernie Fiedler's Riverboat—on the stage, not in the kitchen. It was a triumphant performance, establishing Mitchell as an artist in her own right and a songwriter whose material possessed a distinct Canadian quality. Songs like "Urge for Going," "Winter Lady" and "Come to the Sunshine" that she performed that week were rich in imagery. Each painted a vivid portrait of the changing seasons and owed much to her origins on the Saskatchewan

Prairies. Like Tyson and Lightfoot before her, Mitchell was writing songs with a unique sense of place.

Her Riverboat performance was a turning point. Afterwards, Mitchell left her husband and moved to New York where, she hoped, bigger things lay in store. Settling in Manhattan's Chelsea district, she turned her one-bedroom apartment into what she called her "magic princess" retreat, with bedroom walls covered in tinfoil and door frames lined with crêpe paper. There she began writing as many as four songs a week, including the buoyant "Chelsea Morning" (for which U.S. president Bill Clinton and his wife, Hillary, later named their daughter). "I Had a King" detailed her marriage break-up with its lines about the man who "carried me off to his country for marriage too soon." With $400 in the bank, she told *Rolling Stone*, she thought she was "filthy rich."

*Joni, triumphant at the Riverboat*

But Mitchell was about to become much richer, very quickly. While performing for $15 a night at New York's Café Au Go-Go, then the hottest club in the city, her new friend Buffy Sainte-Marie brought along her manager Elliott Roberts to see her. Although Roberts remembers Mitchell as "a jumble of creative clutter with a guitar case full of napkins, road maps and scraps of paper—all covered with lyrics," he was astonished at her talent—so much so that he promptly quit managing Buffy to handle Joni exclusively.

Meanwhile, David Clayton-Thomas was realizing

that the United States was the place for an aspiring musician, something Joni had already figured out. Without a strong Canadian recording industry or radio stations that were truly committed to playing Canadian music's new sound, there was nothing to keep him in Canada. After his Bossmen went bust, Clayton-Thomas saw an opportunity to head south. One night at the Riverboat, he was sitting in with legendary blues musician John Lee Hooker. After the show, Hooker explained to him that his guitarist usually doubled as his chauffeur. Would Clayton-Thomas drive him to New York? Clayton-Thomas jumped at the chance.

*Lightfoot with CHUM DJ Bob McAdorey*

But when they arrived in the Big Apple, the pair ran into trouble. A prostitute whom Hooker knew stole his car and he took off after her, leaving Clayton-Thomas high and dry. The Toronto singer began scuffling around Greenwich Village, looking for work.

Meanwhile, the sheen was coming off the Big Apple for The Sparrow. Their New York producers were pushing them for more of a lightweight pop sound, while The Sparrow were much more bluesy. John Kay and the group sensed it was time to move west, where more experimental sounds were in the air. Arriving in Los Angeles in late '66, The Sparrow ran into Buffalo Springfield. Bruce Palmer and Neil Young were happy to see them, both curious to hear about the Yorkville scene. The Sparrow got their first gig at It's Boss on Sunset Boulevard. After setting up their gear at the club, they checked into a nearby motel. When they returned to the bar for the gig, their guitars and amplifiers had been ripped off. But friends came to the rescue. Palmer and Young loaned The Sparrow equipment so the band could keep its gig.

The Sparrow's stay in L.A. was cut short by the Sunset Strip riots. Clashes between teenagers hanging out on the Strip and city authorities enforcing anti-loitering laws turned ugly as police responded with brutal force, hitting demonstrators with truncheons and throwing them into paddy wagons. After witnessing the riots on TV, Stephen Stills was compelled to write "For What It's Worth," soon to become a major hit for Buffalo Springfield and an anthem for the times.

The riots closed many clubs on the Strip. Suddenly, there was nowhere to play. Migrating north, Sparrow (no more "The") arrived in San Francisco in January '67, just in time to catch the "Human Be-In" at Golden Gate Park. Organized by the Diggers, a Haight-Ashbury group of hippie social activists, the Be-In was the first mass gathering of the Bay Area counter-culture. In a crowd of 20,000, John Kay was blown away by the acid-rock sounds of Jefferson Airplane and The Grateful Dead. Says Kay, "I've been lucky to be in a number of places just as they exploded—Yorkville, Greenwich Village, Sunset Strip during the riots and then San Francisco, where we blundered into the peace, love and brotherhood of the first Be-In, which spawned the Summer of Love and the whole 'San Francisco, please be sure to wear a flower in your

**CHUM CHART TOP TEN JULY 18, 1966**

*Pied Piper*
Crispian St. Peters

*Hanky Panky*
Tommy James & Shondells

*Sweet Pea*
Tommy Roe

*Lil' Red Riding Hood*
Sam the Sham

*Solitary Man*
Neil Diamond

*Brainwashed*
David Clayton-Thomas

*You Don't Have to Say You Love Me*
Dusty Springfield

*I Saw Her Again*
Mamas & Papas

*Mother's Little Helper/Lady Jane*
Rolling Stones

*Billy & Sue*
B.J. Thomas

*Troiano, at Mandala's peak in '67*

hair' thing. I wouldn't trade those memories for anything."

While his contemporaries were testing American waters, Lightfoot was content to remain in Canada, savouring his newfound celebrity status. During the summer of '66, he had continued to pack the Riverboat, although with a new look and a slightly different sound. "Some of the jammed-in crowd were jolted by the short-sleeved flowered shirt, mod tie and Lightfoot's new Caesar-style hairdo," the *Toronto Telegram* reported. But Lightfoot's voice was as strong and vibrant as ever as he began to move away from his country-tinged sound to a more pop-ballad style.

It was at a Riverboat gig that Lightfoot first met Cathy Smith. Bernie Fiedler had hired her as a waitress after Smith came looking for work to support herself and her "band baby," Tracey Lee. One night, after finishing his sets at the Boat, Lightfoot and a friend partied with Smith and one of her girlfriends. Lightfoot and Smith wound up in a bedroom together and Lightfoot's affair with Smith would continue off and on for the next four years.

One fall afternoon shortly thereafter, the phone rang in Lightfoot's spacious duplex in midtown Toronto. Bob Jarvis, a producer from CBC TV, was calling. The network was planning a big special to celebrate Canada's upcoming centennial. Would Lightfoot be willing to write a song? He agreed. Today, Lightfoot recalls how the song came about: "Part of their special had a segment about railroading and they wanted a song from me to build a scene around. Bob

Jarvis sent me over to the library and I got out a book on Van Horne, the railroad's chief engineer. That's where I got the word 'navvy' from. Then I thought about how I was going to structure the thing, so I borrowed from a [U.S. folk singer] Bob Gibson format. I wrote the slow part in the middle and the fast parts at each end, just as he did in his 'Civil War Trilogy.'"

Lightfoot's "Canadian Railroad Trilogy" debuted on CBC's "100 Years Young" on New Year's Day and was a stunning success. From its mood-setting opening, "There was a time in this fair land when the railroad did not run," and its stirring chorus about navvies "swinging [their] hammers in the bright blazing sun," to the chilling closing about "when the green, dark forest was too silent to be real," the song worked on many levels. It conveyed the vastness of Canada and the striking beauty of its landscapes. It somehow also achieved what historians, journalists and politicians had failed to do: bring the country together with a proud sense of its past.

Armed with a four-song demo tape of The Paupers, Finkelstein flew to New York in the winter of 1966–67 in search of a record deal. On the advice of Harvey Glatt, the Ottawa promoter and owner of Le Hibou coffee house, he arranged a meeting with MGM Records. MGM had started a label called Verve Forecast featuring Richie Havens, Tim Buckley and The Paul Butterfield Blues Band. Cool company, Finkelstein thought, for a folk-rock band like The Paupers. To his surprise, MGM were interested and signed the band to the company's Verve Forecast label right on the spot. With the signing, The

Paupers became the first Canadian rock group to snare a fat American recording contract.

Flush with confidence, Finkelstein ventured into Greenwich Village and looked up Howard Solomon who ran the Café Au Go-Go. When Solomon learned where The Paupers were from, he suggested they open for Ian & Sylvia at the club, making a nice, all-Canadian bill. Finkelstein demurred. "What else have you got?" he gambled, somewhat boldly. "Well, there's a date in March with this band called Jefferson Airplane," said Solomon, "but they've never played outside California." Finkelstein, whose band had never played outside Canada, had heard of them. "We'll take it," he said.

Back in Toronto, The Paupers were enjoying a medium-sized hit with the folk-flavoured "If I Call You by Some Name," which was getting airplay on local radio. Meanwhile, the group prepared for their New York debut by stepping up their already rigorous rehearsal schedule. Singer Adam Mitchell remembers one particular twenty-two-hour session which left his fingers bleeding and his voice hoarse. Prokop, who was well used to brutal practising from his days as a Canadian champion drum-corps competitor, joined Finkelstein in pushing the band to polish their material. By the time the group's members flew down to the Café Au Go-Go, they knew exactly what they were doing. "We had no fear," recalls Prokop. "We were a well-oiled machine."

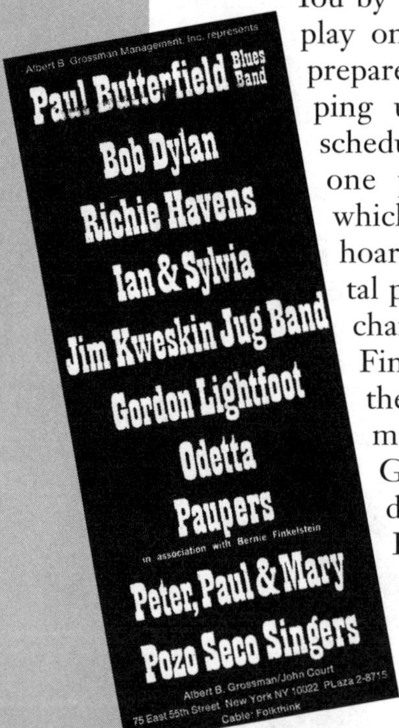


Like Prokop's Paupers, Domenic Troiano's The Mandala seemed destined to break into the United States. "The Mandala are about to take off," gushed pop critic Jack Batten, now a well-known mystery writer, at the time. "And when they do they're going to take a lot of Canadian rock groups up to the top with them. They're going to make the Toronto Sound big. Big—that's big like in the Mersey Sound. Big sound, big money, big everything."

Fuelled by the hype, The Mandala's manager hooked the band up with the William Morris Agency, the top booking agency in the States, and secured a gig at L.A.'s trendy Whiskey A Go-Go. After generating a buzz at their Whiskey show, The Mandala opened a three-week gig at Hollywood's Hullabaloo club where they eventually drew a capacity crowd of 1,400 by word of mouth. During the second week, singer George Olliver was mobbed by young girls as he fled the stage after the last number. And by the third week, according to one newspaper account, "the group had to cut short its finale, as teeny-boppers thronged the stage clutching at Olliver and dragging drummer Whitey Glan off his perch."

The Mandala returned home as heroes and played standing-room-only shows. One night, the band was performing at the Hawks' Nest while bluesman Bo Diddley was in at the Le Coq D'Or. During a break, Diddley came upstairs to hear these so-called blue-eyed soul wonders. Impressed by what he heard, the man who put the jungle-beat back in rock 'n' roll returned home to Chicago and mentioned The Mandala to the people at his label, the legendary Chess Records. A few weeks later, producer Marshall Chess flew up to catch Troiano and his band perform at the YMCA in Hamilton. He promptly signed them.

**CHUM CHART TOP TEN AUGUST 8, 1966**

*Summer in the City*
Lovin' Spoonful

*I Saw Her Again*
Mamas & Papas

*Wild Thing*
The Troggs

*Lil' Red Riding Hood*
Sam the Sham

*Where Were You When I Needed You*
Grass Roots

*I Couldn't Live Without Your Love*
Petula Clark

*Somewhere My Love*
Ray Conniff Singers

*The Merry Ploughboy*
Carlton Showband

*Hanky Panky*
Tommy James & Shondells

*See You in September*
The Happenings

Troiano and his mates were ecstatic. Chess was the home of Muddy Waters and many of their other heroes. In Chicago, The Mandala recorded the first of three singles that rank among the best to come out of Canada in the 1960s. Troiano's "Opportunity," especially, captures the exuberance of the band. With a spirited introduction drawn from their California sojourn—"We came three thousand miles from Canada to L.A., to tell you exactly how we *feel*"—the song, all sass and syncopation, zoomed up the CHUM chart to number three in February of 1967. The opportunities seemed limitless.

It was a chilly March morning when The Paupers flew into New York for their Café Au Go-Go gig. Spring was still nowhere in sight and a cold wind hit Greenwich Village that night like a rude slap in the face. Inside the club, however, the temperature was warm with body heat. The village had been abuzz for days with talk about the group from Haight-Ashbury, led by a striking singer named Grace Slick, that was making its East Coast debut. Now the Au Go-Go was packed with the elite from both the media and music worlds, a who's who of the hip.

Finkelstein did a quick tally of the heavyweights. There were record company executives from RCA and United Artists and many of the top agents and managers in the business, from The Beatles' Brian Epstein to Albert Grossman, who was already managing Dylan, Peter Paul & Mary,

Ian & Sylvia and Lightfoot. Some of the leading critics and photographers of the day were also crammed in, including the *Village Voice*'s Richard Goldstein and Linda Eastman (the future Linda McCartney). All of them had come to see the super-hyped Airplane.

*Murray McLauchlan*

When The Paupers stepped out onto the darkened stage just after nine o'clock, they planned to simply give the Au Go-Go audience the same set they delivered every night at El Patio. As the lights came up and the band kicked into percussive assault, slashing guitar and fuzz bass that opened "Think I Care," an electric surge raced through the crowd. Who were these guys? Prokop's crisp drumming was flawless. Mitchell's vocals hit all the right notes. Beal's looped guitar brought shrieks of excitement. And Gerrard's bass solos, especially the one on "Dr. Feelgood," were nothing short of stunning.

By the time The Paupers finished with the anthemic "Magic People," the Café Au Go-Go—indeed, the whole village—was theirs. "We absolutely tore the place apart," admits Adam Mitchell. Added Prokop, "People went berserk. They hollered, screamed and pounded. It was absolutely outrageous."

As they reached their dressing room, The Paupers were greeted by Epstein and Grossman. The *Voice* and *Esquire* demanded immediate interviews. And Eastman, then one of New York's leading freelance pho-

tographers, was acting like a groupie and wanted to shoot the group the very next day. (She later underscored the point by delivering several joints to Finkelstein at his hotel.) The Paupers were blown away by the response. The poor Airplane hadn't just been upstaged. They'd had their Haight-Ashbury asses well and truly kicked.

In the *Voice*, Richard Goldstein raved about this group that had "swooped out of nowhere, from a scene nobody knew about." The Paupers, he added "descended on New York like electronic thunder...their music makes the average combo sound like a string quartet doing Wagner...they have a power and discipline I've never seen before in performance." Finkelstein was summoned to Grossman's plush apartment overlooking Central Park. There, he recalls, Grossman and his partner John Court got him incredibly stoned on grass and made him a lucrative offer to co-manage his band. Laughs Finkelstein: "I was ridiculously high. Plus, I was so excited that I might get to meet Dylan through Grossman, that I just wanted to do the deal."

By mid-summer, The Paupers would release their debut album, *Magic People*. Featuring the snarling, fuzz-drenched "Think I Care" and the dreamy, drum-driven title track, the album would offer a good taste of The Paupers' kaleidoscopic, "pre-psychedelic" sound. With Grossman's muscle behind them, the group began getting major bookings all across America, including a May date—opening again for the Airplane—this time at Bill Graham's Fillmore theatre in San Francisco.

No other Yorkville folk singer was more deeply influenced by Dylan than Murray McLauchlan.

Visually, with his Robinson Crusoe cap and curly hair, he resembled Donovan, himself the quintessential Dylan imitator. But musically, he perfectly captured Dylan's literary bent and sympathy for the underdog, expressed in his early songs like "Sylvia Shaw," about a kind-hearted hooker, and "Hard Angel," about a fading swinger. "Until I heard Dylan," says McLauchlan, "I thought songs were only about stupid stuff. The real power, I thought, was in literature. But suddenly I realized songs didn't have to be stupid. They could express ideas and draw from literature. It was an amazing revelation."

Although he initially sounded like a Dylan wannabe, McLauchlan quickly found his own voice. Increasingly, his songs took on a more individual perspective as McLauchlan started writing directly from personal experience. "Child's Song," written about his leaving home, stood out as a moving declaration of independence. And "Sixteen Lanes of Highway," about Toronto's urban sprawl, was McLauchlan's poignant response to seeing his outdoor playground covered with asphalt.

Bernie Fiedler knew McLauchlan from Riverboat hoot nights. McLauchlan was always in his face asking for a chance to perform at the club. But in 1966, the folk singer had still not impressed Fiedler enough to get his own billing. McLauchlan remembers taking his girlfriend Patti Sockwell to the Riverboat one night that year to hear Phil Ochs. They sat in one of the club's red vinyl–cushioned booths and watched as Ochs performed his biting protest tunes and "Changes," the bitter-sweet love song he'd reportedly written on the Riverboat's back steps. In a little

**CHUM CHART**
**TOP TEN**
**OCTOBER 10, 1966**

*Last Train to Clarksville*
The Monkees

*Wipeout*
Surfaris

*See See Rider*
Eric Burdon & Animals

*96 Tears*
Mysterians

*Girl on a Swing*
Gerry & Pacemakers

*Spin Spin*
Gordon Lightfoot

*Hooray for Hazel*
Tommy Roe

*Cherish*
The Association

*Reach Out I'll Be There*
Four Tops

*Born a Woman*
Sandy Posey

over a year, McLauchlan would be performing there himself.

## DISCS TO DISCOVER

*Creeque Alley: The History of The Mamas & the Papas* (2 CD set): The Mamas & the Papas (MCA, 1991)

*The Lovin' Spoonful Anthology:* The Lovin' Spoonful (Rhino, 1990)

*Too Much Too Soon*: The Ugly Ducklings (Pacemaker, 1997)

*Made in Canada: Our Rock 'n' Roll History, Vol. 3, Eclectic Avenue* (1965➔): various artists (BMG, 1990)

# 8

# Love-itis

The San Francisco Be-In that John Kay had dropped in on was a cultural earthquake. The word about the "Gathering of the Tribes," some 20,000 strong, quickly spread into Canada. With it came the news of the flowering Haight-Ashbury culture, the new sounds of Jefferson Airplane and Grateful Dead, the hippie costumes of kaftans, peacock feathers and army-surplus gear and the mind-altering effects of acid—especially the primo stuff produced in the Bay Area lab of amateur chemist Augustus Owsley Stanley III, who was best known by his middle name Owsley.

By the spring, San Francisco–style Love-Ins were happening in Vancouver, Saskatoon, Montreal and Toronto. More than 4,500 gathered in Toronto's Queen's Park on May 22, blowing bubbles, burning incense and dancing barefoot to the beat of such bands as Montreal's The Rabble and Toronto's Isabella Blues Band. Some in the crowd entertained themselves, sitting in circles, playing bongos, Indian drums, bells, flutes and even sitars. In

*Buffy Sainte-Marie at the Toronto Love-In, Queen's Park, May 22, 1967 (lawyer Clayton Ruby is front row, centre, wearing glasses)*

some parts of the park, the air was thick with pot. At least one group smoked banana peels, thinking that it produced a mild, marijuana-like high.

The crowd listened politely when the great Canadian poet Earle Birney, then writer-in-residence at the University of Toronto, read his work. They applauded more enthusiastically when Leonard Cohen stepped on to the stage, announcing that "spring called me here." Dressed in a brown suede jacket and turtleneck, Cohen was the prince of cool as he sang before his largest audience to date. But the gathering saved its most effusive greeting for Buffy Sainte-Marie. When the raven-haired Cree singer performed her stirring protest anthem "Universal Soldier" and her touching love song "Until It's Time for You to Go," the event was declared an unqualified success. The only casualty of the day was half a bed of hippie-picked yellow tulips.

**At least one group smoked banana peels, thinking that it produced a mild, marijuana-like high**

The Love-In had been organized by an offshoot of Haight-Ashbury's Diggers. But the Toronto Diggers were more than concert promoters. Led by Brian (Blues) Chapman and David DePoe, son of CBC newsman Norman DePoe, they were hippie Samaritans who dispensed free food and clothing to the hundreds of kids who were flocking into Yorkville that summer. At the same time, the Diggers supplied volunteers to the Trailer, a medical and counselling clinic on Avenue Road run by the Jewish Family and Child Services agency.

But the swelling numbers also brought an increased police presence—and tension—to Yorkville's streets. Kids started getting hit by a sudden rash of drug and vagrancy charges. To advise kids on their rights, the Diggers, with lawyers Clayton Ruby and Paul Copeland, set up a Yorkville legal aid clinic. And the summer was only beginning.

*The Raja were part of the nehru shirt contingent*

Meanwhile, a love-in on a national scale had broken out with the previous month's opening of Expo 67 in Montreal, a massive event that lasted all summer long. Timed to coincide with the country's centennial celebrations, Expo 67 brought the world—literally 50 million tourists—to Canada's doorstep. Basking in the international attention, Canada proved it had more to offer than wheat and hockey. From the diverse exhibitions of the individual provincial pavilions to stunning architecture of Moshe Safdie's Habitat housing experiment (described by author Robert Fulford as stacked "blocks in a child's higgledy-pig-

*Buffy Sainte-Marie; Leonard Cohen at the Toronto Love-In: "spring called me here"*

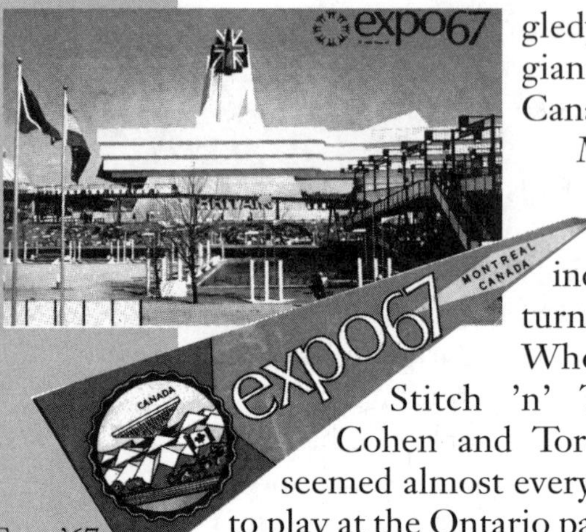


*Expo '67: a love-in on a national scale*

gledy pyramid"), Expo 67 was one giant birthday party that made Canada feel good about itself.

Musicians from every corner of the country found a stage to perform on at Expo, including Vancouver's The Nocturnals, Winnipeg's The Guess Who, former Maritimers The Stitch 'n' Tyme, Montreal's Leonard Cohen and Toronto's Gordon Lightfoot. It seemed almost every band in Yorkville got invited to play at the Ontario pavilion. There were also cross-cultural exchanges. Jay Telfer of Toronto's A Passing Fancy remembers jamming with a Montreal group called Les Têtes Blanches. "We taught them some of our songs in English and we learned one of theirs in French," says Telfer. He added, laughing, "Our performances together may have been a bit feeble, but they were a lot of fun."

Meanwhile, Bobby Gimby's "Ca-na-da," the cheery, government-sponsored singalong became a nationwide hit, both for Gimby's Young Canada Singers and for The Sugar Shoppe, a Mamas & Papas–style vocal group that included Victor Garber, now a respected actor. Both versions of the song, with its exuberant boast "now we are twenty million," sold an astonishing 300,000 copies.

*A Stitch 'n' Tyme at Expo with "internationally renowned beauty" Greta Thyssen*

Although he'd inhaled (deeply) the dizzying smell of success with Albert Grossman, Bernie Finkelstein was bummed out. Being a partner in the most powerful management company in the world was great, but Finkelstein found himself no longer in control of his own band. Plus, he had to admit, he was doing way too much dope. "I kind of lost my way in New York," Finkelstein now admits. After several months, he sold his interest in The Paupers to Grossman for $20,000 and moved back to Toronto.

With music-industry heavyweight Grossman at the helm, bigger things lay in store. First, Grossman began boasting that The Paupers were going to be the biggest thing since The Beatles. Then he landed the group a prestigious booking at the Monterey International Pop Festival south of San Francisco. The first rock festival of its kind, Monterey coincided with the June release of The Beatles' revolutionary *Sgt. Pepper's Lonely Hearts Club Band* album, which was played during intermissions throughout the weekend. The festival featured dozens of performers, including Jefferson Airplane, Janis Joplin & the Holding Company and Otis Redding. In particular, Monterey was the North American launching pad for two acts: The Who and Jimi Hendrix, who gave his now-legendary, guitar-blazing (literally) performance.

Denny Doherty was there, along with his fellow Mamas & Papas (Papa John Phillips was one of the organizers). It was to be one of their last appearances before getting lost in a dizzying world of martinis, fast cars and heavy dope. And although Buffalo Springfield also appeared, neither Neil Young nor Bruce Palmer was with them. Palmer had been deported back to Canada after a marijuana bust in New York, while Young quit the band temporarily in an artistic snit. David Crosby of The

*The Sugar Shoppe: A Mamas and Papas-style vocal group that included actor Victor Garber (second from left)*

Los Angeles Free Press July 21, 1967

ARE PAUPERS DESTINED TO SURPASS BEATLES?

BILL KERBY

world: Mike Flagfield's Electric Bloomers and the Paupers. Everyone who has ever heard a Dylan or a Butterfield record

so precise, so deft, because they know about thirty-five hours per week more than most groups. This internal discipline has honed

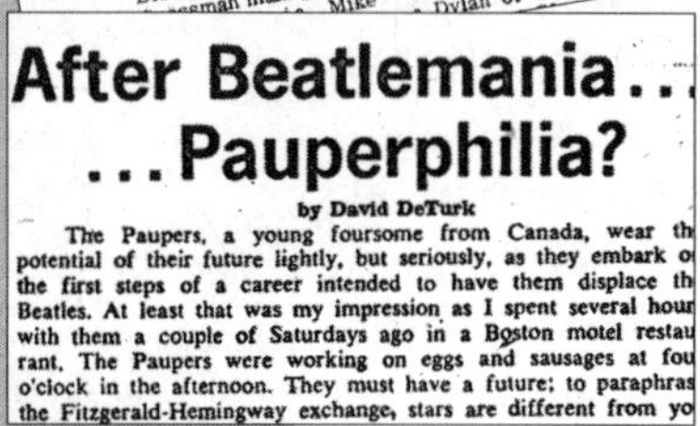

After Beatlemania...
...Pauperphilia?

by David DeTurk

The Paupers, a young foursome from Canada, wear th potential of their future lightly, but seriously, as they embark o the first steps of a career intended to have them displace th Beatles. At least that was my impression as I spent several hour with them a couple of Saturdays ago in a Boston motel restau rant. The Paupers were working on eggs and sausages at fou o'clock in the afternoon. They must have a future; to paraphras the Fitzgerald-Hemingway exchange, stars are different from yo

Byrds stood in for Young.

Monterey was a big deal for The Paupers after their Café Au Go-Go show-stopper. The group spent two weeks rehearsing for the festival, working out a strong, twenty-minute medley of their best numbers. The chance to blow away the competition looked good when the band was scheduled to follow mellow popsters The Association. David Crosby hyped The Paupers in his rave introduction, calling them the best thing he'd ever heard. "Just watch," he told the crowd of 30,000, "you're going to be amazed."

The minute The Paupers kicked into their set, everything seemed to go terribly wrong. First of all, guitarist Chuck Beal's amp crapped out, then came back on, emitting an odious, sputtering noise. To make matters worse, Denny Gerrard's bass playing seemed strangely out of sync. The problem may possibly have been a batch of LSD circulating at Monterey, likely Purple Haze tabs from Owsley's infamous lab. According to Pauper Adam Mitchell, Gerrard had dropped some acid just before going on-stage, and wound up marching to the beat of his own drummer. Says Mitchell: "Denny was probably the best bass player who ever lived, certainly at that time. But on this particular day, he totally fucked up."

Many of the Monterey acts

*Spot the differences?*

16 MAGAZINE

5 ERRORS CONTEST

SHAZAM! Look at Canada's contribution to the pop-rock scene! They call themselves the Paupers and they have one of the newest sounds around! Run right down to your local record store and pick up a copy of their smash Verve-Forecast LP *Magic People* and you'll be a Pauper fan too – quicker than you can say "Abracadabra"! But hey – what's goin' on *here*?!

The top drawing is fine, but the bottom drawing contains five errors. Can you spot them? If you can, just draw a circle around each error with a pen or pencil, fill in the coupon below, tear the page along the dotted line and mail the coupon to: Five Errors Contest, *16* Magazine, Box 104, Brooklyn, N.Y. 11202.

To each of the first five readers who can correctly identify all five errors, *16* will award $10 in cash. All coupons will be dropped inside a revolving barrel and Gloria Stavers, *blindfolded*, will pick the winners – so everybody has a chance!

*Go to work right away – and good luck!*

RIGHT

WRONG

5 ERRORS CONTEST DEC. 1967

NAME... MY AGE IS...

STREET...

CITY... ZIP CODE...

STATE... ARE YOU A SUBSCRIBER?

MAIL TO "5 ERRORS CONTEST" • 16 MAGAZINE • BOX 104 BROOKLYN, N.Y. 11202 blew people's minds. The Paupers simply blew it. Ralph Gleason, influential music columnist with the *San Francisco Chronicle*, called the band one of the festival's real disappointments. (Gleason had already been a champion of Gerrard's talents in *Playboy*, where the musician had twice been voted top bassist in the magazine's annual jazz poll.) And, perhaps most significantly, the group's performance was not included in *Monterey Pop*, the seminal rockumentary by D.A. Pennebaker that helped to make superstars out of Hendrix and Joplin.

Meanwhile, John Kay and Sparrow were starting to make some noise, opening for acts like The Doors and Big Brother & the Holding Company at the Fillmore. Then, just as Sparrow was on the verge of success, Dennis Edmonton changed his name to Mars Bonfire and quit the band to become a songwriter. But Kay was determined to keep the band alive. Landing a deal with Dunhill Records, home of Denny Doherty's Mamas & Papas, Kay lured Jerry Edmonton and Goldy McJohn back. With two American recruits rounding out their ranks, Kay and company adopted the name Steppenwolf (after the popular novel by Hermann Hesse). The group's edgy, blues-rock sound suddenly seemed perfectly suited to the mood of the times.

*The Sparrow do the Avalon thing with The Doors*

It was Judy Collins who invited Leonard Cohen and Joni Mitchell that summer to the Newport Folk Festival, where she was hosting a singer-songwriter workshop. In the car en route to Newport, a nervous Cohen confessed to his lawyer Marty Machat

*Joni and Leonard at Newport '67*

that he had doubts about his singing ability. "None of you guys know how to sing," replied Machat. "When I want to hear singers, I go to the Metropolitian Opera." Yet Cohen, who would not record his debut album *Songs of Leonard Cohen* until later that year, stole the show at Newport from Joan Baez and Pete Seeger with his poetic ballads of romantic despair.

Meanwhile, backstage, there was an instant attraction between Cohen and Mitchell. Their love affair lasted for part of the summer as their paths crisscrossed on the festival circuit. Ultimately, Mitchell would write two songs about their brief affair—"The Gallery" and "That Song About the Midway"—both of which would appear on Mitchell's *Clouds* album. On "Midway," Mitchell wrote of Cohen, "You stood out like a ruby in a black man's ear." She would later refer to Cohen, along with Dylan, as her only real "pacerunners" when it came to songwriting.

There was no Lovin' Spoonful at Newport that year, although the popular jug band had been the hit of the previous year's festival. The Spoonful's Zal Yanovsky and Steve Boone had been busted for pot in the summer of '66. In the cop shop, Yanovsky was threatened with deportation if he didn't name his dealer. The nineteen-year-old guitarist caved in under the pressure. The news that the two had "squealed on

their dealer"—a cardinal sin of the sixties—led to a public outcry calling for a boycott of their concerts and records. Once the group's source of fun and spontaneity, Yanovsky became increasingly bitter and despondent, effectively killing the chemistry he'd helped to create. In June, John Sebastian had the unenviable task of kicking his buddy "Zally" out of the band. Although the Spoonful carried on for another year, the magic was gone. Yanovsky would drift in and out of the music world for the next several years, re-emerging with a wildly eccentric solo album *Alive and Well and Living in Argentina*. In fact, he was back in Canada and, sadly, would soon turn his back on music altogether.

In Yorkville, Bernie Finkelstein sat at an outdoor café and planned his next move. What he really wanted to do was put together a new band, one that stretched musical boundaries the way Jefferson Airplane was doing. With half of his $20,000 Paupers buyout from Albert Grossman in hand (he claims that Grossman, who died in 1986, never did pay him the other half), he had the capital to launch such a group. Now, to find the right players.

Finkelstein had already met Keith McKie, originally from Sault Ste. Marie, whom he considered

Yorkville's best new songwriter. It didn't hurt that McKie could also sing and had the sort of dark, sultry looks of a Mick Jagger; he was the perfect frontman. Finkelstein and McKie then spent several afternoons casting about for the right mix of musicians. Both of them knew Gene Martynec, a former guitarist with Bobby Kris & the Imperials who often brought down the house at the Avenue Road Club. Martynec was in. Their drummer was right under their noses, hanging out in Yorkville and looking for a band himself. Not only could sixteen-year-old Jimmy Watson drum up a storm, he could also play a bit of sitar (it didn't hurt that he was also Van Morrison's cousin). All they needed now was a bass player. McKie suggested his old pal from the Soo, Alex Darou, then living in New York. Darou, a talented older musician, was lured back to Toronto by the promise of a new, experimental band.

Calling themselves Kensington Market after Toronto's funky, ethnic street market, the band made its debut on June 4, 1967, at Yorkville's Night Owl. *The Toronto Star*'s Sid Adilman immediately declared them "the brightest and most inventive band ever grouped together in Toronto." Peter Goddard, then writing for *The Globe and Mail*, caught the Market a few weeks later at Boris's Red Gas Room and applauded the group's poetry

*Luke & the Apostles*

and its "impressions of cacophonous Toronto streets and drawn-out solos of jazz-like origin." Goddard was also impressed that, "unlike many West Coast–oriented groups (Jefferson Airplane, The Grateful Dead etc.), the Market's primary concern is with music and not its supposed mind-expanding aftereffects."

Psychedelic-rock came to Canada in July on the wings of Jefferson Airplane. Flying high with its *Surrealistic Pillow* album and its edgy, cinematic hits "Somebody to Love" and "White Rabbit," the Airplane arrived in Toronto on July 23 to perform a free outdoor show at Nathan Phillips Square, and a week-long gig at the O'Keefe Centre with The Grateful Dead.

More than 50,000 attended the outdoor concert. Those who did remember it as the day the old Toronto Sound died, as the love affair with r & b was replaced by the kaleidoscopic sounds of acid-rock. It was a glorious day, full of sunshine, dancing and general grooviness. Joints were passed, munchies shared and everyone basked in the freaky sounds coming from the stage. Luke & the Apostles had opened the show and came away with an enviable invitation. Promoter Bill Graham, impressed by the band's electrifying set, asked the group to join the Airplane–Dead line-up at the O'Keefe.

The O'Keefe concerts took place from July 31 to August 5. Each band would perform atop a platform on wheels; when the curtains opened, stage hands would push the platform out just as the musicians struck their first chords. On opening night, Luke Gibson and his group had a case of the jitters. Just before they were to go on, Graham visited them in their dressing

**CHUM CHART TOP TEN APRIL 24, 1967**

*Something Stupid*
Frank & Nancy Sinatra

*Happy Jack*
The Who

*Sweet Soul Music*
Arthur Conley

*Looking at a Baby*
Collectors

*Sit Down I Think I Love You*
Mojo Men

*The Happening*
Supremes

*If You're Thinking*
Dino, Desi & Billy

*I'm A Man*
Spencer Davis Group

*My Back Pages*
Byrds

*I Think We're Alone Now*
Tommy James & the Shondells

*Christopher's Movie Matinee by Three's a Crowd*

room. "OK, gentlemen," he told the group, "as you're being pushed out tonight, I want you to urinate towards the audience." There was a momentary silence as the Apostles looked at the mercurial promoter and then each other. "We broke out laughing when we realized he was kidding," says Gibson. "He was trying to loosen us up, and it worked."

The shows went over so well that the *Toronto Telegram*, in an article entitled "Flower Power Takes Over," declared the event a "cultural revolution." Critic Barrie Hale marvelled at the visceral effects of the psychedelic light show and the insistent, pulsing sounds which had audiences up and dancing on the stage and in the aisles—previously unheard of at the staid O'Keefe. The concerts ended with Luke & the Apostles joining the Airplane and the Dead for an extended jam, making it a triumphant week for the local band. Gibson's group decided to make it their swan song and go out on a high note. "Everyone was ready for a change," recalls Gibson. "I had grown tired of playing the blues by that point. I was getting interested in original material." Within a few days, he'd be invited to join Kensington Market, Canada's answer to the Airplane.

Mariposa was something of a love-in itself that summer. Joni Mitchell and Leonard Cohen continued their not-so-secret affair there at Innis Lake north of Toronto. With Mitchell, Cohen, Buffy Sainte-Marie and Murray McLauchlan (making his Mariposa debut), there was a heavy emphasis on Canadian singer-songwriters, now becoming a strong national tradition. But the festival also featured a wealth of blues-oriented artists, including Ritchie

Havens, Reverend Gary Davis and Buddy Guy, who performed a thrilling folk-festival first. Nearly a

**They wore epauletted jackets, Indian beads and hip-hugger pants**

decade before punk musicians began surfing mosh pits, Guy leapt into the audience with his electric guitar still plugged in and continued playing, without missing a lick.

Mariposa '67 further stretched the definition of "folk" by adding the electrified sounds of Three's a Crowd and Kensington Market to the line-up. By now, Three's a Crowd had added singer David Wiffen, drummer Richard Patterson and bassist Ken Koblun, Neil Young's former partner in The Squires. The group had just finished recording its first album, produced by Mama Cass Elliot. *Christopher's Movie Matinee*, which would be released the following year, featured numbers by two little-known songwriters—Bruce Cockburn and Murray McLauchlan.

With their electronic effects and adventurous song structures, the Market brought a heavier vibe to the festival, and with their epauletted jackets, Indian beads and hip-hugger pants, a funkier look. And the group's Keith McKie took part in a songwriters' workshop hosted by Cohen, joining such hip company as Mitchell, Sainte-Marie and McLauchlan.

Back in Toronto, Luke Gibson added a bluesier, soulful voice to the Market's artfully crafted sound. Although the group had already released a single, the McKie-penned "Mr. John," its big break didn't come until the members jammed one night with Zal Yanovsky. Knocked out by the band's sophisticated sound, Yanovsky went down to New York where he raved about them to Felix Pappalardi, already one of the hottest new U.S. record producers with The Youngbloods and Cream to his credit. Pappalardi flew up to Toronto in October to check them out. Before he left the band's warehouse rehearsal space that night, Pappalardi had signed the group to a two-record deal and made plans to make the Market the "next big thing."

The Summer of Love was filled with music, drugs and a euphoric sense of hope and idealism about the future. Kids across North America were searching for a different way of life, shaking off the confining fifties values about work and education they'd grown up with, and adopting the hippie ethos of "turn on, tune in, drop out." Hippies everywhere were in the vanguard of the revolution that The Beatles sang about, the change that was surely just around the corner.

But while the Haight-Ashbury freaks tripped out on the splendour of their Pacific Ocean paradise, Yorkville's hippies found themselves choking on exhaust fumes from bumper-to-bumper traffic. Reduced to curiosities for the passing, pointing motorists, many resented the way their community was being taken over by tourists gawking at the longhairs. Kids started demanding that Yorkville's streets be closed to cars. The Diggers seized on this and the issue became the hippies' new mantra.

Yorkville had been a thorn in the side of Toronto the Good for some time. But in the heat of that summer, the problems came to a head. Cops in the village started hassling kids with a "move-along, move-along" attitude. Politicians, meanwhile, railed against the presence of runaway youths, calling for curfews and stricter by-law enforcement. In August, city controller and former mayor Allan Lamport invited Yorkville's hippies down to city hall to discuss the situation. David

*Allan Lamport and David DePoe: "generational gap"*

DePoe, for one, took him up on it.

A charismatic twenty-five-year-old with long dark hair, wide-brimmed black hat and a Fu Manchu mustache, DePoe told the older, balding Lamport that the heavy traffic on the one-way street was creating pollution and safety problems for pedestrians. The patronizing politician suggested that maybe this was a good reason for the kids to leave. When confronted, Lamport's agenda for Yorkville became clear. "Frankly, I'd like to see it become a shopping centre," he told DePoe. "But it'll have to be cleaned up first."

*The Yorkville sit-in, August 20*

News about the stand-off brought even larger numbers into Yorkville that weekend. Needing a break from the crowds, a large group of hippies split to a "happening" in a downtown warehouse. When cops arrived to bust up the party, the hippies headed back to Yorkville and spontaneously sat down on the street, preventing any cars from entering the village. "Close our street," they chanted, "close our street." As their numbers swelled, the police sent in the paddy wagons.

The August 20th sit-in was dealt with swiftly and aggressively by Metro Toronto's finest. Police, many in plain clothes, struck girls in the face, kneed guys and kicked fallen and limp kids. The clashes went on for three nights before the Diggers called off the sit-in. By the end of the skirmish, sixty-one had been arrested including Pops, a sixty-seven-year-old eccentric known as Yorkville's oldest hippie, June Callwood, then a young freelance journalist, and DePoe himself. So much for the Summer of Love.

When lawyer Clayton Ruby bailed DePoe out of Toronto's Don Jail, much of Yorkville's hippie community was waiting for him at a Queen's Park rally. They weren't disappointed. The leader of the Diggers had lost none of his political fire. He organized a series of "sleep-ins" for Nathan Phillips Square that week to

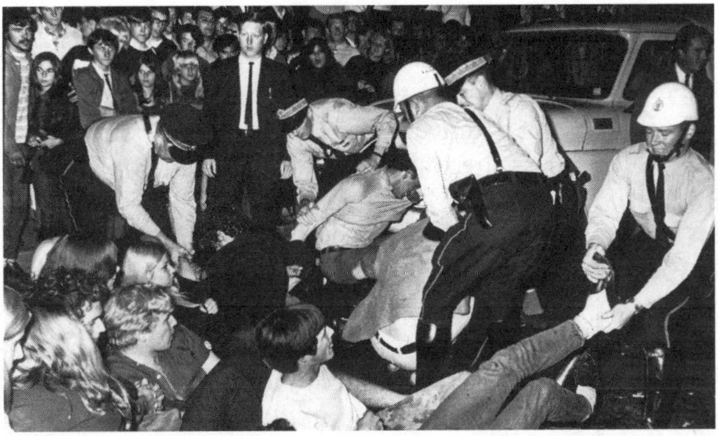

*The sit-in was dealt with swiftly and aggressively by Metro Toronto's finest*

pressure Mayor William Dennison to listen to the villagers' demand to close the street to cars. After considerable, often raucous debate and strenuous objections from Lamport, the Board of Control eventually allowed DePoe to address the issue. But it was clear that the city had no intentions of closing Yorkville Avenue. "What we've seen here," DePoe told the board in an articulate, reasoned speech, "is a striking example of what might be called a generational gap."

*Cockburn: more into pot than protest*

Bruce Cockburn was at the warehouse happening that sparked the Yorkville sit-in. At the time the musician was more into pot than politics. "I remember hearing about the sit-in," he says, "but I really wasn't involved in things like that then, so I didn't make the connection."

After The Children broke up in the spring of '67, Cockburn had come to Toronto to play in a band called The Flying Circus, managed briefly by John Craig Eaton, the same department-store magnate who had invested in Neil Young's Mynah Birds. Cockburn and the rest of The Flying Circus would lug their equipment to Eaton's stately Rosedale mansion where the rock philanthropist invited the group to rehearse. It was not clear whether Eaton's wife shared her husband's musical taste. Cockburn remembers her looking askance at the hippies on her shag rug. "I guess she wasn't used to having people like us in her house," he laughs.

**CHUM CHART TOP TEN AUGUST 28, 1967**

*Cornflakes & Ice Cream*
Lords of London

*Ode to Billy Joe*
Bobby Gentry

*Reflections*
Diana Ross & Supremes

*The Boat That I Row*
Lulu

*Heroes & Villains*
Beach Boys

*It's the Little Things*
Sonny & Cher

*Fakin' It*
Simon & Garfunkel

*There Is a Mountain*
Donovan

*Come Back When You Grow Up*
Bobby Vee

*All You Need Is Love*
Beatles

Like The Children, The Flying Circus gave Cockburn another opportunity to advance his guitar playing and showcase his songwriting (one song from this period was "St. Martha's Earthworm"). Although the group never amounted to much, The Flying Circus did get to perform its psychedelic-rock sound in memorable opening slots for Wilson Pickett and Jimi Hendrix. By late '67, Cockburn was thinking about flying solo. "I'd accumulated a body of original material that I liked singing alone better than with the band," he says. "Plus, I was getting a little sick of self-indulgent, noisy rock."

During the Summer of Love, Murray McLauchlan and Patti Sockwell married and moved into a communal house in the heart of Yorkville. They shared the house with Moses, one of Yorkville's most colourful characters and the secretary-treasurer of the Vagabonds motorcycle gang. Although he looked every bit the part of a hulking, intimidating biker, Moses was also a charismatic, self-educated sort, a Marxist who read *The Daily Worker*, loved poetry and listened intently to McLauchlan's songs—in short, an amiable, if unusual, house-mate.

"People in the village attached a certain kind of glamour to bikers in those days," recalls McLauchlan. But he was under no illusion about what Moses and his cronies were up to. "They knew there was money to be made in Yorkville, with a healthy market in grass and speed." He adds wryly, "Make no mistake about it, your average motorcycle gang *is* a criminal organization."

**The sound of Donovan's cautionary "Season of the Witch" had an eerie resonance**

Change was in the air in Yorkville. The exotic smells of patchouli oil and incense had been supplanted by the suffocating scent of defeat. Yorkville's denizens had bravely squared off with City Hall during the August protests, standing face-to-face with The Man—and lost. To make matters worse, many of the community's leaders, including DePoe and Callwood, faced a bureaucratic labyrinth of endless court appearances following their arrests.

The villagers' demand to turn Yorkville Avenue into a pedestrian mall was, in hindsight, entirely reasonable. There was even a petition from Yorkville businesses in support of the idea. But that was forgotten in all the hysteria. What City Hall really objected to was that the demand was coming from a bunch of longhairs and lefties who had the gall to think that the neighbourhood was somehow theirs. Lamport was already working quietly behind the scenes with a growing number of developers who had other plans for Yorkville.

The police presence was almost constant that fall. Foot patrols monitored the crowds, and a 10 p.m. curfew kept anyone under eighteen out of the village. Weekends were especially tense as a paddy wagon, routinely parked at the corner of Hazelton and Yorkville, seemed to say "don't even

*The Ugly Ducklings: raw energy*

*think* about it." To the hippies hanging out across the street at the newly opened Upper Crust café, the sound of Donovan's cautionary "Season of the Witch" had an eerie resonance.

But at the same time, more upbeat sounds could be heard on the airwaves. In August, The Lords of London were the first Canadian group to score a number-one hit on CHUM since Ritchie Knight & the Midnights topped the charts in July 1963 with "Charlena." The Lords' song, "Cornflakes and Ice Cream," was a pseudo-psychedelic pop tune that brought the young group a fanatical teenage following. Then in October, The Ugly Ducklings found their way to the top of the charts with "Gaslight," the band's anguished tale of a heartless girl who was "everybody's flame."

Like Montreal's The Haunted and Vancouver's Painted Ship, the Ducklings captured the transitional mood of the period that straddled the Summer of Love. With psychedelic-laced punk (best heard on the band's last single, the spacey, backwards-recorded "Epilogue"), the Ducks offered an edgy, adventurous alternative to the pop-oriented sounds of the day. "We weren't very good musicians," admits Roger Mayne, "but what we had was this raw energy and attitude. That's what made us create rather than imitate."

The secret to that "raw energy" was the creative tension that existed between Bingham and Mayne,

who co-wrote most of the band's material. "Dave and I were always at war," admits Mayne. "One night, we were playing at the Hawk's Nest and I got so mad that I hit him right in the face while we were on stage. His nose started to bleed and he walked off." Mayne laughs, "We had to play instrumentals for half an hour afterwards." Canada's godfathers of punk broke up not long after Mayne left the group.

The Ugly Ducklings left an impressive history. Their performances are still talked about with something approaching awe. The band's vinyl legacy, recordings that bristle with a palpable, pre-punk rage, inspired new generations of garage bands. And the Ducklings' album and all of their singles are considered classics of the genre, commanding hefty prices on the international record collectors' circuit.

By the end of '67, The Mandala's album had still not been released and singer George Olliver had given up and quit the band, leaving Domenic Troiano deeply frustrated. *Soul Crusade* finally saw the light of day in the spring of '68 when Atlantic Records' chief, Ahmet Ertegun, acting on a tip from producer Phil Spector, bought out the group's contract from Decca. The Mandala's big hit "Opportunity" wasn't included on the album. But "Love-itis," featuring new vocalist Roy Kenner and a big, brassy horn arrangement, became the group's next hit, making it to number nine on the CHUM chart. Like "Opportunity," the song became a much-loved soul anthem of the late '60s, blasting out of speakers at high-school dances all across the country.

## DISCS TO DISCOVER

*Buffalo Springfield*: Buffalo Springfield (Atco, 1990)

*Retrospective*: Buffalo Springfield (Atco, 1987)

*Songs of Leonard Cohen*: Leonard Cohen (Columbia, 1990)

*The Best of Leonard Cohen:* Leonard Cohen (Columbia, 1987)

*Magic People* (vinyl only): The Paupers (Verve Forecast, 1967)

# 9

# avenue of broken dreams

Robbie Robertson and the rest of the Hawks sat out the Summer of Love, holed up in a large pink house in the wilds of upstate New York. Big Pink had been their retreat ever since Dylan broke his neck in a motorcycle accident and brought his '66 world tour to a premature end. It was perfect for woodshedding—a place where they could hone their talents in total isolation. They used their time well, resting up, communing with nature and later, with Dylan, recording some laid-back but wonderfully eclectic music that would later emerge on the brilliant *Basement Tapes* album.

Robertson lived down the road a few miles in a cabin with his girlfriend Dominique, a Montreal journalist he'd met in Paris. Each day, Robertson would go to Big Pink to work out songs and play football with the other Hawks. Although they now enjoyed a give-and-take relationship with Dylan, the group was clearly ready to go it alone. With Albert Grossman's help, they landed a recording contract with Capitol and work began on the first album in January '68. The eleven tracks the Hawks recorded that spring included several collaborations with Dylan and one Robertson classic, "The Weight." Now, to prepare for the album's release, all they had to do was come up with a new name for the group. After toying with self-deprecating names like The Crackers and The Honkies—both terms for Southern white trash—they settled on the plainest one they could think of: The Band.

*Joni at Mariposa*

When The Band's debut album, *Music from Big Pink*, came out in August '68, it was immediately hailed by critics everywhere. *Life* magazine praised its "clear, cool, country soul that washes the ears with a sound never heard before," while *Rolling Stone*, which began publishing in late '67 as the counter-culture's own magazine, described it as "that good old intangible, can't-put-your-finger-on-it 'White Soul.'" Along with Dylan's *John Wesley Harding* and The Byrds' *Sweetheart of the Rodeo*, The Band's debut signalled a return to quieter, acoustic music.

Meanwhile Ian & Sylvia, who had fallen out of favour as folk's popularity waned, staged a comeback with a brand-new hybrid sound. Having recorded two country-flavoured albums, *Nashville* and *Full Circle*, the couple was now ready to add the intensity of a rock-and-roll rhythm section. First, they recruited former Dirty Shame Amos Garrett, a guitarist who Ian reckoned rivalled Eric Clapton, no less. Then they hired bassist Ken Kalmusky and drummer N.D. Smart II. The line-up was rounded out with steel player Buddy Cage, a teenage veteran of Toronto's honky-tonks. The Great Speckled Bird was born.

A cross-border cousin of The Band, Great Speckled Bird helped to forge the counrty-rock sound at a time when that type of music was still in its infancy. With Ian & Sylvia's trademark harmonies, Garrett and Cage's raging string duels and the group's kick-ass rhythm section, the Bird came up with a unique variation on the formula. And when the band's album, *Great Speckled Bird*, was released in 1969, featuring evocative songs like Ian's "Long Long Time to Get Old" and Sylvia's "Trucker's Cafe," it reaffirmed the duo's stature as respected pioneers of Canadian music.

**CHUM CHART TOP TEN JULY 22, 1968**

*Born to Be Wild*
Steppenwolf

*You've Had Better Times*
Peter & Gordon

*Hello I Love You*
Doors

*Hurdy Gurdy Man*
Donovan

*Everyday Housewife*
Glen Campbell

*Classical Gas*
Mason Williams

*Dream a Little Dream*
Mama Cass

*People Got to Be Free*
Rascals

*Halfway to Paradise*
Bobby Vinton

*You Keep Me Hangin' On*
Vanilla Fudge

After the summer of '67, Joni Mitchell left behind her "magic princess" castle in Chelsea to become a lady of California's Laurel Canyon. Immediately, she began work on her first album, with singer David Crosby producing. Crosby remembers "a willowy blonde with blue eyes and high cheekbones, singing art songs in a bell-like soprano with a Canadian accent and accompanying herself on acoustic guitar and dulcimer...not anyone's idea of the next big thing."

But Joni surprised everyone. The self-titled album was a quiet, sparsely produced chronicle of the past year of her life. Side one was titled "I Came to the City" (meaning New York), while side two, featuring songs like "The Dawntreader" about life on Crosby's boat, was called "Out of the City and Down to the Seaside" (presumably the Pacific Ocean). The album established Mitchell as an artist in her own right. In December she performed at the Miami Pop Festival before 100,000 people, on a bill with Marvin Gaye, Fleetwood Mac, Canned Heat and Three Dog Night. The same month, Judy Collins's version of Mitchell's "Both Sides Now" became a major hit.

**It was a raging road anthem, full of power chords, pounding drums and raw, pedal-to-the-metal vocals**

In February '69, she was to make her debut at Carnegie Hall. A lone figure on the massive concert stage, she thrilled the Carnegie crowd as her pure voice filled the hall, accompanied only by the rhythmic, open chording of her acoustic guitar. But more than anything else, it was her romantic, confessional lyrics that stayed with the audience that night. Mitchell continued writing those intense, diary-like songs while touring that year as an opening act for friends Crosby, Stills and Nash.

The airwaves during the summer of '68 belonged to Steppenwolf. Under John Kay's direction, the band quickly forged their distinctive, hard-rock sound and began making a big noise on the California concert scene. But it wasn't until the group took a song from former Sparrow Mars Bonfire and pumped up its tempo and volume, that Steppenwolf really took off. The song was "Born to Be Wild." Bonfire had written it as a tribute to his first car, a second-hand Ford, and the freedom he felt driving it. In Steppenwolf's hands, however, the song was transformed into a raging road anthem, full of power chords, pounding drums and raw, pedal-to-the-metal vocals.

That spring, Dennis Hopper had heard "Born to Be Wild" and thought it a perfect song for the movie he was then filming with Peter Fonda about a biker's drug-laced misadventures on the road. Hopper, making his directorial debut, decided to include it on the movie's soundtrack. When *Easy Rider* hit movie screens that summer and became a runaway, counter-culture hit, it was "Born to Be Wild" that captured the film's rebellious spirit. By July, the song had roared all the way up to the top of the charts across North America, selling more than a million copies. The image was so successful that Kay found it impossible to escape. Although he tried to take Steppenwolf in new directions—and even disbanded the group at one point in frustration—he learned to accept that there would always be an audience hungry for Steppenwolf's thrilling road anthems.

The association with *Easy Rider*, combined with John Kay's fondness for wearing leather and sunglasses, gave Steppenwolf an instant image as a biker band. Steppenwolf's next hit, Kay's "Magic Carpet Ride," with its crunching chords, syncopated beat and, especially, the lyric "heavy metal thunder," only added to the band's biker mystique, and helped popularize the term "heavy metal."

**CHUM CHART TOP TEN FEBRUARY 15, 1969**

*These Eyes*
Guess Who

*Games People Play*
Joe South

*Dizzy*
Tommy Roe

*Build Me Up Buttercup*
Foundations

*I'm Living in Shame*
Supremes

*Can I Change My Mind*
Tyrone Davis

*This Magic Moment*
Jay & Americans

*Crimson & Clover*
Tommy Jones

*Things I'd Like to Say*
New Colony Six

*Hang'em High*
Booker T.

Heavy drugs, especially speed and heroin, arrived in Yorkville in the summer of '68 with the Vagabonds, who saw the village as their turf and worked quickly to make it theirs. Living in rooming houses around Yorkville, Vags, as members were known, hung out at the Upper Crust, always parking their choppers in front. There, they conducted their not-so-secret trade in grass, hash and, increasingly, speed. The bike

*A Vagabonds-style Christmas*

gang's leader was a colourful character named Ed Johnson (Edjo for short) who drove around in a red '58 Cadillac convertible.

The Vags were Yorkville's unofficial police force. "They were like our bodyguards down in the village," recalls The Ugly Ducklings' Roger Mayne. "They'd always be around." He adds, laughing, "Because of them, we never had any security problems." But singer Dave Bingham remembers it differently. "We had problems with a couple of them at Boris's in the Red Gas Room one night," says Bingham. "These two got into real spacey drugs, doing speed balls—speed and acid mixed together. Suddenly, they just freaked out and started throwing things around the room and beating up on people. I had to unscrew the microphone and threaten them with the stand if they didn't stop. It was pretty heavy."

Former Yorkville waitress Jeanine Hollingshead and singer Tannis Neiman shared a house with the Ducks during that time. "All us girls had to walk home at two in the morning," says Hollingshead. "The guys cruising Yorkville that late, mostly creeps from the suburbs, would give us a hard time. 'Hey, baby, free love over here,' that sort of thing. The Vags told us, 'Tell them you belong to Edjo.' We felt safer when we mentioned his name."

Murray McLauchlan, who knew the Vagabonds better than most, believes that he and other villagers were blind to the bike gang's darker side. "Hippies romanticized bikers as just another form of counter-culture," says McLauchlan. "People were looking at the style, not the stealing, dope dealing, gang rapes and all the other shit that these guys were into. We used to use the phrase 'pulling train' as if it was a joke, when it's an expression for when one girl gets fucked by twenty guys. The reality never hit us. We thought it was all a myth." June Callwood agrees: "At first, the bikers were a colourful addition. I didn't know how sinister their presence was. Then I began to hear about rapes and strikers (new biker initiates) finding girls and taking them down alleys to gang rape them. The bikers then started bringing in the heavy drugs, like speed and heroin. It became a very bad scene."

As if City Hall, the cops and bikers weren't enough, Yorkville faced a threat from a different source. Volunteers at the Trailer began to see an alarming number of sick kids. Youth workers began circulating leaflets warning of potentially fatal hepatitis. By early August, there had been more than fifty cases reported at three downtown hospitals. All but two of the victims were regulars in Yorkville. Several doctors jumped the gun and labelled the situation an epidemic although the city's medical officer demurred. "Calling it an epidemic would mean by definition that we're dealing with the infectious hepatitis," said Dr. G.W.O. Moss at the time, "and we just can't pin it down that closely. We don't know what is causing it." He added that it could simply be "hippie hepatitis," so called because that form was passed on via dirty dishes and unwashed residents of Haight-Ashbury, where it was first reported.

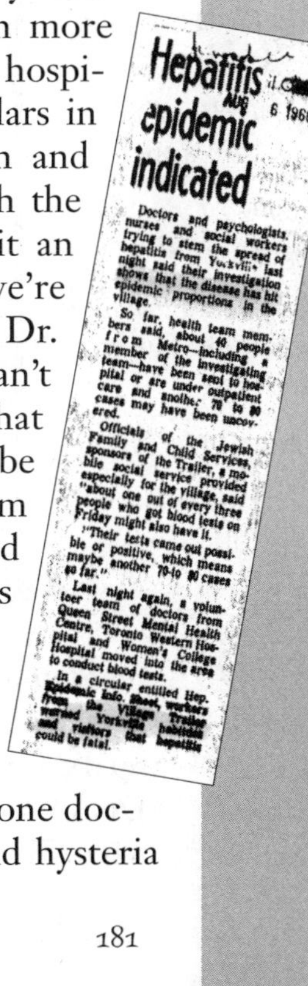

# Hepatitis epidemic indicated

AUG 6 1968

Doctors and psychologists, nurses and social workers trying to stem the spread of hepatitis from Yorkville last night said their investigation shows that the disease has hit epidemic proportions in the village.

So far, health team members said, about 40 people from Metro—including a member of the investigating team—have been sent to hospital or are under outpatient care and another 70 to 80 cases may have been uncovered.

Officials of the Jewish Family and Child Services, sponsors of the Trailer, a mobile social service provided especially for the village, said "about one out of every three people who got blood tests on Friday might also have it.

"Their tests came out possible or positive, which means maybe another 70-to 80 cases so far."

Last night again, a volunteer team of doctors from Queen Street Mental Health Centre, Toronto Western Hospital and Women's College Hospital moved into the area to conduct blood tests.

In a circular entitled Hep. Epidemic Info. Sheet, workers from the Village Trailer warned Yorkville habitués and visitors that hepatitis could be fatal.

The Trailer volunteers moved quickly. Vaccine shots were administered on Yorkville's sidewalks and the disease was contained. But *The Globe and Mail*, quoting one doctor, had already declared it an epidemic and hysteria set in. People fled from Yorkville and stayed away for weeks. The once-teeming village looked like a ghost town. Bernie Fiedler gave one measure of the effects of the scare—the Riverboat lost $15,000 in a six-week period. Was it an epidemic? "We'll never know," says Callwood. "It was the epidemic that never happened. But with the casual lifestyle of the kids, there was a good danger it could've become one."

**CHUM CHART TOP TEN JULY 5, 1969**

*Spinning Wheel*
Blood, Sweat & Tears

*Israelites*
Desmond Dekker

*Good Morning Starshine*
Oliver

*What Does It Take*
Jr. Walker

*My Pledge of Love*
Joe Jeffrey

*Color Him Father*
Winstons

*Baby I Love You*
Andy Kim

*Chrystal Blue Persuasion*
Tommy James

*One*
Three Dog Night

*When I Die*
Motherlode

The Paupers never really recovered from their Monterey disaster. Bassist Denny Gerrard became increasingly preoccupied with psychedelic drugs, and alienated from the rest of the group. While experimenting with a remote device for his bass at a band rehearsal in Yorkville, Gerrard stepped outside the club to test its range—and didn't come back. Passers-by claimed they saw him wandering down Avenue Road, still playing. While touring through Pennsylvania one night in drummer Skip Prokop's station wagon, Gerrard asked to stop for a pee break, and went AWOL again. Singer Adam Mitchell heard from him three days later by phone. "Adam, it's Denny," a worried-sounding Gerrard said. "Where am I?" After Mitchell suggested he look out a window for clues, the bassist realized he was somewhere in Philadelphia.

By 1968, Gerrard's chronic drug use became impossible to deal with. Prokop, Mitchell and guitarist Chuck Beal fired him, replacing him with Brad Campbell. A good bass player, Campbell was certainly able to learn all of Gerrard's parts. But according to Chuck Beal, he "lacked Denny's drive." Added Beal, "Denny did for the bass what Hendrix was doing for the guitar. Nobody had seen anything like this. Of all of us, he had the most raw talent. But with that talent came the problems that led to his drug use. He got into drugs a lot sooner than the rest of us. Anything Denny did, he did to extremes."

*Janis Joplin's Full Tilt Boogie*

The Paupers were a lesser force without their inspired, maniacal bassist. When their second album, *Ellis Island*, came out that summer, diehard Paupers fans were mystified. Gone were the trademark sounds of thundering rhythms and sunny melodies. In its place was a hodgepodge of styles, from darker, heavier numbers like "South Down Road" and "Yes I Know" to the theatrical "Cairo Hotel" and the country-and-western parody "Another Man's Hair on My Razor." The album badly lacked coherence. Only the breezy pop rave-up of "Julliana" seemed to bear any relation to the beloved sound of old. And, without Gerrard, it wasn't long before The Paupers started coming apart at the seams.

First Prokop left, drawn to lucrative session work (he had already played on Peter, Paul & Mary's "I Dig Rock and Roll Music"). Although deeply frustrated, he had not given up on the music business. Mitchell and Beal, faced with $40,000 in debts, kept The Paupers going for another year. But by then the band was effectively finished. As for Brad Campbell, his time in The Paupers got him the gig of his dreams. Along with several other former Ronnie Hawkins side men, he formed Janis Joplin's Full Tilt Boogie Band. And Prokop was already hatching plans for a new band—and another shot at breaking into the Canadian scene.

By the summer of '68, Mike McKenna was a Canadian guitar hero. Unaware of his stature, he placed a classified ad in *The Toronto Star*, asking for like-minded blues musicians to call him. One of the respondents was a gruff-voiced guy who immediately chastised him for putting his name in the paper. "You shouldn't have to do that," he told McKenna. "You're a well-known guitar player." So it was that Mike McKenna met the tough-talking iconoclast known as Joe Mendelson.

Although their paths had never crossed before, Mendelson had also been around Yorkville since the mid-1960s. A burly bear of a man, Mendelson had played jug-band music with the equally eccentric Daisy Debolt, a singer-accordionist who would later become part of the successful duo Fraser & Debolt. But at the time McKenna met him, Mendelson was a belt maker, tooling leather goods and selling them around town, and playing rugged, Robert Johnson–style acoustic blues in coffee houses. Recalled McKenna, "He sang very hard and just ripped the strings off his guitar. I thought, 'This guy is the real thing.'"

*Mainline, flanked by Mike McKenna (left) and Joe Mendelson (right)*

Teaming up, the two soon conscripted another local hero, former Paupers bassist Denny Gerrard, and Tony Nolasco who had played drums with The Spasstiks. After many late-night rehearsals, the McKenna Mendelson Mainline landed themselves a gig at the Night Owl. By November, their gut-wrenching blues sound took them to the Rock Pile, where they backed blues giant John Lee Hooker in a hugely successful show. But Mendelson was unimpressed. "Hooker was a fuck-up," he later told a college newspaper. "He wanted a cheap back-up band. He was just interested in making money; he didn't even care about his own music or McKenna Mendelson Mainline. We made him a star at that gig."

*Canada's answer to Jefferson Airplane*

That sort of cockiness took Mainline out of Toronto in the winter of '68, across the Atlantic and all the way to England, drawn by the British blues boom led by John Mayall's Bluesbreakers and Eric Clapton's Cream. But it was also a matter of sheer pragmatism. "At that time, Canadians could get six-month work visas in England as British subjects," says McKenna. "Getting U.S. visas, on the other hand, was almost impossible." To finance his way over, the newly married McKenna sold all but one of the twenty guitars in his collection. The trip was really a matter of survival. According to McKenna, "Joe really felt that if we stayed in Toronto at that time, we were going to die a bad death. He was right."

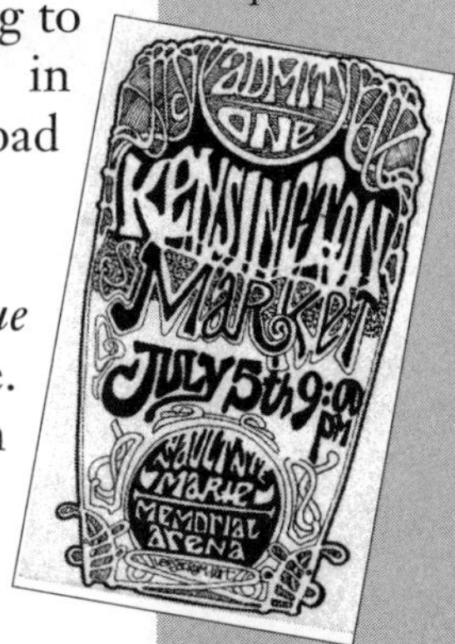


Kensington Market's 1968 debut album, *Avenue Road*, had more than lived up to its promise. "Probably the finest album ever cut by a Canadian group," declared *The Globe*'s influential pop critic Ritchie Yorke. Softer and subtler than the band's live show, the recording was full of strings, horns, bells, shifting time signatures and complex imagery. Its psychedelic overtones quickly established the Market as the acid-rock dealers of the North.

MDA, a hallucinogen, known as the "love drug," became the psychedelic substance of choice for members of Kensington Market. "Everyone was doing drugs in those days, audiences and bands alike," says the Market's Luke Gibson. "It was all about expanded

consciousness—anything for revolution, including mental revolution. A lot of people would drop MDA and go see the Market. I guess our band became to MDA what the Dead was to LSD."

None of the Market's members performed on hallucinogens. "I never found I could operate an instrument while stoned on the stuff," says Gibson, laughing. But many of the band's songs were clearly influenced by them. Gibson says that his "Speaking of Dreams," one of the first songs he ever wrote, is about an acid trip. The drug-induced creativity produced plenty of new material, and plans were made to return to the studio with producer Felix Pappalardi.

Meanwhile, Warner Bros. had not done much with the debut album. First they took issue with the title. Although the group thought *Avenue Road* a fitting name, reflecting its Toronto roots, label executives were perplexed by its seeming redundancy (must be some stoned-out hippie's idea of a joke, they figured). Nor was the record company thrilled with the cover photograph of the quintet huddled together in another typically Canadian setting—a blinding January snowstorm.

**He had his first psychedelic trip during the making of the album**

The Market's second album, *Aardvark*, was recorded at Yorkville's Eastern Sound Studios and captured all of the Market's experimental eclecticism. Songs like the majestic "Side I Am" and the plaintive

Kensington Market, on CBC's "Through the Eyes of Tomorrow"

"Help Me" stood out as among the band's best tunes. To go along with the horns and strings, the group added the unearthly strains of a Moog synthesizer—one of the first bands anywhere to do so. Played by new member John Mills-Cockell, the Moog gave the Market a much wider palette from which to paint their increasingly vivid pictures.

Finkelstein looks back on the recording as the Market's finest moment. "*Aardvark* was a psychedelic experience," he says. "It was recorded in Yorkville, where we were all living, so you'd walk out of the studio and you were right there. It was all pretty seamless." Producer Pappalardi was also blown away by *Aardvark*. He had his first psychedelic trip during the making of the album.

High on *Aardvark*, the Market flew to San Francisco in September '69 to play the Fillmore, the acid-rock capital of the world. But when they arrived, they found themselves billed to play with retro-rockers The Steve Miller Band and Chuck Berry. It was a classic case of being on the wrong show at the wrong time. "We bombed big time," recalls Market guitarist Gene Martynec. "Nobody seemed to get what we were doing. But then Steve Miller came out, playing stuff we'd all been playing years earlier, and everyone loved it. It was really strange."

Finkelstein with the Market

Ultimately, the hallucinogens that inspired the group also led to its demise. "It was a pretty intense band to begin with," says

*The Market: dazed and confused*

Gibson. "But after *Aardvark* came out, we all started going a little crazy. There was a lot of paranoia, mostly drug related. In the end, all that tension simply blew the band apart."

The decision to break up Kensington Market had tragic consequences. Bassist Alex Darou withdrew to his apartment above Yorkville's Grab Bag in a deep depression. Despite attempts by band members to get him help, Darou refused to come out. When his friends finally broke down his door, he was dead. The official cause of death was malnutrition, but everyone knew that Darou, who was heavily into mysticism, had lost touch with reality. He'd probably gone too far during a fast, and had starved himself to death.

The Guess Who's fortunes forever changed the day they met Jack Richardson. A former jazz musician turned jingle producer, Richardson handled the Coca-Cola account for the Toronto advertising company McCann-Erickson. Seeing an untapped market, he suggested using Canadian rock groups in jingles to help sell kids Coke—not a popular idea with the American multinational. But he convinced the soft-drink giant to let him record some acts. Richardson went even further. Why not have kids save bottle-cap liners to trade in for albums as a sales incentive. A successful promotion using pop star Bobby Curtola's album proved the point. Then, in early 1968 Richardson released *A Wild Pair*, an album evenly divided between songs by Winnipeg's Guess Who and Ottawa's Staccatos. It sold a staggering 85,000.

Immediately, Richardson and The Guess Who went to work on a full album. Toronto's Hallmark

Clayton-Thomas (front right) with Blood, Sweat & Tears

Studios proved inadequate so Richardson, showing unstinting support for the group, mortgaged his suburban house in order to finance a trip to New York. There, the band recorded a collection of original songs by Burton Cummings and Randy Bachman for an album they called *Wheatfield Soul.* As Cummings explained, it was a term he came up with in self-defence. "We used to go to Toronto and get looked at as Prairie hicks, farmers and country bumpkins," said Cummings. "We were really white bread compared to all the Toronto boogaloo bands. So I just said, 'Hey, you can call us down all you like but we've got wheatfield soul.'"

The first single, a Cummings-Bachman collaboration called "These Eyes," had hit written all over it. The instantly catchy pop ballad should have shot straight to the top of the Canadian charts when it was released in late '68, but according to Bachman, Canadian radio shied away from it. "We were incredibly frustrated," Bachman recalls, "because everyone was telling us what a great song it was. But CHUM wouldn't touch it. It wasn't until it had gone gold in the U.S. that they jumped on it." He adds, laughing, "CHUM tried to say they broke us, but they were eight months after the fact." Still, after Canadian radio finally did embrace "These Eyes," The Guess Who could do no wrong.

Clayton-Thomas (middle, with hat)

Domenic Troiano's Mandala was one of the Toronto "boogaloo bands" to which Cummings was referring. The Mandala broke up in early '69, another great band of unfulfilled promise. Out of its ashes rose Bush, an innovative funk-rock band formed by Troiano, with ex-Mandala members Roy Kenner on vocals and Whitey Glan on drums joining Prakash John on bass. That band recorded one brilliant, but overlooked, funk album, before Troiano went on to lend his guitar skills to The James Gang and a later version of The Guess Who.

One day late in 1968, David Clayton-Thomas got a phone call from Bobby Colomby, a jazzman he'd met in Greenwich Village. Colomby had formed the band Blood, Sweat & Tears and recorded one album. But the group's singer Al Kooper had quit, leaving Colomby searching for a replacement. He remembered Clayton-Thomas. Would he be interested?

It was exactly what Clayton-Thomas had been waiting for. In many ways, Blood, Sweat & Tears' jazz-rock fusion was an extension of the sound he'd experimented with in The Bossmen. Flying down to New York, Clayton-Thomas brought not only his rugged blues vocals but a briefcase full of his own compositions. Standing between classically trained musicians and hardened jazz players, the singer ultimately became the glue that held Blood, Sweat & Tears together. "Spinning Wheel," one of several songs he'd written in Toronto, became a Top Five hit the following year, spurring sales of BS&T's self-titled album to 3 million copies.

Just as Clayton-Thomas was joining Blood, Sweat & Tears, Skip Prokop was hooking up with the band's previous singer, Al Kooper, and getting into the jazz-rock fusion thing. Prokop played with Kooper and guitarist Mike Bloomfield on one of their "Super Session" projects and listened intently to Bloomfield's bluesy, horn-driven band Electric Flag, then stretching the boundaries of rock.

*(from left) Duke Ellington with Lighthouse's Prokop and Paul Hoffert*

Prokop was excited by the prospects. While playing his last gig with The Paupers at New York's Electric Circus, he met Toronto jazz keyboardist Paul Hoffert, then working in the Big Apple. Prokop talked about forming a freewheeling rock orchestra. To Prokop's surprise, the jazzman was open-minded, even enthusiastic, about the idea. "Great," he told Prokop. "If you do it and you do it in Toronto, call me."

Expanding on the BS&T jazz-rock formula, Prokop wanted to add strings to the mix, allowing the band to duplicate on the stage the orchestral sounds so many groups were attempting in the studio. What about it? he asked Hoffert. Sure, but how to amplify violins and cellos? Hoffert wondered. Prokop didn't have a clue. He naively suggested mounting pick-ups, unaware that the very thought would make most classical musicians apoplectic. Eventually, the band would develop some of the first electric violins and cellos, but in the meantime, Prokop and Hoffert had to find the right players.

First Prokop used his Yorkville connections to

recruit Pinky Dauvin and Grant Fullerton from The Stitch 'n' Tyme. Then Hoffert, who had also written for various string ensembles, went seeking jazz and classical musicians. According to Hoffert, "Toronto was known throughout North America at that time as a source of high-quality musicians. Skip was able to tap into Yorkville's rock scene and I knew I could call the Toronto Symphony and get four string players under the age of twenty-five who were totally into rock and roll. And I had no trouble finding horn players of that calibre either. It all came together very naturally."

*Woodstock Music and Art Fair*

Lighthouse, thirteen members in all, made its hasty debut at Toronto's Rock Pile in March 1969. The group got a call. Could they fill in for Kooper and Bloomfield who'd cancelled out at the last minute? The Rock Pile was an auspicious debut and Lighthouse was enthusiastically received at three separate shows before a total of 3,000 people. At the same time, the group enjoyed a chance encounter with Duke Ellington who was in town performing at the Royal York Hotel. Before the year was out, Lighthouse had also appeared at New York's Carnegie Hall and recorded *three* albums, no less.

That August, Lighthouse was invited to perform at the Woodstock Music and Art Fair. Held on farmer Max Yasgur's 600-acre farm in Bethel, New York, Woodstock—billed as "Three Days of Peace and Music"—had great promise. Everyone, short of the Beatles and the Stones, was booked to perform. But Prokop, hearing advance reports predicting overcrowding, inadequate supplies and the threat of LSD-spiked drinking water, decided that his group would pass—a decision he deeply regrets to this day.

Nor did Joni Mitchell perform at the Woodstock weekend. Mitchell, who'd released her second album,

*Clouds*, featuring songs that others had already made famous, was scheduled to appear on Dick Cavett's popular talk show in Manhattan and her manager didn't think she'd have time to get back for the show's Monday taping. Mitchell did, however, capture the event in her song "Woodstock," which became a number-one hit for Crosby, Stills, Nash & Young.

Canadians who appeared at the historic festival included members of The Band, Neil Young (playing with Crosby, Stills & Nash in the aftermath of Buffalo Springfield's break-up) and David Clayton-Thomas fronting Blood, Sweat & Tears, then riding high with "Spinning Wheel." But the experience was far from satisfying for Clayton-Thomas. "We didn't feel it was the right place for us," recalled the singer. "We had so many subtleties in our arrangements. Playing music by [French classical composer] Erik Satie in a huge outdoor festival, where all they want you to do is whack out your hits, seemed a little futile." Still, the high-profile appearance did help BS&T cross over to a mainstream audience, and for the next two years the band was one of the hottest touring acts in the world.

Although Woodstock had its problems—torrential rain, bad trips, dehydration and three deaths (two drug overdoses, one ruptured appendix)—the festival assumed mythic importance simply because it wasn't the disaster authorities were predicting. A crowd "half a million strong," as Joni sang, had gathered for fun and music and safely emerged as the "Woodstock Nation."

If Woodstock was the peaceful mother of all festivals, then December's Altamont was the nightmarish antithesis. While The Rolling Stones sang "Sympathy for the Devil" in front

Developer Richard Wookey

of 300,000, Hell's Angels security guards at the California festival savagely beat audience members with loaded pool cues. All of the hope and optimism of Woodstock was instantly shattered with the vicious injuries and the brutal murder of a black man at the hands of some bike-gang thugs, captured in the disturbing documentary *Gimme Shelter*.

More than bikers and drugs were responsible for Yorkville's decay. June Callwood, who was instrumental in setting up a hostel for homeless Yorkville youths, blames land speculators for allowing properties to get run down. "Nobody was keeping up the houses along Yorkville and Hazelton," she recalls. "They were letting kids live in places with broken windows, dangerous wiring and plumbing that didn't work. It had been rumoured that someone was hoping to drive down property values and buy all those houses cheap." The rumours were well founded.

**If it hadn't been bikers, bad dope and opportunistic developers, something else would have brought an end to Yorkville**

One of the biggest land assemblers was Richard Wookey, who had started buying places as early as the mid-sixties. Wookey bought up no fewer than seventy houses in the area and set about refurbishing them. Eventually, he would build the chic retail complex Hazelton Lanes, now one of Toronto's toniest addresses. But his ultimate move was finessing a land deal that saw the thirty-two-storey Four Seasons Hotel go up at the corner of Avenue Road and Yorkville.

The Riverboat's Bernie Fiedler, always a man with one eye on the ledger sheet, noticed the jump in property values right away. "When I first went into Yorkville, you could've bought any one of those beautiful Victorian houses for $30,000," said Fiedler. "By the time I left in the '70s, the same houses were worth half a million dollars." He added: "My landlord, Harry Jordans, had bought the entire row from Hazelton right down to the Riverboat. Then all the boutique people moved in."

Yorkville was controlled by big-league players now, and the few hippies who hadn't moved, mostly over to nearby Rochdale College, were powerless to stop them. But if it hadn't been bikers, bad dope and opportunistic developers, something else would have brought an end to Yorkville. By then, the village had served its purpose. It had spawned a cross-fertilization of styles, a community of bands that shared members and experiences for years to come. A veritable breeding ground, Yorkville had produced almost a decade's worth of memorable music—and the first evidence of a Canadian sound.

## DISCS TO DISCOVER

*Clouds*: Joni Mitchell (Reprise, 1990)

*Hits*: Joni Mitchell (Reprise, 1996)

*Neil Young*: Neil Young (Reprise, 1990)

*Everybody Knows This Is Nowhere*: Neil Young (Reprise, 1987)

*Music from Big Pink*: The Band (Capitol, 1987)

*Born to Be Wild: A Retrospective Steppenwolf* (2 CD set): Steppenwolf (MCA, 1991)

*Blood, Sweat & Tears*: Blood, Sweat & Tears (Columbia, 1996)

*What Goes Up! The Best of Blood, Sweat & Tears* (2 CD set): Blood, Sweat & Tears (Columbia Legacy, 1995)

*Great Speckled Bird*: Great Speckled Bird (Stony Plain, 1994)

*The Guess Who: The Ultimate Collection* (3 CD set): The Guess Who (RCA, 1997)

*Avenue Road* (vinyl only): Kensington Market (Warner Bros., 1968)

*Christopher's Movie Matinee* (vinyl only): Three's a Crowd (RCA, 1968)

*Soul Crusade* (vinyl only): Mandala (Atlantic, 1968)

# 10

# Back to the Land

Just as hemlines had been up and then down, and Beatle boots and bangs had been replaced by paisley and polka dots, so music by the late '60s had been through a succession of changes—from acoustic folk and electrified folk-rock to psychedelic-pop and blues-based rock. Tired, perhaps, of the excesses of music—the feedback, distortion and the sheer volume of it all—many people in the aftermath of the acid-rock era longed for a return to a simpler, gentler sound. So, in 1969, the pendulum was swinging back to folk and more roots-oriented rock.

The Band had already been doing this. *Music from Big Pink* had gone against the grain of prevailing rock music, emphasizing ensemble playing over solos with music steeped in country and blues–based sounds. A hugely influential album, *Big Pink* set the stage for the release of the group's 1969 album titled simply *The Band*. Rich in Americana, Robbie Robertson's songs—drawn

from his love affair with Southern culture which began when Ronnie Hawkins called him down to Arkansas—unabashedly celebrated rural life. The music, too, had a down-home, old-time feel. Combined with photos of the group looking like Civil War survivors in beards, hats, waistcoats and wing collars, the whole image was deeply and lovingly rooted in the past.

Similarly, by the end of the decade, many hippies were rejecting city life and its values in favour of a rural, communal existence. Suddenly, macrobiotic diets, organic vegetables and geodesic domes were in fashion, while *The Whole Earth Catalogue*, the bible for the back-to-the-land movement, celebrated all things rural and rustic. A number of Yorkville residents headed to the country to a 500-acre commune south of Algonquin Park near the town of Killaloe. Among them were Bernie Finkelstein and Luke Gibson.

Killaloe offered an escape from the insanity that followed the break-up of Kensington Market. "We were all going crazy," says Gibson, referring to himself and his bandmates. "We'd been living in airplanes and hotels and, meanwhile, the village was going downhill. Everyone's reality was being ripped apart. So I got a tent and my raincoat and took off."

For Finkelstein, the trek to Killaloe was a life-saving move. "Toronto had gotten strange," he says bluntly. "Yorkville deteriorated when the motorcycle gangs moved in and heavy drugs like speed took over. I was in a real descending spiral, snorting a lot of pure meth. I decided to get myself straight." When they arrived, Gibson and Finkelstein found the commune a bit strange. "It was all very ritualistic," recalls Finkelstein. "Everyone sat around the dinner table and had to smell the bread with their eyes closed. People were reading too much Tolkien or something. They had a council of people, sort of like a tribe, and Luke and I had to state why we wanted to join the commune and what we could contribute. They weren't sure about us, but said we could stay down by the lake in our tents." Ultimately, Finkelstein and Gibson passed on the commune's tribal experience in favour of a nearby farm, which they bought later that year.

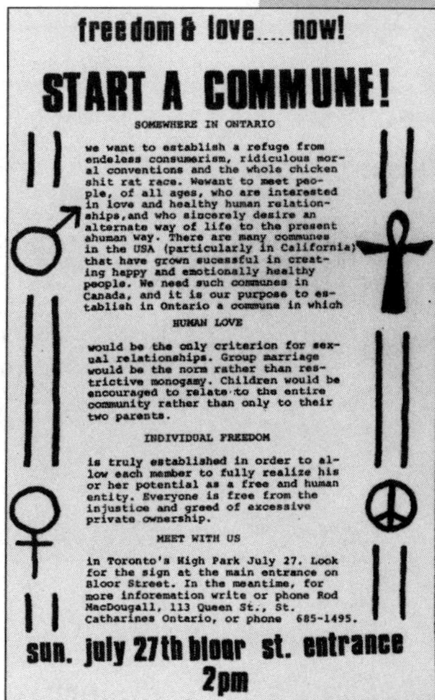


Back in Toronto the new acoustic sound was coming on strong, particularly from Bruce Cockburn and Murray McLauchlan. The two musicians had kept in touch ever since they first met at Ottawa's Le Hibou. They played on the same bill at Mariposa '68 and when Cockburn decided to go solo, McLauchlan put in a word, getting Cockburn his first Riverboat gig in May 1969.

Once in the same city, Cockburn and McLauchlan, although quite different in personality and interests, became fast friends. When McLauchlan and his wife Patti moved away from Hazelton, leaving biker Moses and an increasingly speed-riddled village behind, they joined Cockburn and his wife Kitty in a flat above a Queen Street pawnshop. "He had a fresh sort of intensity, a very youthful quality," says Cockburn of McLauchlan. "He had great songs, good lyrics and music, played guitar well and sang beautifully. On top of that, he had a lot of charisma. What wasn't there to like?"

The respect was mutual, but McLauchlan found Cockburn sometimes difficult to fathom. "He was an odd buzzard," recalls McLauchlan. "I remember my first exposure to Bruce and thinking he was like a choirboy. In fact, sometimes on stage he used to wear these little Catholic choirboy shirts with a little tie. It was very weird. This was when he was just entering his bucolic phase."

Cockburn explains the difference between himself and McLauchlan: "There were a lot of things that we didn't have in common which became more apparent later. I wasn't really a drinker. I'd get very stoned [on pot] and sit there for an hour not saying anything. I remember once, after a long, uncomfortable silence, Murray saying to me, 'So what's next in the Cockburn theatre of the absurd?' I just wasn't able to communicate very well. Eventually, I stopped smoking dope for that reason."

*Cockburn and McLauchlan, with Aroo*

That summer, Cockburn received a call from Richard Patterson, the drummer of the defunct Children, now with a new version of Three's a Crowd that included David Wiffen, Colleen Peterson and ex-Children member Sandy Crawley. Would Cockburn like to join them? Always in the market for a way to pay the bills, Cockburn agreed. Together, the group taped twenty-six TV shows that Cockburn remembers included some silly episodes. "There's one where I'm playing drums and another where I'm singing 'Shake, Rattle & Roll' and wearing this sparkly shirt and sunglasses," he recalls. "You'd have to have been there to appreciate it." Few people were; only one of the episodes was ever aired.

Before the year was out, Three's a Crowd broke up. At the same time, Cockburn and McLauchlan and their respective spouses began to suspect their Queen

Street flat was haunted. "It was real psychodrama stuff," McLauchlan recalls. "We all woke up one morning and everyone looked pretty rough. Then, over coffee, someone said they'd had a dream where they flew disembodied through the apartment and saw everyone else hacked to pieces, all bloody and disembowelled in our beds. It turned out that all of us had had the same dream. Other strange things started happening. I was sitting alone in a chair reading a book and I felt something grab the back of my head, like a hand. When I turned around, there was nothing there. And Bruce's dog, Aroo, was terrified all the time, cowering and whimpering. It was weird. One cold, rainy night, Patti and I went out for a walk and decided never to go back." As for Cockburn, he and Kitty and Aroo quit the city altogether. They moved into a camper and began travelling across the country. Almost immediately, Cockburn's exposure to Canadian landscapes began to influence his songwriting.

*Three's a Crowd: (from left) David Wiffen, Dennis Pendrith, Colleen Peterson, who died in 1996, Cockburn and Richard Patterson*

Meanwhile, several Canadian artists had found their voices. By January 1969, Neil Young had released his self-titled debut solo album. Taking a break from Crosby, Stills & Nash, Young returned to Toronto the following month to perform at the Riverboat. It was a gig he'd waited a long time to play. "You know all those dirty long-haired kids with no direction in Yorkville?" Young told *The Toronto Star*'s Marci McDonald, "well, I was one of them." He added, "I tried to get work as a folk singer at all the clubs there but they didn't take me

*Neil Young waited four long years to headline the Riverboat*

seriously. They used to say, 'Run along, kid.'"

No doubt Young savoured the rave reviews for his week-long engagement. That year, he recorded another album, *Everybody Knows This Is Nowhere*, featuring "Cinnamon Girl," "Down by the River" and "Cowgirl in the Sand," with the band Crazy Horse. Two years later, the singer-songwriter had a critically acclaimed album—*After the Gold Rush*—and such hits as the classic "Only Love Can Break Your Heart." But John Craig Eaton had the last laugh when Young returned to Toronto to play Massey Hall in early 1971. Remembering the money Young owed him for The Mynah Birds' equipment, Eaton used a court-approved garnishment to reclaim it from the box-office receipts. Young, by then one of rock's mega stars, could hardly object.

By 1969, Gordon Lightfoot realized that Massey Hall was the perfect venue for his performances. The large hall could accommodate his many fans, and its intimate atmosphere and fabulous acoustics made it an ideal replacement for the Riverboat. Lightfoot's Massey Hall spring concerts were to become an annual tradition which continues nearly three decades later, as much a sign of the changing seasons as the return home of the Canada geese.

At the same time, Lightfoot's canny manager Albert Grossman had just secured him the Warner Bros. recording contract that had eluded him four years earlier—an unprecedented deal worth more than one million dollars. With the title track from his first Warner Bros. album *If You Could Read My Mind*, Lightfoot finally reached the pop stratosphere. The song, based on an "old-time movie about a ghost from a

*Savouring his Riverboat triumph*

wishing well," soared to the top of the charts and was eventually covered by more than a hundred artists including Barbra Streisand. "That put him in a whole other category," concluded former producer John Court. "Gord hasn't been hungry since." Wanting to handle his own affairs, Lightfoot formed Early Morning Productions that year.

Joni Mitchell was herself hugely successful by the end of the decade. *Clouds* won the singer-songwriter her first Grammy Award, for Best Folk Performance, and took her on the road for much of the year. Then in January 1970, Mitchell made the surprise announcement that she was quitting touring, cancelling an important gig at Carnegie Hall. She used the time off to travel in Europe and the

**Deeply haunting, Mitchell's masterpiece *Blue* defined a whole new genre of music—confessional songwriting**

Caribbean, writing songs about the experience that would show up on her exquisite *Ladies of the Canyon* album, a recording that also reflected her new life in California.

With 1971's *Blue*, Mitchell created her masterpiece. Deeply haunting, the album defined a whole new genre of music—confessional songwriting. Mitchell had dramatized her relationships, writing about Graham Nash in "Willy" and James Taylor whom she had met at Mariposa '70 in "Blue." Her love affairs became a source of constant fascination for her fans, who hunted for evidence of them in her lyrics like sleuths on the trail of some tabloid-style

*The magnificent misfits that made up Mainline*

scandal. The tawdry speculation about her romantic relationships with famous musicians hit rock bottom in 1971 when *Rolling Stone* voted her "Old Lady of the Year" and "Queen of El Lay." It would be a decade before Mitchell would speak to the magazine again.

Although the members of McKenna Mendelson Mainline found England's dark, damp winter depressing, the relocation quickly paid dividends. With the help of an English manager, the group joined an agency that began booking the band into clubs around London. One particular gig, with several bands including progressive rockers Yes at London's Marquee club, proved especially fruitful. The shows turned out to be an audition for London-based Liberty Records, whose executives were impressed enough with Mainline to finance a demo recording, and then excited enough by what they heard to sign the group to an album deal. But before the record was released, a homesick McKenna returned to Toronto. Mendelson and the others trooped home shortly afterwards.

Back in Canada, news of Mainline's success in England had quickly spread. When the band made its homecoming appearance at the Rock Pile in July 1969, simultaneously releasing their debut album *Stink* and first single "Better Watch Out," fans greeted the group like conquering heroes. Mendelson immodestly told *The Globe and Mail*: "Being good musicians in England was easy. We tried to compete but there was no one to compete with. We expected to see unbelievable things from groups there but we were really disap-

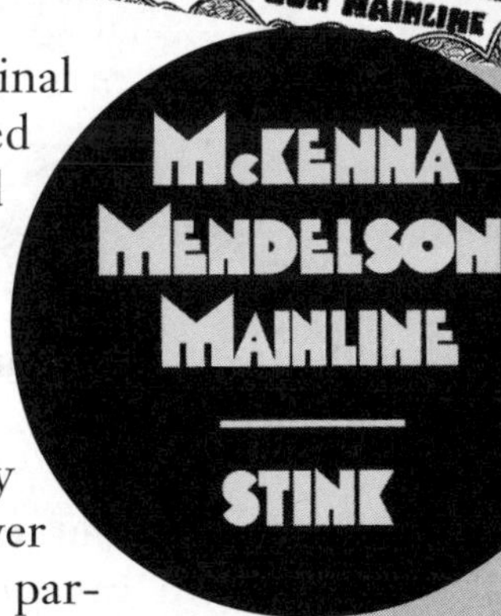


pointed. It was a big bummer." He added, "Our music is as original as it can be. We don't sound like any band that's ever played."

Mendelson got that right. *Stink* was as good as his boast. Bristling with coiled energy and raw emotion, the album had a ferocity never heard before—at least not on a Canadian recording. Featuring eleven original songs by Mendelson who pounded piano, blew harmonica and grunted vocals in his inimitable way, *Stink* also showcased the inspired guitar work of McKenna, who could rip through an incendiary lead solo or pull off a chilling slide riff with equal aplomb. Quickly the bluesy album with the all-black cover became standard equipment at house parties—as indispensable as a two-four of beer or an ounce of weed on a Saturday night. A note inside the jacket read, "Here's some honest music from London—play it loudly."

Boosted by the success of the dark, edgy single "Better Watch Out," *Stink* became a genuine Canadian hit, enjoying sales of more than 30,000 copies in its first year alone. Meanwhile *McKenna Mendelson Blues*, recorded before they left for England, was released on the fledgling Paragon label. Then, just as Mainline were touring universities throughout Eastern Canada and seemed destined for an international breakthrough, Mendelson began to have misgivings. Inexplicably, he called it quits in December, leaving McKenna adrift. Afterwards, McKenna joined a reformed Luke & the Apostles, but the band imploded a few months later.

Though they passed on Woodstock in August '69, Lighthouse accepted a gig at the prestigious Atlantic City Pop Festival that same month on a bill with Jefferson Airplane and Creedence Clearwater Revival. It was a high-profile appearance in front of 70,000 rock fans, and the band was understandably nervous. Just as Lighthouse was about to go on, the festival's sound system broke down, delaying the concert as techies frantically tried to get it up and running. With the crowd starting to turn ugly, promoters sent Lighthouse leader Skip Prokop out to try and talk them down. Someone in the crowd called out, "Do you guys up in Canada get drafted?" No, we don't, Prokop answered. A suddenly quiet crowd, with Vietnam weighing heavily on their minds, then engaged Prokop in a forty-minute dialogue about Canada's politics and its attitudes towards draft dodgers.

"It was incredible," recalls Prokop. "The tension suddenly lifted as this giant, sort of town-hall meeting took place." With the sound system fixed, Prokop's group easily won over the audience—especially with its Beatles medley of "A Day in the Life," "All You Need Is Love" and "Give Peace a Chance." *Rolling Stone* dubbed Lighthouse "the Canadian peace band."

The band's anti-war opinions, however, did not go down nearly so well with the U.S. authorities. Prokop recalls getting a visit shortly afterwards from federal agents. "These guys came backstage to one of our shows," says Prokop. "I can't remember whether they were from the FBI, the CIA or national security. But these dudes made it pretty clear that if I wanted to continue getting an H1 (work) visa in America, I'd better learn to shut my mouth. It was really heavy."

After the group's triumph at Atlantic City, Lighthouse jumped at the chance to perform a free August concert in Nathan Phillips Square at Toronto's city hall. The free appearance, however, quickly became a hassle for the group, which was scheduled to appear at the new Electric Circus on Queen Street East just four days later. The promoters of the ticketed Lighthouse show, fearing poor attendance because of the free city hall appearance, threatened to sue the band. Modelled after the New York nightclub of the same name, Toronto's Electric Circus had been opened by Stanton Freeman, the playboy investor who'd set up The Sparrows' success in New York. Concerts at the new club were a big deal, with expensive, state-of-the-art sound equipment and psychedelic light shows. Lighthouse refused to back down and, riding a wave of popularity, the band not only brought out thousands to city hall but sold out the Electric Circus gig as well.

Lighthouse's first three albums—the self-titled debut, *Suite Feeling* and *Peacing It All Together*—were not nearly as successful as Mainline's *Stink*. Rambling and unfocused, they suffered from what Paul Hoffert calls the folly of self-production. "Skip and I made the mistake of thinking we could do it ourselves," says Hoffert. "To make matters worse, we chose to consult each band member in the studio at the mixing stage. The result, of course, was that every musician had his own idea of what it should sound like. We lost all focus." Hoffert adds, chuckling, "All the pot smoking didn't help either."

**CHUM CHART TOP TEN JULY 26, 1969**

*In the Year 2525*
Zager & Evans

*Baby I Love You*
Andy Kim

*Sweet Caroline*
Neil Diamond

*Spinning Wheel*
Blood, Sweat & Tears

*When I Die*
Motherlode

*What Does It Take*
Jr. Walker

*Good Old Rock 'n Roll*
Cat Mother

*Ruby Don't Take Your Love to Town*
First Edition

*Yesterday When I Was Young*
Roy Clark

*Color Him Father*
Winstons

By late 1969, Bernie Finkelstein had had enough of the country life and returned to Toronto. Anxious to catch up on the music scene, he sought the advice of his old buddies. Former Kensington Market guitarist Gene Martynec suggested he catch folk singer Bruce Cockburn at the Pornographic Onion, a coffee house on the Ryerson campus. Finkelstein remembered Cockburn from the night The Children and The Paupers opened for The Lovin' Spoonful at the Gardens on December 11, 1966. But when Finkelstein heard Cockburn's gentle, evocative songs at the Porno Onion, he was really impressed. In particular, he was struck by "Going to the Country," a cheerful Cockburn tune that not only reflected the back-to-the-land movement, but Finkelstein's own experience in the wilds of Killaloe.

Not long after, Finkelstein and Cockburn forged a partnership. In early 1970, Finkelstein formed True North Records, a pioneering independent label dedicated to releasing new Canadian music. Cockburn became his first artist. Cockburn's self-titled debut album, recorded at Yorkville's Eastern Sound Studios and produced by Martynec, was released that spring. The album's ten songs were all Cockburn originals. "Going to the Country" and the carefree, piano-driven "Musical Friends," which celebrated the joys of making music over glasses of wine and pipes of pot, contrasted with the quieter, more cerebral songs like "Man of a Thousand Faces" and "Thoughts on a Rainy Afternoon." The latter included the plaintive line, "O Jesus, don't let Toronto take my song away."

*Cockburn at the keys*

Filled with droning notes and bell-like sounds, the album drew at least some of its musical influences from medieval styles. And Cockburn dressed the part. According to writer Jack Batten, "He dresses like a splendid survivor of Robin Hood's merry men, in russet colours and leather jerkins, boot-high moccasins and swirling scarves." Cockburn's preoccupation with the wilderness, expressed in soft, sparse songs like "The Thirteenth Mountain," reinforced the outdoors image. Space, he told *Saturday Night* interviewer Myrna Kostash, was what distinguished his songs and those of other Canadian songwriters from American

**The gentle singer in the Cowichan sweater and granny glasses became Canadian pop's new poet laureate**

music. "Space may be a misleading word because it is so vague in relation to music," he explained, "but maybe it has to do with Canadians being more involved with the space around them rather than trying to fill it up as the Americans do. I mean physical space and how it makes you feel about yourself."

Cockburn's early songs were intensely introspective, a quality he shared with his contemporaries Joni Mitchell and Neil Young. But Cockburn's compositions also expressed a spiritual calm that made him seem wise beyond his years. For many people, the gentle singer in the Cowichan sweater and granny glasses became Canadian pop's new poet laureate.

While Cockburn's solo career seemed to be on the rise, McLauchlan's was stuck in a rut. Although he'd received money after Tom Rush recorded two of his compositions, "Child's Song" and "Old Man's Song," things were going nowhere fast. Late in '69, bummed out and broke, McLauchlan sought a chemical solution to his woes. Dropping two tabs of MDA, McLauchlan spent several blissful hours in a state of giddy, cartoon-like euphoria. But then paranoia struck deep and McLauchlan became convinced that his tooth enamel was going soft and the skin on his face was flaking off. Freaked and fatigued, he and Patti spent the night on Finkelstein's living-room floor. Finkelstein knew the guy had talent, but he already had his hands full with Cockburn. He urged McLauchlan to try his luck in the United States where prospects for a music career seemed brighter. McLauchlan took Finkelstein's advice and he and Patti headed to New York. The plan was to meet with Tom Rush's guitarist Trevor Veitch, formerly of Three's a Crowd, and start a band. The group never panned out and McLauchlan wound up, with eleven dollars in his pocket, at Albert Grossman's office. Grossman and his partner Bennett Glotzer, who managed Tom Rush, offered McLauchlan

*McLauchlan: back on the street*

$1,400 for his catalogue of forty-odd songs. He took it. Grossman and Glotzer also set McLauchlan up with a desk job, writing songs for their stable of artists. At night, he performed around New York at places like City College and Cooper Union Hall.

Living at the seedy Albert Hotel, however, took its toll on McLauchlan. By the spring of 1970—tired of his desk job, suffering from pneumonia and finding New York increasingly claustrophobic, McLauchlan and Patti decided to return to Toronto. They found an apartment in the city's Kensington Market and McLauchlan began writing again. Hanging out at Grossman's Tavern, a neighbourhood watering hole, he began soaking up the gritty stories of the bums and bikers, the artists and the hucksters. Soon he had a new batch of songs. Full of piss and vinegar, McLauchlan called up Bernie Finkelstein.

With Cockburn's debut already out and doing well, Finkelstein was now in a position to expand his artist roster. He had begun working with Luke Gibson and Keith McKie, singer-songwriters he knew well from his Kensington Market days. But when McLauchlan called, Finkelstein realized this was opportunity knocking a rare second time. Quickly he signed him to a management and recording deal.

Although he was still performing acoustic music, McLauchlan was looking for a tougher sound to convey his songs about life in a hard-rock town. Influenced by the blues bands like Downchild that McLauchlan had heard at Grossman's, he started jamming and recording demo tapes with various local musicians.

McLauchlan's debut album signalled the arrival of a powerful new songwriter. Working with musicians like Bruce Cockburn's friend Dennis Pendrith on bass, former Passing Fancy frontman Jay Telfer on drums and producer Gene Martynec, McLauchlan recorded ten songs. They ranged from early classics like "Child's Song" and "Sixteen Lanes of Highway" to wry, tough-minded rockers like "Jesus Please Don't Save Me (Till I Die)" and "Honky Red," an affectionate tale of a streetwise wino. But of all the songs, "Back on the Street" best summed up McLauchlan's new outlook in the lines, "I used to be a vagabond, it's a life that's hard to beat / but in my mind I think it's time to be back on the street."

Although it didn't fit the soft-rock format of then-popular albums by James Taylor or Carole King, *Song from the Stree*t was an auspicious debut. The calibre of the songwriting was enough to propel McLauchlan to the forefront of Canadian pop. He became the flip side of the coin shared with Cockburn—the urban street singer to Cockburn's rural balladeer.

## DISCS TO DISCOVER

*The Band*: The Band (Capitol, 1987)

*To Kingdom Come* (2 CD set): The Band (Capitol, 1989)

*Bruce Cockburn*: Bruce Cockburn (True North, 1995)

*Ladies of the Canyon*: Joni Mitchell (Reprise, 1990)

*Stink:* McKenna Mendelson Mainline (Capitol, 1994)

*McKenna Mendelson Blues*: McKenna Mendelson Mainline (Pacemaker, 1995)

*Aardvark* (vinyl only): Kensington Market (Warner Bros., 1969)

# 11 The Freak Flag Flies

It was the late sixties and The Guess Who had just returned to Canada from a gruelling tour of the United States, where they'd had their eyes opened. "We'd never seen ghettos in Winnipeg before and suddenly we're in Savannah, Georgia, witnessing real poverty." says guitarist Randy Bachman. "Then we almost got drafted. We had green cards and had to run away from selective service—that's how badly they were looking for young men to serve in the war."

The band was in Kitchener, Ontario, playing that most Canadian of concert venues—a hockey arena. In the middle of a number, Bachman broke a string. "This was in the days when I could still only afford one guitar," he explained. The group had to take a break. Singer Burton Cummings, bassist Jim Kale and drummer Gary Peterson all left the stage while Bachman changed his

*The Guess Who at home in Winnipeg, January 1968*

string. As he was tuning up, Bachman started playing an edgy, urgent riff. Taking it as a call to arms, Kale and Peterson jumped back on stage and began jamming with Bachman. Cummings, then out in the parking lot, was oblivious to all of this until someone asked why he wasn't up there with the rest of the band. Rushing in, Cummings jumped on stage and asked what was going on. "We're jamming in E," yelled Bachman. "Play something." After Cummings had run out of harmonica, piano and flute solos, Bachman yelled, "Sing something." And Cummings, looking out over an audience of fresh-faced Canadian girls and thinking back to where the band had been, sang the first phrase that came into his head: "American woman stay away from me, American woman mama let me be."

The jam had driven the Kitchener crowd into a frenzy. The Guess Who knew it was a tune with undeniable power, but as a song it needed more words. Drawing on their U.S. experience, Cummings added more images—"war machines and ghetto scenes" and "coloured lights can hypnotize, sparkle someone else's eyes"—to round it out. By the time "American Woman" was released in the spring of '70, the song had been transformed into a raging, fuzz-guitar powered anti-war anthem—timed perfectly to coincide with rising opposition to the American presence in Vietnam. The song shot straight to the top of the U.S. charts, helping to make The Guess Who one of the best-selling acts of the year. In fact, the Winnipeg band sold more singles in 1970 than any act *in the world* (including The Beatles) and more

records than *all* Canadian artists *combined* (including Gordon Lightfoot and Anne Murray).

The success of "American Woman" underscored how much things had changed—both politically in the United States and practically in the fortunes of Canadian bands. Four years earlier, David Clayton-Thomas's anti-war song "Brainwashed" had been banned by U.S. radio, denying him a much-deserved U.S. breakthrough. Now, suddenly, The Guess Who's more explicit protest song was being embraced across America—even U.S. president Richard Nixon's daughter Tricia loved the band. However, when The Guess Who were invited to perform at Tricia's birthday party at the White House in July, the group complied with an official request not to play their hit.

By the end of the decade, Canada was teeming with musical talent. The West Coast rocked with a host of popular bands, with imaginative names like Mother Tucker's Yellow Duck, Papa Bear's Medicine Show, The Hydro Electric Streetcar, Crosstown Bus and Chilliwack (formerly The Collectors). The Retinal Circus, a club on Davie Street, was the focal point for the rock scene. And Tom Northcott, a veteran Vancouver folkie who had started the city's independent label New Syndrome and scored hits with songs like "1941," "Sunny Goodge Street" and "Girl from the North Country," had created the largest independent production company on the West Coast with Studio 3 Productions. All that was lacking in the burgeoning scene was a major outlet for airplay.

As Chilliwack's Bill Henderson told Ritchie Yorke, "What we needed in Vancouver was a really powerful radio station like CHUM in Toronto."

Montreal was experiencing a similar boom. Along with a flourishing francophone rock scene, the city produced a number of promising English-language acts, including MG & the Escorts, The Rabble, The Haunted and Mashmakhan. The Haunted, who had beaten out David Clayton-Thomas & the Shays in a Battle of the Bands at the Montreal Forum to win a recording deal with Quality, scored a national hit single with "1-2-5." Taking a unique approach to psychedelic music, the band also recorded such other classics as "I'm Just Gonna Blow My Little Mind to Bits" and "Vapeur Mauve," a French version of Jimi Hendrix's "Purple Haze."

Mashmakhan, named after a drug, had its origins in a mid-1960s band called The Triangle, singer Trevor Payne's back-up group. While Payne put together The Young Ones, an early Afrocentric jazz-rock group that thrilled audiences at Yorkville's Penny Farthing, Pierre Senecal went on to form Mashmakhan, which scored a million-selling hit in 1970 called "As the Years Go By."

There were other isolated Canadian hits in the late 1960s, such as "Half Past Midnight" by Ottawa's The

Staccatos (later The Five Man Electrical Band) and "Which Way You Goin' Billy?" by Vancouver's Poppy Family. One of the biggest North American hits of 1969 came from Toronto's Motherlode, a band whose members were drawn from two talented outfits—Grant Smith & the Power and The Soul Searchers, a dynamic r & b group that backed singers Eric Mercury and Diane Brooks. Motherlode's Steve Kennedy, William "Smitty" Smith, Ken Marco and Wayne Stone could scarcely believe that their song "When I Die," which topped the charts that summer, went on to sell more than half a million copies.

But even with those breakthroughs, a lot of Canadian music was still falling on deaf ears. The problem was a general lack of support from radio stations and record companies. Few of the foreign-owned major labels operating in Canada were signing local acts. Radio stations, taking cues from U.S.-based consultants, were programming with a heavy bias towards American music. Small wonder that The Band, Joni Mitchell, Neil Young, David Clayton-Thomas, Steppenwolf, Zal Yanovsky and Denny Doherty had all

**The flag-waving trade journal began advocating government intervention to force broadcasters to play Canadian records**

pulled up stakes and headed south. Something had to change.

There had been attempts to improve the airplay situation for Canadian artists. In an influential series of articles in 1968 titled "Legislated Radio," *RPM*

*Weekly*, the flag-waving trade journal published by Walt Grealis and Stan Klees, had begun advocating government intervention to force broadcasters to play Canadian records. *RPM* had also been responsible for establishing the Maple Leaf System (MLS), an attempt to coordinate the playing of indigenous discs by twelve major radio stations across the country. But the member stations eventually disbanded and MLS was shelved due to lack of interest.

Canadian broadcasters, in fact, resisted all efforts by outsiders to influence what they played. Funnily enough, the mere threat of legislation actually helped to boost the Canadian quotient on the airwaves for a while as stations attempted to put a more patriotic face on their programming. This, in turn, led to a flurry of domestic signings by several of the major labels, especially Capitol Records, where Paul White was a major supporter of Canadian talent. When Pierre Juneau, chairman of the CRTC, the government's regulatory body for broadcasting, proposed legislation requiring AM stations to play thirty percent Canadian content in early 1970, battle lines were drawn right across the Canadian music industry: artists and record companies were in favour of the legislation, while broadcasters were vehemently opposed.

Meanwhile, live music was thriving—especially at the outdoor rock festivals that sprang up across Canada in the late 1960s and early '70s. These festivals, financed by young, high-risk entrepreneurs, provided memorable communal experiences for music lovers and important showcases for countless bands. In 1969, promoters John Brower and Ken Walker were responsible for two of the year's most successful festivals: the Toronto Pop festival and the Toronto Rock 'n' Roll Revival show, which included John Lennon's Plastic Ono Band.

But the most magical of all such events was the Transcontinental Pop Festival, held in the summer of '70. Promoted by Walker—without Brower but with significant cash infusion from George and Thor Eaton, scions of the T. Eaton Company and brothers of John Craig, the festival was a phenomenal, million-dollar rock show on wheels. Some of the biggest names in popular music, including The Band, Janis Joplin and The Grateful Dead, travelled across the country on twelve Canadian National train coaches. With "Festival Express" painted in orange and black ten-foot letters on the baggage car, the train and its rock-star passengers made stops with performances at stadiums in Toronto, Winnipeg and Calgary. Among the Canadian acts on board were Mashmakhan, Cat and Ian & Sylvia with Great Speckled Bird, including Amos Garrett.

The Speckled Bird's ace guitarist claims he remembers precious little about the historic trip. "The amount of alcohol consumed aboard that train is legendary," laughs Garrett. "We partied morning, noon and night." The promoters had thoughtfully provided two lounge cars, outfitted with electrical outlets so the musicians could plug in and play their instruments, which they did at all hours of the day and night, says Garrett. "In fact," he adds, "people were almost reticent to get off the train to go out to the stadiums to play the shows because there were so many amazing jams happening."

Garrett has one vivid memory of Janis Joplin whom he met for the first time on the trip. "I remem-

ber how incredible she was on stage," he says, "yet how totally worn out she was afterwards, with nothing left at all." Well, almost nothing. Joplin flew into action when the train ran out of booze in the wilds of Saskatchewan. The singer commanded the train to stop on the outskirts of Saskatoon (unaware they were in Joni Mitchell's old stomping grounds) and led the entire cast of musicians and crew members on an expedition in search of a government liquor store. When they found it, the musicians proceeded to buy up nearly half the stock. Recalls Garrett, "So here's this contingent of stoned freaks, led by Janis Joplin, followed by Jerry Garcia and the rest of us, filing back through town, carrying cases of beer with bottles of wine and liquor stacked on top. Within minutes, we were gone. The townsfolk who witnessed it all must've thought *they* were hallucinating." The Express carried Joplin to one of her last performances; she died of a heroin overdose in October in Hollywood's Landmark Hotel.

At the festival's final stop in Calgary, Ian & Sylvia, Delaney & Bonnie (another husband-and-wife act), The Band's Rick Danko and the Dead's Jerry Garcia performed together in one memorable jam session. All sorts of musical barriers were broken. "We thought you were just California freaks," Danko told Garcia afterwards, "but you're just like us." The relaxed, free exchange of musical ideas was felt by the train's whole entourage of 140 musicians and associates. Said the Dead's manager Rock Scully, "The train made friends of everybody. We rarely come across each other for

*(from left) Great Speckled Bird's Ian Tyson, Sylvia Tyson, Ken Kalmusky, Amos Garrett (top), N.D. Smart II and Buddy Cage*

any length of time, rapping, playing music especially. Music most of the time has to be hammered out, it isn't in the air, as it was on the train."

The festival was not without its share of controversy. Walker and the Eaton brothers had to contend with protests from the May 4th Movement (M4M), a radical coalition of students and street people based at Toronto's Rochdale College. Targeting the promoters as capitalist exploiters, M4M tried to discredit the festival with the slogan "Stop the Rip-Off Express" and a propaganda campaign that demanded free admission along with "free dope and no cops." After a meeting with the coalition, Thor Eaton concluded, "These people have a loose grip on reality." Still, the smear campaign hurt ticket sales and the festival lost $350,000. It was the last time the Eaton brothers would venture into the tumultuous world of rock 'n' roll.

Meanwhile, Ronnie Hawkins was still pumping out the old hits on Yonge Street. But he was also continuing to groom new musicians, working them hard until they could play better than most. Hawkins's latest band was a group led by singer Kelly Jay and harmonica player Richard Newell that rehearsed twelve hours a day for six months until the Hawk, in his inimitable way with words, declared them "tight as a frog's mouth stretched over a boxcar." Hawkins had nicknamed the blues-blowing Newell "King Biscuit Boy" after a radio show back in his home state of Arkansas. He'd also called the group "dumber than a crowbar." Both names stuck. After Jay, Newell and company played New York's Fillmore East, nearly upstaging Joe Cocker, the group—like predecessors The Band and Full Tilt Boogie—decided to break away from Hawkins and go it alone.

*Crowbar, with Kelly Jay (second from right), outside Bad Manors in Hamilton, Ont.*

In May 1970, the same month they left Hawkins, King Biscuit Boy recorded his debut album with Crowbar. *Official Music*, featuring eight blues standards and three Newell originals, was the first release of a newly formed Canadian indie label started by their manager Frank Davies. Surprisingly, Hawkins wasn't the least bit bitter—and in fact joined Davies and other investors in launching a whole chain of companies to handle the band: Daffodil Records, Love Productions, Love Management, Freewheeled Music and Daffodil Design. The investment began to pay off in September. The group stole the show at the Strawberry Fields rock festival east of Toronto, and the album's "Corrina, Corrina" hit the charts all across the country.

But Newell wanted to continue playing blues while the rest of the band preferred to move in a looser, rambunctious rock direction. "Richard was into more of a purist thing," explains Jay. "The rest of us were enamoured of the audience reaction we got from playing good-time rock 'n' roll. We loved bringing the house down with fast, freewheeling numbers." After an amicable parting, Crowbar set up house in a six-bedroom, 100-year-old mansion that sat on twenty-five acres on Hamilton Mountain in Ancaster, Ontario. Communal life in the gloomy mansion, which the band called "Bad Manors," allowed them crucial woodshedding time to polish their axes and hone their chops.

In the end, Mainline's dissolution proved only temporary. Mendelson called McKenna in the summer of '70 and asked if he'd like to join him, Nolasco and a new bassist, Zeke Sheppard, at an outdoor festival in east Toronto called Scarborough Fair. Performing on a bill with fellow blues acts Downchild and Whiskey Howl and several rock bands including Nucleus, the reunited Mainline went over so well that its members decided to try it again.

With a new manager, Wayne Thompson, the band set out in search of another record deal. But Mendelson's personality detonated things just as they were looking good. Sitting in the New York office of Capitol Records' president Dick Asher, Mendelson and his father Harry, who was acting as the group's lawyer, insulted the record executive. This brought negotia-

*Mendelson in drag*

tions to an abrupt close—the group was actually thrown out of the building. Recalls Thompson, of the volatile meeting, "I sat there and watched a $50,000 advance with a major U.S. label go up in smoke."

Although a Capitol deal eluded them, Mainline did land a lucrative recording contract with GRT Records. Under the shrewd direction of Thompson, an economics graduate from the University of Toronto, the group quickly became one of biggest money-earners on the Canadian rock scene. While other bands demanded $750 for high-school and university shows, Mainline worked for union scale (then around $125) but with one significant condition: they also received ninety percent of the gross receipts. Thompson had the group working up to three school shows a day and readily admits they raked it in. "There were times when I left a school concert with shopping bags absolutely stuffed with cash," said Thompson. "I felt like a mobster."

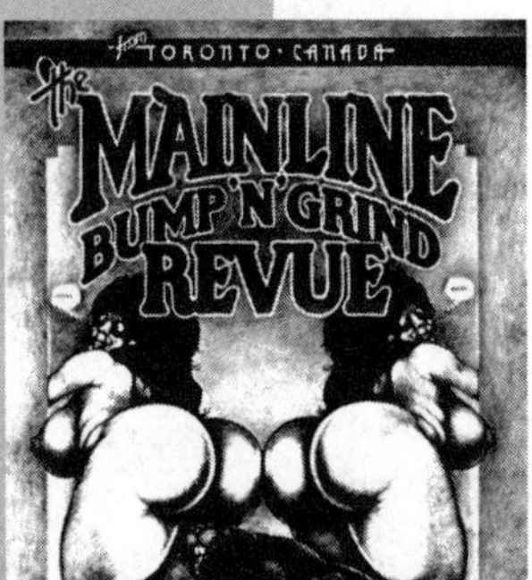


With Mainline's 1971 album *Canada, Our Home and Native Land*, came a distinctive new sound and image. Gone was the primitive blues of their two previous albums. The album, produced by ex-Pauper Adam Mitchell and recorded in Los Angeles with the Tower of Power horn section, was a wild and woolly mix of folk, rock and whimsical show tunes, mostly penned by Mendelson. According to Thompson, "Joe had lost interest in the blues thing. He wanted to turn Mainline into an art band." The art concept carried through to Mainline's logo, posters, buttons and album jackets. Designed by artist David Andoff, with direction from Mendelson, the Mainline look was both patriotic and mildly pornographic—Canadian flags and beavers mixed with cartoon images of women with gargantuan breasts and bums. In retrospect, the group's marketing was years ahead of any other band working in Canada at the time. "We were never shy about being Canadians," says McKenna, "but I think Canada was shy about us."

Indeed, Mainline's raunchy image and Mendelson's prickly personality made the group unpalatable for some in the Canadian music industry. Although "Get Down To" from *Canada*, did receive AM airplay, the band found a more comfortable home on the new FM stations that sprang up in the late 1960s and early '70s. Meanwhile, Mainline found itself embraced by a new niche audience: bike gangs. Locally, the Vagabonds adopted the band as its own, even granting the group rehearsal privileges in its downtown club house. And when Mainline arrived in Australia after the release of *Canada*, which included the song "Motorcycle" (Mendelson himself rode a Norton Black Shadow), the band was greeted at the airport by a hundred members of the local Hell's Angels who gave the group an escort to downtown Sydney. McKenna recalls, "The Angels looked like something out of *Mad Max*, really tough with primitive choppers and everything. But we were treated like the second coming."

The band's controversial arrival in Australia made for great headlines, according to Thompson, who also remembers Mendelson and Nolasco hanging moons out the window of their limousine. More difficult was the fallout from Mendelson's admission to one newspaper reporter that he regularly consumed a quarter-ounce of hashish every day. When the group checked into a

**CHUM CHART TOP TEN APRIL 11, 1970**

*Let It Be*
Beatles

*Easy Come Easy Go*
Bobby Sherman

*You Me and Mexico*
Edward Bear

*Shilo*
Neil Diamond

*American Woman/No Sugar Tonight*
Guess Who

*ABC*
Jackson 5

*Gotta Hold on to This Feeling*
Jr. Walker & All Stars

*Love or Let Me Be Lonely*
Friends of Distinction

*Spirit in the Sky*
Norman Greenbaum

*Reflections of My Life*
Marmalade

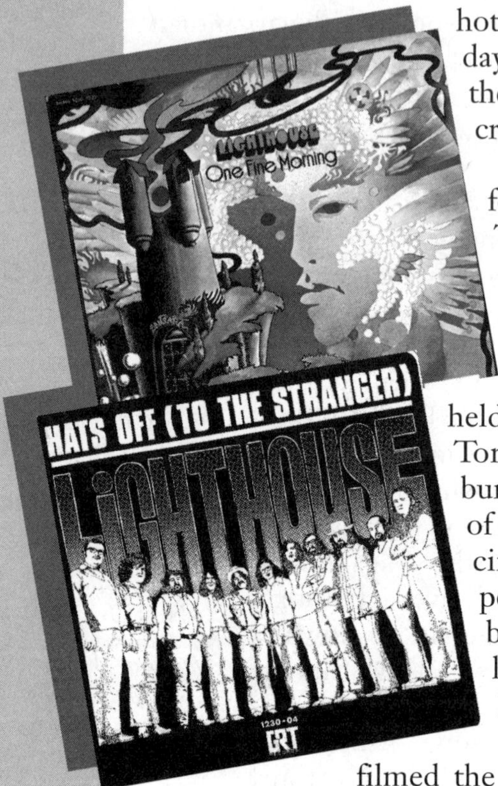


hotel in Melbourne the next day, the police were waiting for them to search every nook and cranny of their luggage.

The band's bawdy side found its fullest expression in The Mainline Bump 'n' Grind Revue, which produced both a live show and a recording of the same name. The first Revue, held on New Year's Eve 1971 at Toronto's infamous Victory burlesque theatre in the heart of Chinatown (now a Chinese cinema), featured Mainline performing in drag with a bevy of strippers with names like Mother Superior and Heaven Lee. Future media mogul Moses Znaimer filmed the X-rated concert to broadcast live on his CityTV station, while TVOntario, the government-funded educational channel, aired a tamer version of the show earlier in the night. A little sheepishly, McKenna chuckles, "It was a helluva show."

The Bump 'n' Grind Revue was either Mainline's zenith or nadir, depending on your moral yardstick. But regardless, the show was also the band's swan song. Too stoned to take work seriously, beset with problems, the group called it quits. Drugs and alcohol were in fact Mainline's ultimate downfall, according to Thompson, who says he watched the band blow its earnings—as much as $2,500 a week—on combustibles. McKenna, for his part, admits that the most he had to show for all the money Mainline made was a Jaguar XKE he bought for himself and a Triumph

TR-7 for his wife. Says Thompson, "Joe was a tough guy to deal with, dictatorial to a point, with wild mood swings. He always felt he could bulldoze his way through any situation. Finesse was not an art form he mastered. But he was—and is—brilliant. A true artist."

Lighthouse on stage at the start of the '70s was a sight to behold. With a long-haired Prokop stationed dead centre behind his drum kit, surrounded by multiple strings and horns, it looked like some kind of large, technicoloured sea creature, all tentacles and suction cups. Hoffert, Paul McGrath reported, played "musical shaman in fake African dress, exhorting the crowd to communion with the musical elements." Its sound, however, was truly revolutionary for the times—a synergistic alchemy of classical strings and jazzy brass combined with pop vocals and a rock backbeat. It spawned countless imitators, including Chicago Transit Authority (later simply Chicago). Lighthouse stretched rock's boundaries by performing with the Toronto, Montreal, Edmonton and Philadelphia symphonies, as well as the Cincinnati Philharmonic. Soon after, England's Procol Harum recorded a best-selling album with the Edmonton Symphony. In April 1970, Prokop stepped out from behind his drum kit to appear before the CRTC hearings on proposed Canadian content regulations for radio. In the banquet room of an Ottawa hotel, Prokop sat and listened as the Canadian Association of Broadcasters (CAB), representing 248 AM radio stations, dominated the CRTC hearings with urgent warnings about the negative effects of a Canadian music quota. "We believe that a thirty percent content

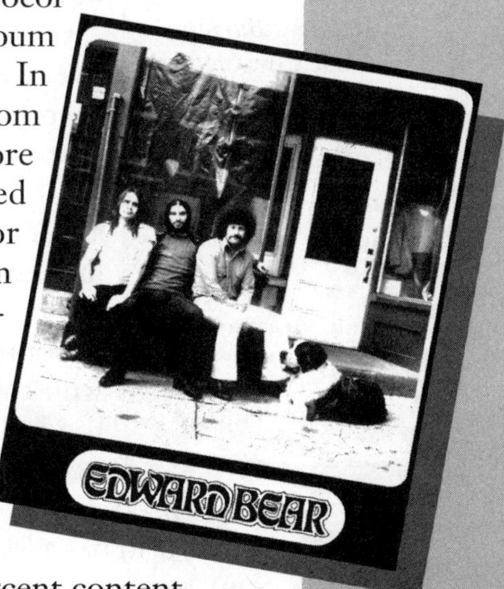

**The lack of a Canadian music industry is the direct result of the lack of exposure of the Canadian product**

**CHUM CHART TOP TEN APRIL 25, 1970**

*American Woman/No Sugar Tonight*
Guess Who

*Let It Be*
Beatles

*ABC*
Jackson 5

*Woodstock*
Crosby, Stills, Nash & Young

*Little Green Bag*
George Baker Selection

*Something's Burning*
First Edition

*Reflections of My Life*
Marmalade

*Easy Come Easy Go*
Bobby Sherman

*Come Running*
Van Morrison

*My Baby Loves Lovin'*
White Plains

is impossible to meet," one CAB spokesman argued. "There is, at present, a decidedly insufficient supply of domestic recorded music." What music is available, another CAB representative added, is inferior compared to American and British recordings. "We would be forced to commence playing a number of works whose performance is poor," he insisted, "since Canadian material, as we know it, varies widely in quality." Prokop, who could list dozens of top-notch Canadian records, was infuriated.

Then the Lighthouse leader had to sit and listen to CAB raise the spectre of dire economic consequences if the quota was put into effect. "It is our belief," concluded one spokesman, "that an implementation of the new proposals will raise the cost of broadcasting to the advertiser, lower the attractiveness of stations to the listeners and thereby, for both these reasons, raise the cost per listener to the point where many stations will cease to be competitive in the advertising market and their incomes will drop significantly."

Prokop was incensed. So, too, was Toronto-based music critic Ritchie Yorke who took the stand. "I am firmly convinced the lack of a Canadian music industry is the direct result of the lack of exposure of the Canadian product," Yorke stated. "Almost every country in the world has a local music industry. Canada has the talent but no music industry. There are two reasons for

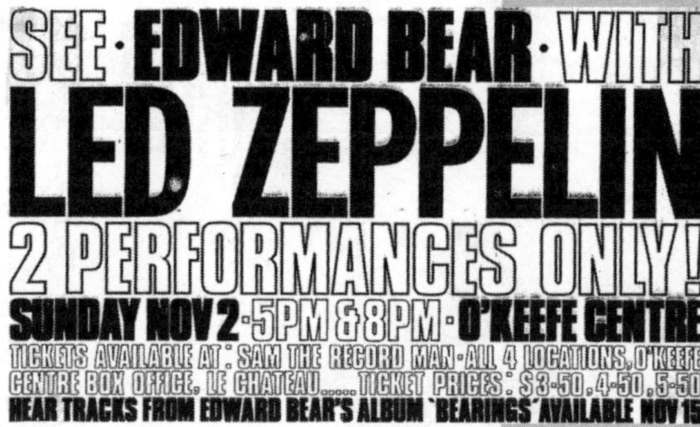


this, I believe: the extreme reluctance of Canadian radio stations to program anything by local artists as if there was somehow something wrong with them. The second reason is that most Canadian record companies are foreign owned and they cannot be bothered sinking valuable profits into making records that few stations will play."

Yorke wasn't finished. "Any broadcaster who played 'Yummy Yummy Yummy (I've Got Love in My Tummy),' that memorable American hit by The Ohio Express, should never get himself involved in a discussion on quality. Radio stations have had fifteen years to get the job done and they have failed miserably. Radio management is just too damn lazy to audition new records. It is easier just to play the Top 40 off the lists sent out by the American music magazines." Finally, Yorke urged, "Create the demand and the supply will be there."

Now it was Prokop's turn. Seating himself in front of the microphone, the celebrated drummer spoke in slow, measured tones. "The thing that I feel," he began, "is that [the quota] will set up a chain reaction. If Canada can get behind this whole thing, there will be a lot more kids who will make it worldwide. First of all, the kids who are recording will start getting hit records. Then Canadian kids will start paying a certain amount of money to go and

see them in concert. This creates the beginning of an industry—you start creating stars within your own country." With the emotion rising in his voice, Prokop concluded, "This is something that Canada has never really had."

Prokop knew what he was talking about. With his previous group, The Paupers, he had enjoyed fleeting fame, both at home and south of the border. And he knew of all kinds of talent that had gone to waste—Domenic Troiano's Mandala, Luke & the Apostles, The Ugly Ducklings and Kensington Market. All of them had come close to breaking through—only to wash up on the shores of a barren Canadian industry. Swayed by Prokop's passionate, pro-Canadian speech, the CRTC voted in favour of the thirty percent quota requirements. In making the announcement, CRTC chairman Pierre Juneau told *RPM* that the

**The prophets of doom and the messengers of mediocrity will be overwhelmed by the new generation of competent, creative, confident artisans**

opponents of the regulations would soon be silenced. "The prophets of doom, the messengers of mediocrity," he predicted, "will be overwhelmed by the new generation of competent, creative, confident artisans and by all those of the preceding generations who have already demonstrated their freshness of mind, their talent and their capacity for inspired leadership." Although he didn't mention them by name, Juneau was referring to established groups like The Guess Who,

*It happened one day in Yorkville: members of Leigh Ashford's Nucleus, Edward Bear—and a few others*

Lighthouse, Mainline and new, up-and-coming bands like Edward Bear, Chilliwack and Crowbar—all of which were busy busting down doors for Canadian music.

Crowbar's debut album, *Bad Manors*, was the first domestic recording to be launched after the Canadian content legislation became law on January 18, 1971. Cancon, as the new ruling became known, helped push the album into heavy rotation at radio stations across the country. Meanwhile, *Bad Manors* quickly earned rave reviews south of the border as well. The album, *Rolling Stone* enthused, "is one of the happiest, raunchiest, freshest emanations of a life energy to pin the grid in many moons." *Creem* magazine was even more ecstatic, gushing, "Mama get your dancing shoes on...then steady yourself for the jivingest rock 'n' boogie band in the land, 'cuz Crowbar is about to smash your body to rock 'n' roll Valhalla." For his part, influential critic Lester Bangs declared *Bad Manors* simply "fantastic."

Crowbar—guitarists John "Ghetto" Gibbard and Rheal Lanthier, keyboardist Jozef Chirowski, bassist Roly Greenway and drummer Sonnie Bernardi—had become the first still-resident Canadian group to

*Prime Minister Pierre Trudeau receiving a Crowbar pendant*

receive critical acclaim from the U.S. rock press, reported Ritchie Yorke. He added that despite The Guess Who's many gold records, the Winnipeg band had still not yet won over the critics south of the border. "While The Guess Who have broken down the chart barriers, Crowbar must get the credit for having torn down the critical walls."

In May 1971, Crowbar's anthem, "Oh What a Feeling," with its crowd-stirring refrain "what a rush," topped the Canadian charts. Two months later, Kelly Jay and the rest of the band were playing a gig in Perth, Ontario. On-stage, Crowbar was a sight to behold, resembling a bike gang crossed with a circus troupe. Bearded Kelly Jay, all six foot, four inches and 250 pounds of him, had a threatening appearance but was in reality a gentle giant, the strong man who performed acrobatics and carried up to three band members on his shoulders at one time. Laughs Jay, "Ghetto would be on my shoulders, Rheal on my back and Roly would be hanging in front of me on Ghetto's legs—and they'd still be playing their instruments. I don't know how we did it."

Among the cheering crowd that day was Pierre Trudeau and his wife, Margaret. After the show, Crowbar presented the prime minister with a plaque that read, "Thank you for making it possible through the CRTC for Canadians to be heard in their own country." According to Jay, two of the band members also handed the buckskin-jacketed Trudeau—an admitted Crowbar fan—something extra. "Roly and Rheal slipped him an envelope with five primo joints of home-grown," chuckles Jay, "telling him, 'here's a little Canadian treat for you and Margaret to enjoy.' Thank God the Mounties didn't intercept it." A new era in Canadian culture, sealed with a spliff.

*The buck-skinned prime minister proudly sporting the pendant*

## DISCS TO DISCOVER

*Blue*: Joni Mitchell (Reprise, 1990)

*After the Gold Rush*: Neil Young (Reprise, 1987)

*Harvest*: Neil Young (Reprise, 1983)

*Decade* (2 CD set): Neil Young (Reprise, 1988)

*Greatest Hits*: Murray McLauchlan (True North, 1978)

*Official Music*: King Biscuit Boy with Crowbar (Stony Plain, 1995)

*Bad Manors*: Crowbar (Stony Plain, 1995)

*The Best of Lighthouse*: Sunny Days Again: Lighthouse (Denon, 1989)

*Made in Canada: Our Rock 'n' Roll History, Vol. 2 Into the '70s* (1969→): various artists (BMG, 1990)

# epilogue

On a hot June night in 1978, Murray McLauchlan stood in the even hotter glow of several spotlights and readied himself for another evening's work. This one, however, would be different. With the sleeves of his epauletted khaki shirt rolled up, the bearded singer-songwriter stepped up to the microphone and looked out into the darkened recesses of the club. "I want to thank everyone for coming down to kiss the old Riverboat goodbye tonight," he told the packed house. "I'm glad we're giving it a decent burial." With those simple words, McLauchlan launched into the first of three sets that closed the doors on Yorkville's most illustrious coffee house—and brought an end to the golden age in Canadian music.

I was there that night. Although I don't remember much about it (proof, as the sixties adage goes, that I *was* there), I do recall that many of McLauchlan's lyrics had a poignant ring to them. "The sun's goin' down on the midway tonight," he sang in "Sweeping the Spotlight Away." His classic "Child's Song" became a bittersweet farewell to the club: "Goodbye to this house...and all its memories." Even his affectionate, fun-loving tribute to

*Bidding farewell to the Riverboat*

Toronto, "Down by the Henry Moore," seemed to underscore the fact that the city—indeed the whole country—was losing one of its cultural landmarks.

It was an emotional evening. After McLauchlan gave the last of many encores, he called Riverboat owner Bernie Fiedler up to the stage and presented him with a silver boat whistle and a black deckhand cap. In accepting the gifts, Fiedler told the audience that he thought that another place like the Riverboat would come along, because, he said, "there'll always be people writing songs and people wanting to listen to them."

The Riverboat, immortalized in the Neil Young song "Ambulance Blues," had become a victim of changing times. After Ontario's drinking age was lowered from twenty-one to eighteen in 1971, Fiedler found it increasingly difficult to compete with licensed clubs like the El Mocambo, which could afford to pay acts much higher fees. At the same time, many of the artists who had got their start in the intimate club had outgrown it by the mid-'70s. For the farewell concerts, McLauchlan and Dan Hill, a Riverboat graduate from another generation, played free to offset some of the losses the club had experienced during its last years. "It was a debt to a scene whose passing I regret," McLauchlan said on the final night, "the free-form club scene."

That scene spawned a wealth of talent—and a tradition that resonates to this day. Canadian singer-songwriters, a natural resource to rival wheat, wood and fresh water, continue to dominate popular music globally. Just as Canada produces comedians with a unique, ironic view of the world, so it seems to regularly turn out singer-songwriters—more per capita than any other country in the world—who have a distinctive personal perspective and a strong sense of place. Ottawa's Alanis Morissette has captivated international audiences with her intense, soul-baring songs, which owe at least some debt to Joni Mitchell. And many of the songs of The Tragically Hip's Gord Downie, with their references to everything from the Group of Seven painters to Canadian hockey heroes, are unabashedly pure Canadiana.

None of that confidence would have been possible without the legacy left by Mitchell or Canada's other great soul searchers, Leonard Cohen, Gordon Lightfoot and Neil Young. Nor could Canadian references have come so unconsciously without the foundation laid by Ian Tyson's "Four Strong Winds" or, for that matter, by Robbie Robertson's "Acadian Driftwood." Recognizing that lineage, many Canadian artists in the 1980s and '90s have paid tribute to their predecessors on stage and on record. When The Band was inducted into the Canadian Music Hall of Fame in 1989, contemporary country-rockers Blue Rodeo backed The Band up on renditions of its biggest hits. Similarly, when Ian & Sylvia received the same honour in 1992, their songs were lovingly covered by the likes of Jane Siberry, Kashtin, 54-40's Neil Osborne and The Skydiggers' Andy Maize.

Tribute albums have seen young Canadian acts lining up to pay homage—some of whom weren't even born when their heroes made their first records. Halifax's power-pop trio Sloan, members of the flannel-shirt brigade for whom Neil Young is the undisputed godfather, recorded a kick-ass version of Mitchell's "A Case of You" on *Back to the Garden*. Calgary's Jann Arden, another devoted Mitchell fan, covered Cohen's "If It Be Your Will" on *Tower of Song*. Toronto's Barenaked Ladies turned Cockburn's "Lovers in a Dangerous Time" into a '90s hit for themselves on *Kick at the Darkness*, while Crash Vegas and Amanda Marshall delivered stirring renditions of Young's "Pocahontas" and "Don't Let It Bring You Down" on *Borrowed Tunes*.

Is there a Canadian Sound to emerge from this songwriting tradition? Yes, but it's as diverse as the country's many regions and not easily summed up in a sentence. Joni Mitchell once heard a similarity between her music and Neil Young's. "There is a lot of Prairie in [it]," she told *Maclean's* magazine. "I think both of us have a striding quality to our music which is like long steps across flat land." Writer Jack Batten has similarly tried to describe Young as having a "peculiarly Canadian touch in his voice, a light, fresh, high sound that suggests wide, clear, open land." Others have simply compared his vocals to the sound of a prairie dog howling, an assessment with which Young's detractors might heartily agree.

Meanwhile, the lilting airs of the Maritimes have imbued a good deal of Canadian music with a decidedly East Coast feel—ever since Hank Snow sang his first country songs in the 1930s. Outside the Cape Breton reservoir that has brought us Ashley MacIssac, the Rankin Family and Natalie MacMaster, you can hear the Celtic connection in the influential songs of Hamilton's Stan Rogers (who died in 1983), in the harp-laden material of Stratford, Ontario's Loreena McKennitt and even in the rollicking tunes of Vancouver's Spirit of the West. If Canadian music is a tapestry, then Maritime sounds are some of its brightest threads.

The blues also runs through Canadian music as distinctly as the sound of a train whistle in the Rockies. From Vancouver's Powder Blues Band to the Maritimes' own Dutch Mason Blues Band, the music has enjoyed a long-standing national following. Today, the torch is carried by the likes of Colin James and Colin Linden, who are broadening the audience for the blues. But none is experiencing more success than Toronto singer Amanda Marshall, whose emotional vocal style owes much to the blues tradition.

Add up these Prairie, Maritime, folk-based, bluesy, garage-oriented traditions, combine them with writerly lyrics that express the loneliness of wide-open spaces, the shifting feeling of the changing seasons and the grandeur of the great outdoors, and you come up with something like...something that can't be defined. The Canadian Sound cannot be reduced to a beaver or a

Mountie cliché. It's a series of sounds that have sprung up and survived, even flourished, in the shadow of the giant American neighbour to the south.

Why has Canadian music thrived in the twilight years of the twentieth century? Ronnie Hawkins will tell you it's because Canadian musicians have to work ten times harder than their American counterparts. Certainly, Canadians have developed a competitive edge in the last thirty years. But besides talent, there are other, more tangible reasons. There are now a host of record companies in Canada—big and small—and all receptive to signing domestic talent. Cancon has meant that after investing time and money in the studio a recording artist can at least expect a fair hearing on radio. Videos and computers, meanwhile, have shrunk the vast expanse of land that once faced a touring musician in the sixties. Indeed, with coast-to-coast exposure on MuchMusic and on the Internet, the legwork involved in breaking a new artist has been reduced to a few managerial steps.

Perhaps the biggest change of the last three decades is the fact that a Canadian artist can now enjoy a successful career at home, without having to go south. With MuchMusic's star-making machinery giving them instant access to the living rooms of the nation and their business plans, marketing campaigns, lawyers and hairstylists busy working to ensure their success, it's easy to forget about a time when music wasn't a video shoot or a career opportunity, when playing in a band was simply an alternative to playing hockey and walking on stage was a trip into the great unknown.

Next time you're watching the videogenic images of Alanis, Céline and Shania, or those of countless other challengers to the throne, remember the early, pioneering careers of Ian & Sylvia, the Hawk, Lightfoot and their sixties colleagues. All of the Canadians shining in today's pop firmament owe some measure of their success to the groundwork laid by those pioneers. The Canadian road to stardom used to run along a short Toronto street called Yorkville. Now it stretches right across the planet.

## APPENDIX 1:

# WHERE ARE THEY NOW?

Randy Bachman (Chad Allen & the Expressions, The Guess Who, Bachman-Turner Overdrive) lives in Vancouver and continues to perform and record.

Dave Bingham (The Ugly Ducklings) lives in Fenelon Falls, Ont., where he works as an auto mechanic.

David Clayton-Thomas (with The Shays, The Bossmen, Blood, Sweat & Tears) lives in upstate New York and recently completed a "back to the blues" album.

Bruce Cockburn recently released his 23rd album, the wondrous *Charity of the Night.*

Leonard Cohen, the perpetual ladies' man, just keeps doing what he does best: putting his haunting, world-weary poetry to song.

David DePoe is a Toronto high-school teacher.

Bonnie Dobson lives comfortably in England, thanks to a steady flow of royalties from The Grateful Dead's version of her "Morning Dew."

Denny Doherty (The Halifax Three, The Mugwumps, The Mamas & the Papas) recently played the harbourmaster in the children's TV series "Theodore Tugboat"; he is currently working on a one-man show about his Papa days.

Bernie Fiedler (the Riverboat) runs an artist management and concert production company in Toronto.

Bernie Finkelstein still manages Bruce Cockburn and continues to run True North Records, Canada's oldest and foremost independent label.

Amos Garrett (The Dirty Shames, Great Speckled Bird) lives in Turner Valley, Alberta; his most recent album, *Off the Floor Live!*, features a brilliant story-song about Yonge Street's musical past.

Luke Gibson (Luke & the Apostles, Kensington Market) lives in Toronto and works as a film set painter.

Sharon Hampson is one-third of Canada's most popular children's musical group, Sharon, Lois & Bram.

Ronnie Hawkins lives in "Mortgage Manor" on Stoney Lake near Peterborough, Ontario; the latest incarnation of his Hawks includes his son, Robin, and his daughter, Leah.

Levon Helm (the Hawks, The Band) is an accomplished actor and continues to tour and record with The Band, albeit without Robbie Robertson or Richard Manuel (who committed suicide in 1986).

Paul Hoffert (Lighthouse) teaches and composes music for film at York University and chairs the Ontario Arts Council.

Rick James (The Mynah Birds) was recently released from Folsom State Prison, where he served time for sexually assaulting a woman, holding her hostage and giving her cocaine.

Kelly Jay (Crowbar) lives in Calgary, Alberta, where he runs a bed-and-breakfast and continues to belt out the blues

Mendelson Joe (Mainline) remains an eccentric talent as both a visual artist (he once painted Brian Mulroney as an anus) and an indefatigible writer of letters to the editor.

John Kay (The Sparrows / Steppenwolf) lives in Franklin, Tennessee, and still regularly performs "Born to Be Wild" in his trade-mark leathers and shades.

Robbie Lane (Robbie Lane & the Disciples) recently released an album entitled *Ain't Dead Yet.*

Gordon Lightfoot, the grand old man of Canadian song, still thrills diehard fans with his annual Massey Hall concerts.

John McHugh (The Penny Farthing) runs a bed-and-breakfast and catering business in Toronto.

Mike McKenna (Mainline) recently released a fine album of blues and Mainline classics.

Keith McKie (Kensingston Market) is raising his eight-year-old son in Toronto and writing songs.

Murray McLauchlan lives in Toronto with his wife, MuchMusic honcho Denise Donlon, and their son; he recently released his 18th album, *Gulliver's Taxi.*

Adam Mitchell (The Paupers) is a Nashville-based songwriter and producer.

Joni Mitchell divides her time between Los Angeles and Sechelt, B.C.

Bruce Palmer (The Mynah Birds) was recently inducted into the Rock and Roll Hall of Fame in Cleveland, Ohio, for his work in Buffalo Springfield.

Skip Prokop (The Paupers, Lighthouse) is an account executive for London, Ont.'s CJBK AM and BX 93 FM.

Chick Roberts (The Dirty Shames) is an actor and cabdriver in Toronto.

Robbie Robertson (the Hawks, The Band), a poster boy for Roots, lives in Los Angeles and is exploring his native Indian musical heritage.

Buffy Sainte-Marie lives in Hawaii with her husband, record producer Jack Nitzsche.

Domenic Troiano (The Mandala) composes music for television and runs his own recording studio in Thornhill, Ontario.

Ian Tyson lives on a 160-acre ranch in Longview, Alberta, rides cutting horses and makes the best, genuine cowboy music in the world.

Sylvia Tyson lives in Toronto and performs and records with the women's vocal group Quartette, which included the late Colleen Peterson (who died in 1996).

David Wiffen successfully battled alcoholism and is writing songs again; he plans to release a new album in 1997.

Zal Yanovsky (The Halifax Three, The Mugwumps, The Lovin' Spoonful) runs Chez Piggy restaurant and a bakery in Kingston, Ontario.

Neil Young (The Squires, The Mynah Birds, Buffalo Springfield, CSNY) is the godfather of grunge.

**APPENDIX 2:**

# 25 top Canadian songs 1961–71

## A PERSONAL SELECTION (IN ALPHABETICAL ORDER)

"American Woman"—The Guess Who
"Been Burnt"—Luke & the Apostles
"Bo Diddley"—Ronnie Hawkins & the Hawks
"Born to Be Wild"—Steppenwolf
"Brainwashed"—David Clayton-Thomas & the Bossmen
"The Circle Game"—Joni Mitchell
"Early Morning Rain"—Gordon Lightfoot
"Four Strong Winds"—Ian & Sylvia
"Gaslight"—The Ugly Ducklings
"Going to the Country"—Bruce Cockburn
"I Would Be the One"—Kensington Market
"Lonesome Mary"—Chilliwack
"Magic People"—The Paupers
"More Often Than Not"—David Wiffen
"Morning Dew"—Bonnie Dobson
"Oh What a Feeling"—Crowbar
"One Fine Morning"—Lighthouse
"1-2-5"—The Haunted
"Opportunity"—The Mandala
"Shakin' All Over"—The Guess Who
"The Stones That I Throw"—Levon & the Hawks
"Sugar Mountain"—Neil Young
"Suzanne"—Leonard Cohen
"Universal Soldier"—Buffy Sainte-Marie
"The Weight"—The Band

## APPENDIX 3

# What's in a Name?

## (some interesting band names from an imaginative era)

### SHAMELESS FLAG WAVERS

Canada Goose (Toronto)
The Five Canadians (Victoria, B.C.)
The Canadian Squires (Toronto, later The Band)
The Canadaires (Toronto, later The Crew-Cuts)
The Canadian Downbeats (Winnipeg)
The Young Canadian Singers
The Forty-Ninth Parallel (Calgary)
The Dew Line (Calgary)
Tundra (Toronto)

### ANGLO À GO-GO

British Modbeats (St. Catharines, Ont.)
The Liverpool Set (Toronto)
Les Merseys (Montreal)
The Quid (Winnipeg)
The Lords of London (Toronto)
The Royal Family (Edmonton)
The Canadian Beatles (Vancouver)
Les Beatlettes (Montreal)

### HISTORICALLY BENT

The Gettysburg Address (Winnipeg)
The Northwest Company (Vancouver)
The British North America Act (Montreal)
The Colonials (Halifax)
Little Caesar & The Consuls (Toronto)
The Boston Tea Party (Winnipeg)
Hudson Bay Company (Toronto)
United Empire Loyalists (Vancouver)

## ARE YOU EXPERIENCED?

The Electric Banana (Winnipeg)
The Reefers (Hamilton, Ont.)
The Trip (Toronto)
Heads of Our Time (Toronto)
Mind Explosion (Winnipeg)
Mashmakhan (Montreal)
Reign Ghost (Toronto)
Paisley Rain (Vancouver)
Plastic Cloud (Bay Ridges, Ont.)
Bent Wind (Toronto)
Strawberry Tangerine Toilet (Halifax)
Professor Fuddle's Fantastic Fairy Tale Machine (Toronto)

## CIVIC MINDED

The Stampeders (Calgary)
The London Town Criers (London, Ont., Valdy's first group)
Bobby Taylor & the Vancouvers
(Vancouver, Tommy Chong's group)
The Vancouver Playboys (Vancouver)
Chilliwack (Vancouver)
Kensington Market (Toronto)
Cabbage Towne (Toronto)
Mountain City Four
(Montreal, Kate & Anna McGarrigle's first group)
Theodore's Smokeshop (Montreal)
Perth County Conspiracy
(Stratford, Ont., actor Cedric Smith's group)
Young Country Boys (Toronto)

## BIRDS OF A FEATHER

Ronnie Hawkins & the Hawks (Toronto, later The Band)
Levon & the Hawks (Toronto, ditto)
Jack London & the Sparrows (Toronto, later Steppenwolf)
The Mynah Birds
(Toronto, included Neil Young, Bruce Palmer and Rick James)
Great Speckled Bird
(Toronto, Ian & Sylvia's country-rock group)

Mojo & the Nighthawk (Winnipeg)
High Flying Bird (Vancouver)
Mother Tucker's Yellow Duck (Vancouver)

## GIVE ME THAT OLD TIME RELIGION

Luke & the Apostles (Toronto)
Abraham's Children (Toronto)
The Preachers (Edmonton)
The Munks (Montreal)

## THE DEVIL MADE ME DO IT

Satan & the D-Men (Winnipeg)
Dante & the Infernos (Winnipeg)
Les Diables Noirs (Montreal)
Les Sinners (Montreal)
The Five Rogues (Toronto, later Mandala)
Those Naughty Boys (Ottawa)
The Scaliwags (Ottawa)
The Bad Cedes (Halifax)
The Scoundrels (Toronto)

## SPELL MUCH?

The Stitch 'n' Tyme (Toronto)
Descendants of Tyme (Vancouver)
The Human Kynd (Winnipeg)
The Luvin' Kind (Winnipeg)
Fludd (Toronto)
Smyle (Toronto)
King Beezz (Edmonton)

### P.R. DISASTERS

Shades of Mediocrity (Winnipeg)
The Sounds of Silence (Winnipeg)
The Very Ordinary Five (Winnipeg)
The Pallbearers (Winnipeg)
The Paint Brushes (Calgary)
The Teenyboppers (Toronto)

### ASK ME NO QUESTIONS

The Guess Who (Winnipeg)
The What Four? (Winnipeg)
The Why? (Winnipeg)

### NUMBERS ON THE BRAIN

Halifax Three (Toronto)
Three's a Crowd (Vancouver)
Three to One (Vancouver)
Four to Go (Toronto, Neil Young's group)
The Five Rogues (Toronto)
The Five Man Electrical Band (Ottawa)
Eight Point Five (Bathurst, N.B.)

### ALL IN THE FAMILY

Brother (Winnipeg)
The Children (Ottawa, Bruce Cockburn's group)
Little Daddy & the Bachelors (Vancouver)
Mother Tucker's Yellow Duck (Vancouver)
Papa Bear's Medicine Show (Vancouver)
Granny (Winnipeg)
The Poppy Family (Vancouver)

### TRANSIT AUTHORITIES

Crosstown Bus (Vancouver)
Hydro Electric Streetcar (Vancouver)
Night Train (Vancouver)
Painted Ship (Vancouver)

Taxi (Sudbury, Ont.)
General Motor (Winnipeg)

### NERDY, JUST PLAIN ODD

Abernathy Shagnaster (Toronto)
Carruthers Emerson (Vancouver)
Melvin D. Burlap (Winnipeg)
The Mugwumps
(New York, Denny Doherty's & Zal Yanovsky's group)
Orville Dorp (Vancouver)

### POLITICALLY INCORRECT

The Honkies
(Toronto, also The Crackers, later The Band)
The Spasstiks (Toronto, later Cat)
Four Niggers and a Chink
(Vancouver, Tommy Chong's group)

### PUNS

Olivus (Toronto, Bruce Cockburn's group)
Just Us (Toronto)
Strolling Bones (Toronto)

### EXPRESSIONS

Three's a Crowd (Vancouver)
Sticks and Stones (Winnipeg)
Footloose & Fancy Free (Winnipeg)
The Good Fortunes (Winnipeg)
The Stitch 'n' Tyme (Toronto)
The Last Words (Toronto)
The Chosen Few (Montreal)
A Passing Fancy (Toronto)
A Foot in Coldwater (Toronto)

### Eastern Vibes

The Raja (Toronto)
The Mandala (Toronto)
The Mantra (Toronto)
Steppenwolf (Toronto/Los Angeles)

### Please Feed the Animals

Cat (Toronto)
The Dawgs (Winnipeg)
Tame Apes (Vancouver)
Rhinoceros (Los Angeles, Toronto)
Walrus (Winnipeg)

### On a Musical Note...

The Tremelos (Montreal)
The Staccatos (Ottawa)
The Crescendos (Winnipeg)
The Two Tones (Toronto, Gordon Lightfoot's duo)
The Del Tones (Montreal)
The Canadian Downbeats (Winnipeg)

### Lost in Space

Les Astronauts (Montreal)
Robbie & the Robots
(Toronto, Robbie Robertson's group)
The Cosmics (Ottawa)
Mike Thornhill & the Rockets (Montreal)
Moon (Winnipeg)
The Galaxies (Winnipeg)
The UFO (Winnipeg)
Expedition to Earth (Winnipeg)

## GONE BUT NOT FORGOTTEN REBELS

The Misfits (Winnipeg)
The Exiled (Winnipeg)
The Condemned (Winnipeg)
The Mongrels (Winnipeg)
The Rabble (Montreal)
The Ugly Ducklings (Toronto)

## ANONYMOUS

The Unnamed (Winnipeg)
The Guess Who (Winnipeg)
Next (Winnipeg)
The Many Others (Winnipeg)
And Many Others (Toronto, later Crowbar)

## MONEY HONEY

The Quid (Winnipeg)
The Nickels and Dimes (Winnipeg)
Big Bob & the Dollars (Montreal)

## WHOSE BAND?

Major Hoople's Boarding House (Cambridge, Ont.)
Mother Tucker's Yellow Duck (Vancouver)
Papa Bear's Medicine Show (Vancouver)
Colonel Popcorn's Butter Band (Hamilton, Ont.)
Faro Wayne's Schmaltz Band (Montreal)
Benson Obermeyer's Fruit Stand Band (Winnipeg)

# acknowledgments

Writing a book about a decade's worth of great music has been a labour of love. But it has also been a monumental task that I could never have pulled off without the help of many supportive and enthusiastic souls.

The generation gap was a giant chasm in the 1960s: the "adults" behind the media viewed "kids'" music with disdain and rarely took the time to document its growth. Consequently, researching the era has been something of an archeological dig, unearthing stories and musical artifacts and memorabilia, mostly with the help of the musicians themselves. Hopefully, material like this can find a permanent home in a future Canadian Rock and Roll Hall of Fame before it is lost forever.

Musicians who dug into their basements and attics to find their personal scrapbooks for me include: Domenic Troiano, Skip Prokop, Keith McKie, Stan Endersby, Mike McKenna, Chick Roberts, Jay Telfer, Joe Lewis, Jim Campbell, Klaas Van Graft, Paul Weldon and Pat La Croix. Former booking agent Ron Scribner, whose vast scrapbook collection represented the motherlode, generously loaned me four crates' worth of clippings, photos, posters and assorted memorabilia. Thanks to Duff Roman at CHUM, along with Richard Maxwell and Brad Jones, for their support.

Bob Stevens at the Mariposa Foundation, whose archives covering nearly 40 years of folk festivals is in dire need of financial aid and restoration, Ottawa's Richard Patterson and CIUT-FM's Ken Stowar were all similarly helpful in providing me with material. David Andoff, Canada's answer to R. Crumb, loaned his original artwork to the book, while Pete Frame and Joe Sherman provided brilliant family trees and maps respectively. Thanks also to Bart Schoales, Sylvia Tyson, John Kay, Bernie Fiedler, Gale Jones, Jane Harbury and Bill Gilliland for sharing valuable personal photos and assorted Yorkville materials. Mike Copas gave copies of his *Ontario Folk* bulletin and Richard Flohil opened his massive Rolodex to me and loaned back issues of *Hoot* magazine.

Others helped me to find rare and, in some cases, never-before-released recordings. Thanks to Rob Bowman, Steve Fruitman and Tom Harrison for the tapes and to Jim Levitt at Discovery Records and Peter Dunn at the Vinyl Museum for hunting down hard-to-find records. Gerry Miskolczi at All That Rocks was extremely generous in loaning precious memorabilia.

Thanks also to Bill Munson, Larry Leblanc, Mitch Potter, Jim Slotek and Robin Selz for their sometimes clandestine assistance on my research mission.

Many friends and colleagues also helped along the way. I am extremely grateful for the support shown by Kirk Makin, Patricia Hluchy, Kim Cooke, Dudley Gibbs, Stephen Berthelot and Janice and the gang at Shaftesbury Films. Special thanks to Ian Pearson and Brian Reagan for reading the manuscript in its various stages, and to Gilbert Belisle, my computer's guardian angel, and to Cate Cochrane, she of great visual taste.

While I was immersed in the manuscript, my agent, Dean Cooke, and his associate David Johnston took care of business. Meanwhile, my publisher was right in my neighbourhood—and always close at hand. Thanks to everyone at Penguin—including Brad Martin, Cynthia Good, Kevin Hanson, Scott Sellers and Karen Cossar—who have been enthusiastic about this book from the day I pitched it to its delivery to bookstores. Special thanks to Martin Gould, Cathy MacLean, Jem Bates and especially Kathy Schleindl, who turned a mountain of memorabilia into a fine-looking book. Finally, to my editor, Jackie Kaiser, who kept me on an even keel through the rough waters between first and second draft: your restructuring advice paid off big time.

As always, my family has been incredibly supportive, including Jean and Roy Hay, who pitched in even on their holiday. Thanks to my mother, Joyce, and father, Cedric, for their love and good counsel, to my sister Christina, for her business acumen, and whose record collection in the '60s was no doubt the genesis of this book, and to my sister Ali, a singer-songwriter herself who will talk about music with me anytime, day or night. I am also indebted to my brother-in-law Paul De Guzman, who loaned me his farm in Hockley Valley, where most of the manuscript was written. To my beautiful boys, Callum and Duncan, who were extremely patient with me and can now sing a frightening number of songs from the '60s: don't worry, I'm back in the present.

Finally, to my partner, Carol Hay, who contributed to this project in countless ways: your flair for the dramatic helped shape this book from beginning to end.

# Photo Credits

*Note: Although every effort has been made to ensure that permissions for all material were obtained, those sources not formally acknowledged here will be included in future editions of this book.*

**PROLOGUE**

3. Mavis Wilson

**CHAPTER ONE**

8. George Brown Management
10. CHUM
11. *Toronto Telegram*, York University, Archives and Special Collections

**CHAPTER TWO**

17. John McHugh
18. Sylvia Tyson
23. City of Toronto Archives
23. Estelle Klein
24. Gerry Miskolczi, All That Rocks
26. CBC Still Photo Collection
27. CBC Still Photo Collection
29. Photographer: Joe Alper; courtesy Sylvia Tyson
30. Ron Scribner

**CHAPTER THREE**

26. Design: Ian Tyson; courtesy Mariposa Archives
37. Mariposa Archives
38. Turkey Scratch Archives
41. Photographer: Clive Webster
43. Photographer: Clive Webster
45. Gerry Miskolczi, All That Rocks
47. Columbia Records
48. Epic Records
49. John Einarson
50. Pat LaCroix

51. Gerry Miskolczi, All That Rocks

**CHAPTER FOUR**

56. Ron Scribner
59. Turkey Scratch Archives
61. Gerry Miskolczi, All That Rocks
62. Duff Roman
63. Insight Productions
64. Vanguard Records
65. Phil Snell
76. Stan Klees
68. Gerry Miskolczi, All That Rocks
69. Ron Scribner
70. *Toronto Sun*
71. John McHugh

**CHAPTER FIVE**

76. Voxx Records (top)
76. Quality/Legend/True North Records
77. Photographer: Herb Nott; courtesy Bernie Fiedler
78. City of Toronto Archives (top)
78. *Hoot*/Mariposa Archives
79. *Hoot*/Mariposa Archives
80. Bernie Fiedler
81. John Einarson
82. Bernie Fiedler
82. Bernie Fiedler
86. Geordie McDonald
87. Mariposa Archives
88. Craig Allen
89. Turkey Scratch Archives (top)
89. Atco Records
92. Richard Patterson
93. Richard Patterson
94. Photographer: Herb Nott; courtesy Chick Roberts
95. Photographer: John Rowland; courtesy Duff Roman
97. Ron Scribner

## CHAPTER SIX

100. *Toronto Star*
101. *Toronto Sun*
102. Gerry Miskolczi, All That Rocks
103. Gale Jones
103. Gerry Miskolczi, All That Rocks
104. Gerry Miskolczi, All That Rocks
104. *Globe and Mail*
105. Duff Roman
106. Geordie McDonald
108. John Kay
109. Gale Jones
110. *Toronto Sun*
111. Photographer: Normunds Berzins; courtesy *Flare* magazine
113. Gale Jones
114. *Toronto Sun*
115. Bernie Fielder
116. United Artists
117. Bernie Fiedler
118. CNE Archives
119. Domenic Troiano
120. Domenic Troiano
121. Atco Records

## CHAPTER SEVEN

124. Warner Bros.
125. Insight Productions
126. Skip Prokop
128. Duff Roman
129. *Hoot*/Mariposa Archives
130. *Hoot*/Mariposa Archives
131. John McHugh
132. Richard Patterson (top)
132. Skip Prokop
133. Photographer: Herb Nott; courtesy Skip Prokop
133. Skip Prokop
134. Skip Prokop
135. Dave Bingham (top)
135. Bill Gilliland

136. Gale Jones (top)
136. CHUM
137. Luke Gibson
139. Luke Gibson (top)
139. Stan Endersby (ex-The Trip)
140. *Globe and Mail*
141. *Globe and Mail*
162. CHUM
144. Domenic Troiano
145. Verve Folkways (top)
145. Domenic Troiano
146. Skip Prokop
149. *Toronto Sun*

**CHAPTER EIGHT**

154. *Toronto Sun*
155. Bill Gilliland (top)
155. *Toronto Telegram*, York University, Archives and Special Collections
155. *Toronto Telegram*, York University, Archives and Special Collections
156. Skip Prokop
156. Popular Culture (pennant)
156. *Toronto Telegram*, York University, Archives and Special Collections
157. Capitol Records
158. Skip Prokop
158. Skip Prokop
159. John Kay
160. Photographer: David Gahr
161. Bill Graham Presents (top)
161. Columbia Records
162. Luke Gibson
162. Luke Gibson
164. RCA Records
164. Mariposa Archives
166. *Harbinger* magazine
167. National Film Board
168. *Toronto Sun*
169. *Toronto Sun*

169. Richard Patterson
171. Gerry Miskolczi, All That Rocks
172. Gerry Miskolczi, All That Rocks
173. Atlantic Records

## CHAPTER NINE

176. Photographer: Bob Stevens
178. Reprise Records
180. *Toronto Sun* (top)
180. Mainstream Records
181. *Globe and Mail*
183. Columbia Records
184. David Andoff
185. Jay Telfer (top)
185. Design: Bart Schoales; courtesy Keith McKie
186. Photographer: Bart Schoales; courtesy Warner Bros.
186. Warner Bros.
187. Photographer: Bart Schoales (top)
187. Photographer: Frank Grant; courtesy *Time* magazine
188. Photographer: Bart Schoales
189. Photographer: Don Hunstein (top)
189. Gerry Miskolczi, All That Rocks
191. Hoffert Communications
192. *Woodstock, the Oral History*
194. *Toronto Star*

## CHAPTER TEN

198. Capitol Records
199. *Harbinger* magazine, North York Public Library
200. Bernie Fiedler
201. Richard Patterson (top)
201. John Einarson
202. Bernie Fiedler
203. John Einarson
204. David Andoff
204. Design: David Andoff
205. *Harbinger* magazine/North York Public Library (top)

205. Capitol Records
206. RCA Records
208. True North Records
209. Photographer: Bart Schoales
209. Photographer: Bart Schoales
211. Photographer: Bart Schoales; courtesy True North Records

## CHAPTER ELEVEN

216. Western Canada Pictorial Service (top)
216. *American Woman*
217. Gerry Miskolczi, All That Rocks
218. Voxx Records
218. Neptoon Records
219. Pacemaker Entertainment
220. Mike Waite, Sam the Record Man
221. Mike Waite, Sam the Record Man
221. Mike Waite, Sam the Record Man
222. Jim Levitt, Discovery Records (top)
222. Artist: Walt Kelly; courtesy Sylvia Tyson
223. Bearsville/Stony Plain Records
224. Frank Davies, The Music Publisher
225. Gerry Miskolczi, All That Rocks
226. Photographer: David Andoff (top)
226. Artist: David Andoff
228. GRT Records (top)
228. Gerry Miskolczi, All That Rocks
229. Paul Weldon
231. Gerry Miskolczi, All That Rocks (top)
231. Popular Culture
232. Frank Davies, The Music Publisher
233. *Toronto Telegram*, York University, Archives and Special Collections
234. Frank Davies, The Music Publisher
235. Frank Davies, The Music Publisher

## EPILOGUE

238. *Toronto Star*
240. Intrepid Records

241. Intrepid Records
242. CARAS

# endnotes

## 1: BOUND FOR MOVING ON

8 "Obnoxious little jerk," Ian Tyson, *I Never Sold My Saddle*, p. 26.
8 "I saw this raggedy-ass kid ... I can too." Martin Melhuish, *Heart of Gold*, p. 44.

## 2: ON THE ROAD

17 "I was wearing brown Bermuda shorts ... blew his mind." Sylvia Fraser, *Chatelaine*, January 1976.
19 "ten months of winter and two of bad sledding." Levon Helm, *This Wheel's on Fire*, p. 48.
"We were exotic ... had ever heard." Helm, p. 54
20 "a clean shaven Vancouverite ... relaxed and easy manner." Sid Adilman, *Toronto Star*, August 20, 1960.
24 "played the fastest ... overwhelming power." Robert Palmer, *Rolling Stone*, November 14, 1991.
27 "The only reason ... sight-reading." Maynard Collins, *If You Could Read His Mind*, p. 51.
28 "unique concept of harmony ... it didn't work." Tyson, p. 24.
"What counts with us ... we discard it." Liner notes, *Ian & Sylvia*, Vanguard Records, 1962.
29 "I'd hear something ... music to me." Helm, p. 71.
30 "You can't go back ... vanish on me." Helm, p. 70.

## 3: HIPSTERS AND HOOTENANNIES

43 "My father didn't understand me ... convenient target." Sheila Gormley, *Star Weekly*, July 31, 1976.
52 "Three singers on one song ... our trademark." Helm, p. 101.
53 "The band was becoming ... only way to explore it." Barney Hoskyns, *Across the Great Divide*, p. 76.

## 4: TICKET TO RIDE

57 "His disciples dressed like him ... stinging staccato

lead guitar style." John Kay, *Magic Carpet Ride*, p. 77.
58 "Each of them had their own little showcase … I had ever seen." Hoskyns, p. 85.
59 "Son, you're gonna have to forget … their money back." Helm, p. 115.
63 "a hint of blues-inflection … or crucial influence." Liner notes, *It's My Way*, Vanguard Records, 1964.
66 "My friends … it must be the same." William Ruhlmann, *Goldmine*, February 17, 1995.
66 "Joni came with her uke … on a Twee." Melhuish, p. 28.
69 "feeling-sorry-for-myself song." *Hoot*, September 1966.

**5: NO DIRECTION HOME**

78 "The thing at the Teachers … something to me." Marjorie Harris, *Maclean's*, September 1968.
80 "lost-love pieces … really did me in." Phil Sutcliffe, *Q*, May 20, 1988.
81 "Neil was playing folk-rock before anybody else." John Einarson, *Don't Be Denied*, p. 120.
83 "Once I began to write … my own voice appeared." Ruhlmann.
83 "I was at an indecisive time … were quickly married." Ibid.
84 "I wasn't very good … I'd bombed." Sankey Phillips & Dave Wilson, *Zigzag*, February 1977.
84 "Brechtian" Larry Leblanc, *Rolling Stone*, March 4, 1971.
85 "absorbing the whistle stops," Sheila Gormley, *Toronto Telegram*, May 5, 1965.
85 "Rangy, curly-haired … he'll make it." *Variety*, July 1965.
90 "Bob needed a group … two needs coincided." Helm, p. 129.
91 "indispensable to his artistic well-being and couldn't be replaced." Helm, p. 137.
91 "It was not a marriage made in heaven … didn't last very long." Ruhlmann.
92 "Van Ronk was saying … that insecure about my

writing." Phillips & Wilson.
95 "rinky-dink, oopsie-doops," Peter Gzowski, *Canadian*, date unknown, c. 1965.
95 "The excited mayor ... stop his gyrations." Peter Worthington, *Toronto Telegram*, September 23, 1965.
96 "Elvis, you're another Elvis ... for the money." *Toronto Star*, November 15, 1965.
97 "Here was a Bob Dylan ... at Maple Leaf Gardens." *Toronto Star*, November 15, 1965.
97 "The whole booing thing ... part of that." Helm, p. 141.
97 "the most decisive moment in rock history." *Time*, January 12, 1970.

## 6: FLOWERS IN A HOTHOUSE

102 "He would go in and collect ... getting a penny." Kay,
p. 128.
104 "more or less a bust ... in her cage." Gary Dunford, *Toronto Star*, August 12, 1966.
109 "It was all slicked ... washed his hair." Kay, p. 130.
109 "gamblers, older guys from Cabbagetown." Kay, p. 140.
111 "Musical LSD ... St. Vitus dance convention." *Toronto Star*, June 4, 1966.
113 "We used to pop amyl nitrates ... middle of a song." Einarson, p. 167.

## 7: A GO-GO '66

130 "This girl has everything ... and soon." *Hoot*, September 1966.
131 "And so you now ... black capes." Fournier, Norris, eds. *Take This Waltz*, p. 25.
139 "the New Orleans of rock ... the Beatles made it." *Toronto Star*, June 25, 1966.
139 "It's kind of whiny ... plays that way." Jack Batten, *Canadian*, December 3, 1966.
139 "They all play ... compared to us." Ralph Thomas, *Toronto Star*, April 1, 1967.
140 "Yorkville with its many clubs ... just to play there."

Thomas.
141 "filthy rich." *Rolling Stone*, July 26, 1979.
141 "a jumble of creative clutter ... covered with lyrics," Brian Hinton, *Both Sides Now*, p. 67.
144 "Some of the jammed ... Caesar-style hairdo," *Toronto Telegram*, June 29, 1966.
146 "The Mandala ... big everything." *Canadian*, December 3, 1966.
147 "the group had to cut ... off his perch." *Toronto Star*, December 12, 1966.

## 8: LOVE-ITIS

155 "blocks in a child's higgledy-piggledy pyramid," Robert Fulford, *This Was Expo*.
159 "None of you guys ... Metropolitan Opera." Ira Nadel, *Leonard Cohen: A Life in Art*, p. 85.
167 "Frankly, I'd like to see it become a shopping centre ... cleaned up first." quoted in *Flowers On a One-Way Street*, National Film Board documentary.
169 "What we've seen here ... generational gap." NFB.

## 9: AVENUE OF BROKEN DREAMS

177 "a willowy blonde ... next big thing." David Crosby, *Long Time Gone*, p. 129.
181 "Calling it an epidemic ... hippie hepatitis," *Globe and Mail*, August 3, 1968.
185 "Hooker was a fuck-up ... a star at that gig." *eye-opener*, November 28, 1969.
189 "We used to go to Toronto ... wheatfield soul." John Einarson, *American Woman*, p. 79.

## 10: BACK TO THE LAND

204 "Being good musicians ... that's ever played." *Globe and Mail*, July 3, 1969.
209 "he dresses like a splendid ... and swirling scarves." Jack Batten, *Maclean's*, January 1971.
209 "Space may be a misleading ... feel about yourself." Myrna Kostash, *Saturday Night*, June 1972.

## 11: THE FREAK FLAG FLIES

218 "What we needed ... CHUM in Toronto." Ritchie Yorke, *Axes, Chops & Hot Licks*, p. 53.
222 "We thought you were just ... like us." David Dalton & Jonathan Cott, *Rolling Stone*, September 3, 1970.
223 "These people have a loose grip on reality." Dalton.
230 "We believe that a thirty percent content ... varies widely in quality." CRTC transcripts, April 1970.
230 "It is our belief ... will drop significantly." CRTC.
230 "I am firmly convinced ... few stations will play." CRTC.
231 "The thing that I feel ...Canada has never really had." CRTC.

## EPILOGUE

240 "There is a lot of Prairie ... across flat land." Interview with Malka, *Maclean's*, June 1974.

# Bibliography

Adria, Marco, *Music of Our Times: Eight Canadian Singer-Songwriters*, J. Lorimer, Toronto, 1990.

Collins, Maynard, *Lightfoot: If You Could Read His Mind: A Biography*, Deneau Publishers, Toronto, 1988.

Crosby, David, and Carl Gottlieb, *Long Time Gone: The Autobiography of David Crosby*, Doubleday, New York, 1988.

Downey, David, *A Dreamer of Pictures: Neil Young, the Man and his Music*, Bloomsbury, London, England, 1994.

Einarson, John, *American Woman: The Story of The Guess Who*, Quarry Press, Kingston, Ont., 1995.

Einarson, John, *Neil Young: Don't Be Denied: "The Canadian Years,"* Quarry Press, Kingson, Ont., 1992.

Einarson, John, *Shakin' All Over: The Winnipeg Sixties Rock Scene*, Winnipeg, 1987.

Fetherling, Douglas, *Some Day Soon: Essays on Canadian Songwriters*, Quarry Press, Kingston, Ont., 1991.

Fournier, Michael, and Ken Norris, eds., *Take This Waltz: A Celebration of Leonard Cohen*, The Muses Company, St. Anne de Bellevue, Que., 1994.

Fulford, Robert, *This Was Expo*, McClelland & Stewart, Toronto, 1968.

Gabiou, Alfrieda, *Gordon Lightfoot*, Gage Publishing, Toronto, 1979.

Gibeault, André, *Canadian Records: A Discography and Price Guide of Canadian 45s and LPs from 1955 to 1975, Underworld Edition*, Montreal, 1987.

Gibeault, André, *Canadian Records: Obscurities and Rarities, A Guide and Discography to the Canadian Punk, Psychedelic, Rock and Pop Music from 1965 to 1972*, Gibeault, Montreal, 1985.

Goddard, Peter, Philip Kamin, eds., *Shakin' All Over: The Rock 'n' Roll Years in Canada*, McGraw-Hill, Toronto, 1989.

Hall, Ron, *The CHUM Chart Book: 1957-1986: A Complete Listing of Every Charted Record*, Stardust Productions, Toronto, 1990.

Hawkins, Ronnie, and Peter Goddard, *Ronnie Hawkins: Last of the Good Ol' Boys*, Stoddart, Don Mills, Ont., 1989.

Helm, Levon, with Stephen Davis, *This Wheel's on Fire: Levon Helm and the Story of the Band*, Morrow, New York, 1993.

Hinton, Brian, *Joni Mitchell, Both Sides Now*, Sanctuary Publishing, London, England, 1996.

Hoskyns, Barney, *Across the Great Divide: The Band and America*, Viking, London, 1993.

Jackson, Rick, *Encyclopedia of Canadian Rock, Pop and Folk*, Quarry Press, Kingston, Ont., 1994.

Kay, John, and John Einarson, *Magic Carpet Ride: The Autobiography of John Kay and Steppenwolf*, Quarry Press, Kingston, Ont., 1994.

Lyons, Don, *Yorkville Diaries*, Elephant Press

Melhuish, Martin, *Heart of Gold: 30 Years of Canadian Pop Music*, CBC Enterprises, Toronto, 1983.

Melhuish, Martin, *Oh What a Feeling: A Vital History of Canadian Music*, Quarry Press, Kingston, Ont., 1996.

Nadel, Ira, *Leonard Cohen: A Life in Art*, ECW Press, Toronto, 1994.

Perry, Charles, *The Haight-Ashbury: A History*, Random House, New York, 1984.

Pevere, Geoff and Greig Dymond, *Mondo Canuck: A Canadian Pop Culture Odyssey*, Prentice Hall Canada, Toronto, 1996.

Randy, Ray, and Mark Kearney, *Canadian Music Fast Facts: Profiles of Cnada, Pop Music Pioneers*, Sparky Jefferson Productions, London, Ont., 1997.

Robertson, John, *Neil Young: The Visual Documentary*, Omnibus Press, London, England, 1994.

Shelton, Robert, *No Direction Home: The Life and Music of Bob Dylan*, New English Library, London, England, 1986.

Smith, Cathy, *Chasing the Dragon*, Key Porter Books, Toronto, 1984.

Tyson, Ian, and Colin Escott, *Ian Tyson: I Never Sold My Saddle*, Douglas & McIntyre, Vancouver, 1994.

Usher, Bill, & Linda Page-Harpa, *"For What Time I Am in This World": Stories from Mariposa*, Peter Martin Associates, Toronto, 1977.

Wallis, Ian, *The Hawk: Ronnie Hawkins & the Hawks*, Quarry Press, Kingston, Ont., 1996.

Yorke, Ritchie, *Axes, Chops and Hot Licks: The Canadian Rode Music Scene*, Hurtig Publishers, Edmonton, 1971.

Young, Scott, *Neil and Me*, McClelland & Stewart, Toronto, 1984.

# index